EXPERIENCE WITH WORKS COUNCILS IN THE UNITED STATES, NO. 50, MAY, 1922

Published @ 2017 Trieste Publishing Pty Ltd

ISBN 9780649579716

Experience with Works Councils in the United States, No. 50, May, 1922 by National Industrial Conference Board

Edited by Trieste Publishing Pty Ltd.
Cover @ 2017

www.triestepublishing.com

NATIONAL INDUSTRIAL CONFERENCE BOARD

EXPERIENCE WITH WORKS COUNCILS IN THE UNITED STATES, NO. 50, MAY, 1922

Trieste

EXPERIENCE WITH WORKS COUNCILS IN THE UNITED STATES

RESEARCH REPORT NUMBER 50
MAY, 1922

National Industrial Conference Board

THE CENTURY CO.
NEW YORK
PUBLISHERS

.Copyright, 1922

National Industrial Conference Board

Foreword

THE present report supplements the two previous publications of the Board dealing with Works Councils, by an analysis of experience with such organizations up to date, as revealed in statements of employers, foremen and employees. In view of the growth in the number of Works Councils during the past two years and of the increasing attention they are receiving from industrial management, it is felt that this report will be of timely and general interest to industrialists and to the public. A larger number of organizations is covered in this report than in any study so far made in this country.

It must be remembered that this investigation concerned itself only with the study of Works Councils and their effects. No attempt was made to deal with the question as to whether other methods might not achieve the same results. The conclusions embraced in the report are not to be interpreted as the opinion of the National Industrial Conference Board as to whether or not Works Councils should be established in industrial concerns. This is a question which only the individual employer, in conjunction with his own employees, can properly determine. It is indeed conceivable that where management takes a personal, intelligent and broad-gauged interest in the questions that arise in the relations between employer and employed in an establishment, no mechanism or plan of any kind may prove to be necessary; but so far as adequate contacts have not been established in other ways between employer and employees, Works Councils, as this report indicates, have demonstrated their value in improving industrial relations.

CONTENTS

PART I

Representative Committee Systems Which Have Been Discontinued

PART II

Works Councils in Operation

Contents—*continued*

PART III

Employers' Opinions as to the Value of Works Councils in Industry

Experience with Works Councils in the United States

INTRODUCTION

In August, 1919, the number of Works Councils in industrial concerns in the United States was 225, according to a survey made at that time by the National Industrial Conference Board for its first report on the Works Council movement, which gave an account of substantially all that were then functioning. Since then, a number of employers have abandoned their employee representation plans, but a much larger number of employers have instituted Councils in their plants, so that in February, 1922, there were approximately 725 such organizations in operation in this country.

The great majority of the Works Councils covered in the Board's first report on the subject[1] had at the time of its publication been functioning on an average for not more than one year. This was a year of business prosperity; production was in demand, labor was scarce and wages were high. Following this came a period of business adversity; the demand for goods fell off, working forces were reduced, and wages declined. Widespread interest was manifest as to how Works Councils would stand the strain of such a period of depression. Were employee representation plans practicable only in times characterized by high wages and high prices? Would employees lose interest in the Councils when wage reductions became necessary? These and similar questions were raised as to the status and value of Works Councils during a period of decreased production and falling wages.

In order to answer these questions adequately, and ascertain the practical experience of employers with their Works Councils during such a period, the National Industrial Conference Board conducted a country-wide investigation. The great majority of the Works Councils treated in the present report have been in operation for periods varying from two to five years. An account of industry's experiences with these Works Councils during that period is presented herewith.

TERMINOLOGY

The term Works Council as used in this report is taken to mean

"a form of industrial organization under which the employees of an individual establishment, through representatives chosen by and

[1]"Works Councils in the United States." Research Report No. 21, Boston, October, 1919.

1

from among themselves, share collectively in the adjustment of employment conditions in that establishment."[1]

Various forms of Works Councils or employee representation plans exist, but they may be conveniently classified into two types:

(1) The "Industrial Democracy" type.[2]
(2) The "Committee" type.

The "Industrial Democracy" Type

This type of Works Council follows the pattern of the United States Government and provides for a Cabinet, Senate, and House of Representatives. In some cases the latter two bodies alone are provided; in others the Senate and House are merged into one joint body of foremen and employees; in others only mass meetings of the employees are provided. Where the plan is in operation in its entirety, the Cabinet is composed of the higher officers of the plant, the Senate is made up of the foremen, and the House of Representatives consists of elected employee representatives. A number of plans of the "Industrial Democracy" type have as an auxiliary feature a "Collective Economy Dividend," which is defined as:

"...a form of bonus paid periodically to the employees of any department which exceeds in production the standard prevailing at the time the plan was introduced. Fifty per cent of any such increase is distributed among the employees, the employer retaining the other 50%."[3]

This "Collective Economy Dividend" while originated in connection with the "Industrial Democracy" plan, is not necessarily a part thereof, and can function without it or with other plans of employee representation.

The "Committee" Type

"This type follows the ordinary committee form of organization, sometimes being a single committee and sometimes comprising a hierarchy of committees. The committee or committees may consist of employees alone, who confer with representatives of the management, or they may be joint committees embracing in their membership representatives of both employees and employer."[4].

"Limited" Works Council

Works Councils which do not include among their activities bargaining over working conditions, hours of labor and wages, are designated in this report as "Limited" Councils.

"Company Unions"

Another kind of Works Council is that which is based upon a "Company Union," that is, a Council subsidiary to an associa-

[1]National Industrial Conference Board. "Works Councils in the United States." Research Report No. 21, October, 1919, p. 1.
[2]The term "Industrial Democracy" has been substituted for the term "governmental" as used in Research Reports Nos. 21 and 26, to avoid confusing this type of Works Council with any governmental agency.
[3]"Works Councils in the United States," *op. cit.*, p. 19.
[4]*Ibid.*, p. 20.

2

tion embracing in its membership part or all of the employees of the establishment. Such a Council may be of the "Industrial Democracy" type or of the "Committee" type.

Shop Committee

Unless otherwise specified the term "shop committee" as used in this report refers to the type of committee introduced into plants by the late National War Labor Board.

SCOPE OF INVESTIGATION

This report embodies the results of an investigation commenced in April, 1921. Various manufacturers' associations and chambers of commerce rendered the National Industrial Conference Board their assistance in making the list of firms with industrial representation plans as nearly complete as possible. The report takes cognizance of practically all Works Councils known to have been organized up to February, 1922. . In most cases the information was drawn from the detailed questionnaires submitted to the manager or other executive of such industrial establishments. This was often amplified by further correspondence where necessary. In about twenty-five cases, embracing the principal forms of Works Council and establishments which have had extended experience, additional information was secured through investigation in the field. Employee representatives, other employees, trade union officials, foremen and other plant executives were interviewed.

GENERAL SUMMARY

The statements of employers, foremen and employees in answer to the inquiries of the National Industrial Conference Board furnish a basis for certain conclusions as to the value of employee representation in industry. These conclusions have been formulated after an impartial examination of the data collected in the present investigation.

In considering the experience in American industry with plans of employee representation, a clear distinction must be made between plans that grew out of, and whose creation was forced by, the war necessity, and those that developed later in consequence of it and by voluntary action of the two parties in the employment relation.

Most of the "shop committees" established by the National War Labor Board, as well as those set up by the Shipbuilding Adjustment Board during the World War, have ceased to function. The explanation of this lies in the fact that the committees were established in plants by order of an outside body and not through a desire on the part of employers and employees. Employers, as a rule, were opposed to this outside intervention and, under such circumstances, the life of the "shop committees" could not be long.

Another factor that militated against any likelihood of constructive work by these committees was that their establishment usually followed a dispute between employer and employees. Due to the fact that they were organized at a time when industrial relations had been severely strained, the committees were usually composed of the radical element among the workers. With employers and employees suspicious and distrustful of each other, genuine cooperation was impossible, and, as a consequence, the committees were allowed to disintegrate.

Some representation plans voluntarily introduced by employers and employees have also been abandoned but these cases are relatively few in comparison with the number of such plans that are still functioning to mutual satisfaction. Various reasons caused their discontinuance. The most common cause seems to have been either the failure of management to "sell" the plan to the employees, or the opposition of trade unions within or without the plant.

Careful investigation has brought out the fact that, whatever changes have been made in Works Council plans, that is in employee representation plans voluntarily organized by management and men, since the time they were first introduced into industrial concerns, they have not altered the essential nature of the Councils. Where there have been changes, these have been

4

mainly minor improvements in operating details to fill requirements which were unforeseen at the time of the formulation of the plans. Conditions to be met have differed in different plants and the changes made in Works Councils plans exhibit, therefore, a wide diversity. The feature which may be said to be common to all the changes is the reason for which they were made; namely, in order better to fit the plans to the organizations in which they operate. How this could best be done was a question that only the employer and the employees jointly in each individual plant could decide.

This experience brings out the important factor, so often lost sight of in the consideration of employee representation plans, that there is no "model" Works Council plan which may be applied indiscriminately to all industrial concerns. It further indicates that rigidity in a plan of employee representation is to be avoided; a Works Council plan should be flexible enough to admit of ready adaptation to new requirements as they arise.

Another major point revealed by the investigation is that usually, when a Works Council is first installed in a plant, there is a tendency for employees to use it chiefly for presenting complaints and grievances. The feature of the plan that appeals especially to the workers is the opportunity it affords of obtaining a hearing and decision in cases where they think they are suffering an injustice. In a few instances this remained the principal use which the employees made of the Works Council plan, even after it had been in operation for a year or more.

Where this had been the case, the explanation was found in the failure of management to take an active interest in the Works Council. Management apparently considered that its responsibility for the success of the plan terminated once the Works Council had been established and employee representatives had been elected. The Works Council was looked upon by management as a safety valve—valuable whether used or not. But little effort was made to enable men and management to arrive at a better understanding of each other's point of view, by holding regular meetings of the works committees at which a free exchange of ideas and suggestions could take place; nor was an effort made to direct the interest of employees upon subjects of a constructive nature. The committees functioned only when the employees had a complaint or grievance to bring before the management.

In times when wages were low and labor plentiful, the workers were naturally more concerned with retaining their jobs than with the correction of minor maladjustments in the plant and the committees lost their effectiveness even as a means for the hearing and adjustments of complaints and grievances. Moreover, the initiative in the choice of subjects with which the Works Council should deal was left entirely in the hands of the

5

employees. When economic conditions imposed a restraint upon the readiness of employees to provide the works committees with subjects for discussion the committees became lifeless.

As the Works Council became better understood, so most employers reported, there took place a gradual decrease in the use which the employees made of the works committees for the presentation of complaints and grievances, and a corresponding increase in the interest which they manifested in general business conditions and plant efficiency. This was, however, not the result of a policy of discouraging the discussion of complaints and grievances, for the employers recognized that, unless complaints and grievances have timely consideration and settlement, they usually lead to serious disturbances and even to strife and strikes. But such matters were not allowed to become the chief topic for the consideration of the works committees, and meetings were not held for this purpose alone. Management took an active, not a passive interest in the Works Council. Periodical meetings providing an opportunity for the discussion of subjects of mutual interest were held in which exchange of opinions and suggestions brought management and workers closer together. Each came to know the other better and to appreciate the other's point of view. Management realized that, to gain the confidence of its employees, it had to provide a means of regular intimate contact with them, and had to strive to obtain their good will. The Works Council was not regarded as an agency, the mere establishment of which would automatically result in obtaining the cooperation of the employees. Where this was appreciated by management, where the attention of the works committees was directed upon definite factory problems of common concern, the result was an increasing interest on the part of employees in the efficient and economical operation of the plants in which the Works Councils functioned.

The extent to which employees take an interest in increasing productivity efficiency appears to be directly related to the extent to which they have confidence in the fairness of management in its dealings with them, and to the degree to which they are convinced that it is to their interest that production be maintained and efficiency kept up. These are objectives difficult of achievement; the statements of employers furnish evidence, however, that employee representation plans have been valuable as instruments for gaining them.

Experience of those firms which have had the most noteworthy success along these lines, indicates that in addition to treating its employees fairly and justly, management must carry on a campaign of education in sound business economics to counteract the teachings of those individuals and groups who preach restriction of production as a real advantage to the workers.

6

Employers who have in their plants Works Councils of the "Industrial Democracy" type with the "Collective Economy Dividend," reported that this feature acts as a direct incentive to employees to assist in economical and efficient production, because it brings to them a direct reward in dollars and cents for their efforts in this direction. There is, however, a tendency for the employees to lose interest in their representation plan when business conditions necessitate the elimination of the "Collective Economy Dividend."

An outstanding feature of the Conference Board's investigation is the fact that proposals for wage reductions or changes in work-hour schedules made by employers have, in every instance of which the Board has learned, been approved and accepted by the employee representatives on the Works Councils, when they were furnished with an explanation of the reasons necessitating such measures. In these instances employers utilized the Works Councils to keep their employees informed of business conditions, as they affected both the companies concerned and the country as a whole; thus they prepared the minds of the employees for retrenchments which were believed necessary. Employers stated that wage reductions or changes in work-hour schedules were put into effect in this way with much less misunderstanding and friction than would otherwise have been possible. This was the case because employees were in a position to realize that the economies which were made did not originate from a ruthless desire on the part of the employers to lower the employees' standard of living, but arose from the pressure of economic forces against which the employer as well as the employee was more or less helpless. Employees expressed appreciation of the manner in which wage reductions or changes in work-hour schedules were handled, because they were told why such adjustments were necessary.

In practically every plant covered by the present investigation the effect of Works Councils upon relations between management and men was reported as beneficial. Statements of employers and employees were in unanimity with reference to this. The improvement in the relations between management and men was attributed to the opportunity afforded by a Works Council for an employer and his employees to come into direct and intimate contact with each other and to learn each other's views. The employees are thus furnished the means of communication with the higher executives of a company and enabled to meet them as "man to man." Where Works Councils are in operation foremen no longer exclusively interpret to the employees the aims and policies of management; employees learn from management itself its attitude toward them.

This exchange of ideas and suggestions and the appreciation of each other's difficulties has had the effect of breaking down

7

mutual suspicion and distrust, and where both parties have been inspired by a desire to be fair, goodwill, confidence and cooperation have resulted. Employers reported that employees appreciated the frank, open policy adopted by management. Their appreciation was manifested in the fairness and impartiality with which they discussed points of difference in the Works Councils meetings, and by the manner in which proposals of economies in wages were received by employee representatives on the Councils. In the few cases in which an unfavorable effect on the relations between management and employees through their Works Councils was reported, the reason was found in the lack of employer interest in the Council.

The information collected by the Conference Board concerning the attitude of foremen toward Works Councils showed a growing tendency on their part to regard the organization with favor. This tendency was based, in general, on the conception that the works committees, by creating better feeling and thus more successful cooperation between foremen and workers, and by relieving the foremen of the onus of settling disputes, would leave them free to devote more time to questions of production.

Where foremen have been antagonistic toward employee representation plans at the time of their installation, it has nearly always proved to be due to ignorance regarding the effect which the plan would have upon the relation between them and their subordinates. With few exceptions, either experience or education has had the effect of changing this non-cooperative attitude on the part of the foreman to one of support and cooperation. The feeling which in nearly every instance induced antagonism on the part of the foreman, was a fear of curtailment of their authority by the Works Councils, but it has been possible, except in a negligible number of cases, to convince foremen that fair dealing with the workers would not result in any wrongful interference with their authority by the Works Councils. Where continued antagonism to employee representation has been reported, the causes have been traced either to the character of the foremen or to the attitude of the higher executives toward the Works Council plan. Since the attitude of foremen tends to reflect that of management, a lack of interest and support of the plan on the part of management tends to produce a like attitude in the foremen.

One of the outstanding benefits of employee representation, according to opinions collected by the Conference Board from employers, employee representatives and foremen, has been the better spirit fostered by it between the foremen and workers. On foremen who had heretofore been arbitrary in dealing with the men under them, the Works Council has been a check in that it has made their decisions subject to review and change by the works committees. This fact has helped to introduce more careful consideration and greater fairness into the foreman's

8

dealings with his subordinates. In cases where a change of this sort has been effected, a corresponding transformation has been noted in the attitude of the workers, manifesting itself in greater contentment and in a spirit of cooperation not hitherto apparent. Employees laid particular emphasis upon this as one of the outstanding benefits of employee representation, namely, the marked improvement in the relations between the foremen and themselves.

Practically all employers reported that in the main very good judgment has been used by employees in their choice of representatives on Works Councils. Men with long service in the company's employ, those of sound judgment, who were fair and impartial in their decisions, those who manifested a desire to assist management in the development of mutual understanding and goodwill—such were the type of men who had mostly been elected as employee representatives. Some employers reported a tendency for the employees to be indifferent or careless at the time of the first elections for representatives, but practical experience with the operation of a plan showed the employees the necessity of electing the best men available. In some cases shop politics, whereby the popular rather than the able man was chosen, were reported to have played their part in the employees' selection. These men were often not the leaders among their shopmates, but the broadening influence of Works Councils deliberations eventually made them leaders and because of their popularity, strong leaders among their fellow employees. Instances of men with radical views having been elected were also reported; usually, however, the responsibility placed upon these men as representatives, together with the education they received in the Works Council meetings, have had the effect of moderating their views.

On account of many other contributing influences, it has not been feasible to determine accurately what effect employee representation plans have had upon labor turnover. Employers in their statements to the Conference Board were of the opinion, however, that although no definite measure of direct influence could be credited to Works Councils, a large part of the credit for reduced labor turnover, where this had occurred, was no doubt attributable to the Councils. Labor turnover was believed to have been reduced as a result of the close contact and better understanding developed between men and management. The elimination of petty, irritating details through discussion and settlement by the works committees was felt to have reduced to a considerable extent the number of workers formerly leaving their employment because of misunderstanding.

Although it is known that organized labor is officially opposed to any system of representative committees that does not provide for full recognition of trade unions, individual members of the union, the investigation has shown, have in many instances

9

heartily supported, and taken an active interest in, Works Councils. Where trade unions have been actively opposed to employee representation plans, this antagonism has expressed itself in various ways. In some cases trade unions' efforts to hamper the effectiveness of Works Councils have been restricted to attempts to ridicule the plans; in others, trade unionists have refused to take part in the Works Councils' activities; in others, strikes have been called against plants in which Works Councils were put into operation, in an effort to break up such committee system. Very little definite information is available as to the success or failure which has attended organized labor's opposition to Works Councils. In a few cases, trade unions have been successful in alienating the employees from their support of the Councils; in others, the employees' confidence in the fairness of management and their belief in the effectiveness of the Works Council as a means for the adjustment of differences and the promotion of mutual understanding, have formed an insuperable barrier to the antagonistic activities of the unions.

The study of the experience with employee representation plans indicates clearly that certain conditions are essential in order for such organizations to function successfully and to bring about a satisfactory degree of cooperation between employer and employee. In the first place, both management and men must be in favor of an employee representation plan as a means for the adjustment of their differences and for the betterment of their industrial relations. The Works Council is an organization that depends for its success upon the active interest and support of both employer and employees. It cannot function with any measurable degree of success where either party is antagonistic or indifferent toward it, no matter how well adapted the plan may be to the establishment within which it operates.

It has been found that both beneficial and detrimental results have followed the introduction of representation plans. This indicates that the success or failure attendant upon such plans is attributable not so much to the plans themselves as to the direction in which their activities are guided. Without the support of the workers and of management, including the supervisory force as well as the higher officials of a plant, a Works Council will not only fail to function successfully, but may become a disturbing element in the relations between employer and employee.

For this reason, therefore, in considering whether Works Councils should be established in industrial establishments, it is of paramount importance to determine first, the attitude of management toward the proposition. Where management is not thoroughly sold to the idea, where it is believed that the desired cooperation and goodwill of the employees can be better

10

obtained in other ways,—experience shows that a Works Council should not be formed.

In the second place, it must be recognized that the machinery of any plan is but a means to an end; the desired objects will be accomplished only if there is present mutual confidence and wholehearted support by those for whose benefit the plan is established. The history of the National War Labor Board "shop committees" furnishes striking proof of the futility of any system of employee representation as a means of bettering industrial relations, unless such scheme has the moral support of both management and men. Joint interest in and support of a plan of employee representation by employer and employee cannot be created by enactment or decree; it must spring from natural desire.

Of the two types of plans, the "committee" type is simpler in form than the "Industrial Democracy" type. As shown elsewhere in this report, a number of employers using plans of the "Industrial Democracy" type found that the business of the Councils was much expedited by the elimination of the "Senate," the body composed of the foremen. In this way there has been an approximation to the "committee" type of plan.

As distinguished from the "Industrial Democracy" type, the "committee" type provides for joint consideration of questions, although provision may be made for the employee representatives to meet apart from those of management following such joint discussion. The "Industrial Democracy" type of plan on the other hand, by setting up separate bodies of representatives of management and men does not provide for joint discussion until after each of the bodies—"Senate" and "House of Representatives"—have formulated their opinion regarding the subject at issue. An exchange of ideas and opinions before a definite stand has been taken by either side is of value, since there is a natural human reluctance to change once such a stand has been taken. From this point of view, the procedure followed in the "committee" type seems to be preferable. However, the experience of some employers has been that it is impossible to obtain full and frank discussion by employees in a meeting at which representatives of management are present. They have found it advisable to form separate bodies of representatives of employees and management, and in this way there has been an approximation to the "Industrial Democracy" type.

It is to be noted that the "Collective Economy Dividend" which is usually a feature of plans of the "Industrial Democracy" type is not an integral part of such plans, and that it may equally be incorporated in plans of the "committee" type.

In the third place, after an unbiased study of the Works Council movement one cannot fail to lay emphasis upon the importance of the manner in which a Works Council is introduced into a plant. The unanimous opinion of the Board's correspondents is to the effect that a Works Council should not be established in a plant without giving the employees a voice in its formulation. The reason given for this is the belief that in this way any suggestion of paternalism or exploitation on the part of management is avoided. Employees are inclined to regard a plan which has been formulated and set up by management alone as a device of the employer "to put something over on them." Where employees are consulted with reference to the structure of the plan before it is adopted, and where they are given an opportunity to decide whether they wish to put it into effect, their active interest in the plan is gained at the outset. This method of introducing a Works Council into an establishment is based upon a recognition of the fact that such an organization is dependent for its success upon the support and interest of employees, as well as of management. It is accordingly considered better to determine whether the employees approve of the Works Council before the plan is set up than to introduce the plan only to find out later that there is no willingness on the part of the employees to utilize it. The best results are likely to develop out of plans which are naturally evolved through carefully conducted experiments. Often some already existing group of employees may well be used as a nucleus with which to make a beginning.

Finally, it must be realized that the employer who looks to the Works Council as a means of gaining the confidence and goodwill of his employees, cannot expect to secure these unless he gives the Works Council constant and sympathetic support. Employee cooperation can only be secured at a price; the employer must keep in close and active touch with the representation plan and must be frank and sincere in his dealings with and through it. Experience shows that where management adopts this attitude toward a Works Council, the latter proves a valuable instrument for securing the cooperation of the workers.

Interest in the Works Council plan on the part of management and the latter's willingness to deal fairly with its employees tend to call forth a corresponding interest on the part of the employees as well as a willingness to be fair and impartial in the consideration of points of difference brought up in the Council meetings. The motto adopted by one firm—"Fairness Begets Fairness"—is applicable to the experience which most employers have had with their Works Councils. But experience shows just as clearly that where management takes no interest in the Works Council after it is introduced into a plant, where it does not "play the game," according to the rules of the plan, the Council becomes at best a mere grievance committee with the probability of its having a destructive rather than a constructive effect·upon the relations between the employees and management.

The increase in the number of employee representation plans in the United States in the last decade to approximately 725 shows a slow but steady growth of this movement with increasingly satisfactory results. This growth is all the more significant when it is remembered that practically all of the "shop committee" plans set up by the National War Labor Board and the Shipbuilding Labor Adjustment Board, are no longer in existence. The increase in the number of Works Councils does not indicate, however, that this movement has assumed really national proportions, for there are many thousands of establishments whose size might warrant the organization in each of a Works Council of one kind or another. But in so far as the movement has progressed, it gives clear evidence of its growing service and value in the employment relation.

Works Councils that have been properly conceived, introduced and conducted have proved a valuable aid in gaining the confidence and goodwill of employees and thus in improving production, reducing labor turnover and other waste, and generally in benefiting alike all those engaged in the common enterprise.

Looking upon the Works Council movement in its broader and more fundamental aspects, the results of the Conference Board's study seem to reaffirm the basic contention that the labor problem within the plant, that is the problem of the relationship of employer to employed, is after all primarily a management problem. From this it follows naturally—and the experiences of employers related in this report are ample evidence of this—that unless management in each individual establishment adopts an enlightened attitude toward the labor problem and concerns itself personally with the various phases of the problem and with their adequate solution, the most elaborate and highly perfected plan will fail of its purpose.

The Works Council is at once an organism and a mechanism; it must, therefore, carry in itself the elements that will make for gradual and definite growth, and it must be guided and operated by an intelligent and understanding mind. But because that mind—management—is supposed to be intelligent and understanding, it must not be expected necessarily to accept and adopt any one employee representation plan as the universal panacea for a set of conditions in which the human equation must always play so large and important a part.

13

PART I

Representative Committee Systems Which Have Been Discontinued

This section deals with "shop committees" introduced into concerns by the National War Labor Board, with Shipbuilding Labor Adjustment Board Committees, and with employee representation plans voluntarily initiated by employers, but which have been abandoned for various reasons. Because the majority of the committees established by both the National War Labor Board and the Shipbuilding Labor Adjustment Board were in existence for a comparatively short period, and because nearly all of them were discontinued three years ago, the National Industrial Conference Board has met with considerable difficulty in obtaining information regarding the value of these committees during their rather brief existence, and the reasons for their discontinuance. This was especially true with reference to the committees formed by the Shipbuilding Labor Adjustment Board.

Questionnaires were addressed to twenty firms in which Shipbuilding Labor Adjustment Board Committees had been formed. In three of these the committee systems established by the Labor Adjustment Board have since been replaced by agreements with labor unions. As trade union committees are not regarded as Works Councils, the committee organizations in those plants do not come within the scope of this report. Six firms in which Shipbuilding Labor Adjustment Board Committees were organized, did not reply to the Board's inquiries; and eight concerns in which the committees have been discontinued wrote that nothing further was to be added to their statements furnished the Conference Board in 1919. The latter were included in the National Industrial Conference Board's first report on the subject.[1] Three firms reported that the committee systems as introduced by the Shipbuilding Labor Adjustment Board had been retained by them with modifications aimed better to adapt the committees to the plants.

Information regarding the results obtained from National War Labor Board Committees and Works Councils voluntarily introduced into plants by employers, showing what the committees accomplished, why they were discontinued, and giving in some instances the employers' opinions as to the advantages or disadvantages of such organizations, is presented in this part of the report.

[1] "Works Councils in the United States," *op. cit.*, pp. 87-94.

CHAPTER I

NATIONAL WAR LABOR BOARD SHOP COMMITTEES

Among "the principles to be observed and the methods to be followed by the National War Labor Board" in exercising the powers conferred upon it by President Wilson in his proclamation of April 8, 1918, was that of the right of the workers to organize and "to bargain collectively through chosen representatives."[1] To make this condition effective in plants where labor unions were not already organized, the Labor Board, commencing in July, 1918, made provision in a large number of its awards for committees of elected employee representatives to deal with their employers. The first firm in which "shop committees" were instituted by the Board was the Pittsfield plant of the General Electric Company. In its award the Board directed that departmental committees should be formed "to present grievances and mediate with the company." From the members of the departmental committees was to be chosen a "committee on appeals" of three members, whose function it was to meet with the management for the adjustment of disputes which the departmental committees failed to settle. Certain regulations were laid down for securing a fair election and the War Labor Board's examiner was to see that minority representation was provided for.

Following the precedent established in the above case, the Board uniformly upheld the right of workers to organize for collective dealing and made provision for it in the majority of its decisions in the following terms:

> "As the right of workers to bargain collectively through committees is recognized by the Board, the company shall recognize and deal with such committees after they have been constituted by the employees."[2]

The Board did not always specify, as in the case of the General Electric Pittsfield plant, the manner of the constitution of the committees. In some instances it merely directed that employers should meet with committees of their employees. In other cases the Board appointed a permanent committee of a specified number of employees which was to adjust all differences that might arise between men and management. In October, 1918, the joint chairmen of the War Labor Board formulated a standard plan for the selection of "shop committees" which was generally but not uniformly stipulated in

[1] National War Labor Board. "Principles and Rules of Procedure," Washington, 1919.
[2] National War Labor Board Dockets Nos. 110, 110a, 110b, 169, 174, 176, etc.

subsequent awards. This plan provided for the election by secret ballot of one member of the committee for each hundred employees in each shop department. Under the supervision of the examiner of the Board the election was to be held "in the place where the largest total vote of the men can be secured, consistent with fairness of count and full and free expression of choice, either in the shop or in some convenient public building." The examiner was to select as his assistants in conducting the election and counting the votes two or more employees from the department in which the election was to be held. An employee named by the employer was to be present to identify the voters as actual employees, but foremen or other officials of the plant were not to be present at the election. Provision was made for reports of the shop committees to their respective constituencies from time to time.

The functions designated for "shop committees" covered a wide field. In some of its awards the Board merely stated that the committees should endeavor to adjust all disputes that might arise. In other awards the Board specifically designated the functions of the committees. In general it may be said that the National War Labor Board Committees were "bargaining committees" dealing mainly with such questions as hours, wages, rates, piecework and overtime.

In studying the accomplishments, and the reasons for the abandonment, of the National War Labor Board Committees, due recognition must be given to the unusual wartime conditions that prevailed when these committees were formed. Moreover, as in almost every instance, the awards of the Labor Board followed disputes between an employer and his employees, the more or less strained relations within the plant were not such as to favor the formation of committees which would have the confidence of both management and workers. The committees were introduced into industrial concerns, not as the result of a slowly developed desire within the plant for such committees, but by order of an outside body which superimposed its will upon both employer and employees. More particularly, this was done at a time when employer and employees were mutually suspicious and distrustful. The plan was not the product of their joint efforts toward finding a means of maintaining industrial harmony. Rather was it imposed upon the organization as a result of the strife that existed. Where this element of coercion was present and where neither the employer nor the employees favored the formation of the committees, it was inevitable that they should fail to function effectively. These seem to be the outstanding reasons for the failure of such a large number of the National War Labor Board Committees.

A study of what was accomplished by the National War

16

Labor Board Committees and why they were abandoned in so many plants confirms these deductions.[1] In the greater proportion of cases the employers in whose plants the National War Labor Board Committees were formed, were opposed to them. This was true, as a whole, of the concerns in Bridgeport, which were party to the award of the Board in November, 1919, providing for the election of employees' committees, under a scheme which became known as the "Bridgeport plan."[2] Although over sixty firms were party to the award of the Board, a number of the employers were so opposed to "shop committees" that they did not set up the committees as called for in the award. A company official of a Bridgeport plant stated regarding the attitude of the employers toward the "shop committees":

"... the plan was practically forced upon the manufacturers, and in many instances against their will and better judgment. Naturally, the moment the armistice was signed, if not before, many of the managements which were not in favor of such a method immediately permitted its disintegration and death."

Another official of a Bridgeport plant which was included in the award of the Board, said that the "shop committees" were

"... really shoved down the throats of the manufacturers of Bridgeport.

"... It is quite apparent that neither the management of the several plants interestedn or the workers were very much in sympathy with the idea, for had they been so, the Works Councils that had been established would not have died out as they have practically all done."[3]

The management of that particular plant, which employed two thousand persons, of whom a large percentage were foreigners, "was not in very great sympathy with the plan at the outset so it died a natural death." It is evident that the conditions which this officer considers essential for the successful operation of an employee representation plan, namely that an interest be taken in it on the part of the management, and that "it should come from the workers themselves, and at least have their major support," did not obtain with respect to the "shop committees" introduced into that plant by the National War Labor Board.

Another Bridgeport employer reported that the plan was introduced into his plant "neither as the result of the employees desiring it, nor the management feeling any particular benefit would be derived from it." It was felt there was no "real

[1]Fifty-nine firms furnished information regarding the success or failure of their National War Labor Board Committees. In forty-nine of these firms the committees have been abandoned. Five only have retained the committees as instituted by the Labor Board. Five other firms in which committees were installed by the Board later voluntarily adopted representation plans.

[2]"Works Councils in the United States," op. cit., p. 10.

[3]Five companies out of the sixty-two that were party to the Board's award in Bridgeport have retained their employee representation plans.

17 .

reason or purpose for an employees' committee." Many other correspondents wrote in the same strain.

The opposition of the employers to the National War Labor Board Committees was in many instances based on their belief that employees' committees were not necessary in their plants because of the close personal contact that already existed between the management and the workers. It was felt that the order of the Labor Board for the introduction of the committees was not based upon a thorough knowledge of conditions within the plant. The employees already had the right of presenting their grievances to the management at all times, and it was not seen that any need existed for committees to secure for the workers what they already possessed. This was the attitude not only of employers, but in many cases of employees.

The president of an eastern machine company wrote that the only reason assignable for the employees' committee never holding a meeting was that

> "... we never employed over 25 men at any time, and as the writer was at all times in personal touch with them so that any grievance could be brought to him direct, the men felt as if there was no necessity for them holding meetings."

In another eastern concern employing seventy workers at the time the "shop committee" was organized by the National War Labor Board, "the employees themselves," wrote an executive, "did not wish for a committee of this character as they have been at all times able to come in direct touch with the executives and in this manner raise any question they had to add to their welfare." This correspondent stated that the employees preferred "individual bargaining rather than collective."

In a plant employing three hundred workers a company official stated regarding the "shop committee" established by the Labor Board:

> "... there seemed to be nothing for it to do and eventually it went out of existence.
> "Our plant is a small one and we are able to keep closely in touch with our people at all times, and we believe that is the cause of a lack of interest among our employees for any kind of a committee."

As already stated, "shop committees" were in most instances established within a plant following a dispute between the employer and his employees or a group of his employees. In some cases the employees had gone on strike. Thus the decision of the War Labor Board, which in dealing with the dispute provided for the election of employees' committees, was made when opposition rather than cooperation existed between management and men. At such a time it was extremely likely that the more radical element among the employees, those who had been the leaders in fomenting trouble, would be elected to the committees. These men, often of the agitator type, viewed

18

industrial problems within the plant chiefly with an eye to what advantages might be obtained for their trade unions, regardless of the cost to the employer or the effect upon the industry itself. Where such was the case, neither their attitude toward the management nor the management's attitude toward them was changed by merely grouping the men into committees. The retention of this hostile attitude toward each other made cooperation impossible. That the relations between management and employees at the time of the initiation of representative committees has a determining effect upon the success of such committees is shown by the experiences of a middle western firm. In this company the National War Labor Board Committee installed, following disputes between management and men which culminated in a strike, was unable to accomplish anything of value, while a Works Council installed at a later date, when relations between employers and employed were more harmonious, has since functioned satisfactorily.

In this plant, a middle western shop with nine hundred workers, the National War Labor Board Committee was formed as the result of a strike by a small group of employees. The committee, composed largely of the radical element that had been the instigators of the strike, was dominated by outside labor interests. The company had no confidence in the committee, nor did the committee trust the company. The result was that the committee accomplished nothing, and was maintained by the management merely in a perfunctory way until the jurisdiction of the Labor Board should cease.

It was, however, the belief of the vice-president of the company that employees' committees elected at a time when no labor difficulties existed and when the matter could be fully explained to the employees, could be made a success. Two years after the establishment of the National War Labor Board Committees, during which time the more radical element within the plant had been eliminated, the company introduced a representation plan under very different circumstances. The relations between men and management were harmonious and the plan was presented to the employees as a sincere effort on the part of the management "to improve the relationship between employer and employee." The company devoted considerable time to an educational campaign among the workers before the plan was introduced, explaining it to them, giving them an opportunity to discuss it, and answering any questions they put regarding it. The employees were then allowed to vote as to whether they wanted the plan or not, and by a large majority they voted to adopt it.

The men elected by the employees to represent them were not of the "firebrand" type, but the recognized leaders in each department, men whom the employees knew they could depend

19

upon, and whom the management found willing to cooperate in securing harmony within the plant. Although fully cognizant of the fact that in its operation there are improvements yet to be made, the management after eighteen months' experience reported the plan to be "working very satisfactorily." Employee representatives interviewed by a field investigator expressed themselves as well satisfied with the way in which the plan is working, and cited several improvements in working conditions that had been obtained through the Works Council. The employees, they said, had confidence in the management because they believed they were being treated "fairly and squarely."

The National War Labor Board Committees initiated by the decree of an outside body against the wishes of the management, at a time when industrial relations within the plant had been severely strained, had failed to function, while the representation plan approved by both parties and formed at a time when the relations between men and management were harmonious, functioned to the satisfaction of all.

The circumstances surrounding the formation of the two sets of committees had their corresponding results. When management and employees distrusted and suspected each other, cooperation was impossible. The representatives elected by the employees to the National War Labor Board Committees, sought to strengthen the influence of outside labor interests irrespective of the effect of such a policy upon industrial relations within the plant. Management learned from its experience with these committees that nothing of a constructive nature could be expected unless the employees were willing to work with it toward a better mutual understanding. Under the representation plan installed later, the cooperation of the employees was obtained at the outset. They were given an opportunity to vote as to whether they wanted the plan, and by a large majority expressed their approval of it. This attitude of the employees was reflected in the kind of representatives elected by them. These representatives, unlike those elected to the Labor Board Committees, devoted their energy to the development of better industrial relations within the plant, and not to increasing the prestige of labor unions.

Several other firms have stated that they found it necessary to discontinue the meetings of their "shop committees" because of the character of the representatives elected. Instead of working to assist the management in the adjustment of disputes and the elimination of strife, it was found that they were endeavoring to stir up trouble. The furtherance of the influence of trade unionism was of more importance to them than the betterment of industrial relations within the plant.

In one firm in the Middle West the representatives on the "shop committee," who "were picked from the strictest union

20

agitators," carried this policy to such an extreme that eventually there occurred between the management and the committee a clash which resulted in a strike. A company official wrote that at the end of three weeks the men came back on the company's terms, and realizing "that the committee they had elected was not one from whom they could expect harmony or constructive work, they denounced the men who had been placed on this committee and abandoned them."

Similar considerations were mentioned by an eastern machine company as the reasons why the activities of their "shop committees" "quickly and promptly ceased." One of the officials of the company stated in the following terms the manner in which the situation was dominated by union influence:

> "We feel that the first and most important policy that assisted in destroying any practical use or effectiveness of these committees, was the personnel of the employees' representatives serving on the shop committees. In the majority of cases, they were the most pronounced agitators in the shop. Some of them were holding positions in the union and the committee's actions and methods of approaching each and every problem was, we feel, based upon definite instructions received from the higher officials of the local union, without regard to the best interests of the public, the corporation, and in some cases the employees, themselves, but to the best interests of the union.
>
> "We found that the shop committees were trying to classify the non-union men lower than union men in our shops, but we, of course, were extremely careful to look after and fully protect the non-union employees. Regardless of what action was taken by the company that resulted in better conditions for the employees, the shop committees would go into great detail explaining that any concessions granted by the company were due to the influence of the War Labor Board and the shop committees."

The propaganda which the labor agitators in the plant directed against the National War Labor Board Committee was given by the president of another eastern machine company as the reason why the committee was "a total failure." After holding one or two meetings, it

> "... was discouraged and brought into disrepute with the rest of the help by a few agitators or radicals, who wished, instead of having a committee to represent the whole of the employees, that a self-elected committee of themselves would dictate to the management and the rest of the help."

Whether acting on the committee, or working within the plant, the influence of this type of men was the same. The committees in their opinion were useful in proportion to the degree that they were instrumental in securing in the plant the application of those principles in which they believed.

Although it is true that the most carefully drawn up plan of representation will fail unless it be supported by the mutual interest of both employees and employer, and although too much emphasis is often laid upon the machinery of the plan, it is nevertheless essential that the plan itself be one that fits the plant or industry in which it is to operate. Obviously it should

21

secure true representation of the employees of that plant, since otherwise the management and the elected representatives will be working at cross purposes.

The results of the failure to provide for such representation in certain of the plans as laid down by the Labor Board, are shown by the experiences of two plants. In each of these the plan called for the holding of the election of representatives outside the plant.

At the time of the award of the Board the management of a western plant expressed their willingness and desire to meet with a committee of employees if this committee were selected within the works and by secret ballot. Instead of this, the committee was elected outside the plant and was composed entirely of union men.

> "... the election was held in the Armory on Sunday afternoon, and as the employees passed into the Armory, they were handed a slip on which was printed the names of seven of our employees who were up for election on the shop committee, and of course, these seven men were elected, so that we felt that it was not a secret ballot."

These representatives of the labor agitator type "spent most of their time in going from department to department and keeping things upset generally." The result was a strike. After the strike the employees asked for the retention of the committee system and this was granted, with this difference, that the elections for representatives were held within the plant.

> "Under this present plan the Conference Committeemen do not feel that it is their duty to go around the plant looking after different things, but have been very willing to bring up suggestions which have been called to their attention, and in all cases have been very fair in all our dealings with them."

A similar instance is that of a middle western canning factory. Under the plan of the Labor Board as applied to this company

> "... the employee elections were held uptown in the union headquarters hall, and those employees who did not belong to the union were not given very much consideration .... Furthermore, the industrial organizers who did not work in the plant were very particular to pick out radical employees and work on the rest of the employees so that these radical ones would be elected to committees, and after this was done, of course, the committees could be controlled and influenced by the outside organizers."

After the jurisdiction of the War Labor Board ceased, this arrangement was changed by the company and elections were held within the plant. A company official wrote that several other changes also were made, because

> "... the representation plan as introduced by the War Labor Board in June, 1918, was so ridiculous and so unfair to our industry."

One of the changes made in the plan of the War Labor Board was the appointment by the management of judges and tellers for counting the ballots at the time of elections. This had been prohibited by the Labor Board. It "allowed the elections to be

22

run by the employees only, and we know the elections were not fair."

Another change was the annulment of that clause in the Labor Board's plan which provided for arbitration by an individual acceptable to both parties in cases where the management and the employees could not settle the matter satisfactorily. The final court of appeal is now the management of the plant.

The War Labor Board in its plan provided that when the management wished to discharge an employee the approval of the "shop committee" had first to be obtained. Under the present plan the right to discharge is entirely within the power of the management.

This official wrote that since the above changes had been made, there had been no friction in the operation of the plan.

A few firms give as the reason for the discontinuance of their "shop committees" the cancellation of their war contracts, at which time their working force was greatly reduced. The same thing occurred in other firms at the time of the signing of the armistice.

The vice-president of an eastern plant wrote:

"The Works Council which we had during the war ceased at the end of the war. The reason for discontinuing this Council was due to our contracts being cancelled."

The number of cases in which this reason was given for the discontinuance of the committees was very small, however, compared to those in which opposition by the employer, lack of interest among the employees, or the character of the elected representatives, was assigned as the cause of the abandonment of the plan.

A few plants reported favorably upon the "shop committees" introduced into their plants by the War Labor Board. An eastern machine company which discontinued its committee because of a change in its business when its working force was considerably reduced, reported "beneficial results" had been obtained while the committee was in operation.

In other cases the favorable account of the activities of the "shop committees" furnished to the Conference Board in 1919 and reported by it in Research Report No. 21, was changed after further experience with the committees into an unfavorable report.

One firm which reported in August, 1919, that the committees selected by the members of the labor union had functioned satisfactorily[1], wrote in August, 1921, that they had been abandoned later because of a strike called by the union men over a proposed reduction in wages.

[1] "Works Councils in the United States," op. cit., p. 85.

23

Another firm which reported in August, 1919, that "the results altogether have been very satisfactory,"[1] wrote in March, 1921, regarding its "shop committee" as follows:

"We did not find any very great advantage from it, and there were some decided disadvantages. At any rate, we allowed the meetings to become less frequent from time to time, and finally entirely dropped the matter."

The "shop committees" established in concerns by the National War Labor Board differ from the Works Councils or employee representation plans discussed in the main body of this report, in the vital respect that whereas Works Councils have been voluntarily initiated by employers, and in most instances with the consent and support of the employees, "shop committees" were organized in plants at the order of an outside body. They were superimposed upon concerns irrespective of the feelings of either the employer or the employees about such committees.

In a following chapter, employers who have achieved success in the operation of employee representation plans lay emphasis upon the necessity of both management and men being "sold" on the idea of employee representation. They point out that no plan, however well drawn up and suited to the industry in which it operates, can function successfully unless both management and employees are enthusiastically behind it. That enthusiastic support was lacking in the case of the "shop committees" of the National War Labor Board. The plans were not set up as the result of a desire upon the part of employers to improve industrial relations within plants; on the contrary, they were regarded either as unnecessary, or as organizations which would result in stirring up more trouble than they allayed. Employees either lost interest in the committees shortly after they were organized, or the more radical element endeavored to utilize them for the furtherance of union policies. Where either of these conditions obtained, the life of the committees was short.

Instead of being based upon a desire of the parties represented to utilize them for the elimination of friction within plants, and for the attainment of a fuller appreciation of each other's problems, the committees were founded upon the decree of an outside organization. The awards of the Labor Board initiated the committees, but the lack of support and interest on the part of the management and employees terminated them.

[1] *Ibid.*, p. 84.

CHAPTER II

WORKS COUNCILS INITIATED BY EMPLOYERS
AND SINCE ABANDONED

Works Councils originally initiated by employers were reported as having been discontinued in thirty-seven industrial concerns. Of these, the Councils were abandoned in fifteen plants because the plants either shut down entirely or ran with such a small staff that the retention of the Works Councils was no longer feasible. Where this was the case the employers usually expressed their intention of resuming the operation of the Councils when business again became normal.

"We expect to again take up employees' representation as our experience has taught us that there is much benefit to employer and employee to be derived from a plan of this nature," wrote an official of an establishment manufacturing heavy machinery, which had discontinued its Works Council when one of its plants was sold.

The experience of this company with its Works Council was described by the same correspondent as follows:

"Our plan when in operation functioned, we believe, to much satisfaction, as it brought questions concerning employer and employee through channels that made it possible to adjust differences more speedily than by any other method, We do not mean however, that these meetings were for the purpose of adjusting grievances only, for the exchange of ideas towards improvement and possible changes in materials and methods was very helpful.

"Representatives chosen by the employees were in most cases those workmen that were above the average and upon whom employees could depend to present their cases in the clearest possible light."

"We have implicit faith in this method of dealing with labor and believe we shall continue this system as soon as business conditions warrant," wrote an official of an eastern company which, because of the reduction of its working force to ten percent of the normal number, discontinued its Works Council. In this company it had. been found that "the representative system was an invaluable aid in avoiding labor troubles...."

An official in an eastern plant reported in April, 1921, that, although the "Industrial Democracy" type of Works Council in his establishment had not been in operation for some time because of the reduction in the number of its employees,

"...we have, however, had such good results in the past with this method of operation, should business pick up we shall certainly continue."

Another eastern official wrote:

"We have used shop committees with much success. At the present time we are not using this method of approach to our employees because our mills have been practically closed for some months.

"It is likely that when business conditions make it possible, we shall be disposed to use the shop committees as heretofore."

A southern lumber company which introduced a plan of the "Industrial Democracy" type into its plant early in 1920, maintained it in operation till December of that year. When the mill was reopened in March, 1921, with a considerably reduced force, the management decided not to re-establish the Council unless the employees asked for it, which they have not yet done. This is to be explained by the attitude of the employees toward the plan, when it was in operation, which was described by the secretary of the firm as "more or less indifferent, although there was never any opposition." The attitude of the older employees was described as one of "good-natured indifference." The same correspondent reported:

"Our experience was that the works committees of employees were for the most part inactive, although some practical suggestions were occasionally made and adopted by the organization."

He also said "the general tone of efficiency is greater at the present time than it was under the 'Industrial Democracy' régime."

As a result of this experience with a Works Council, it is the opinion of this executive that no advantage is to be gained from a Works Council plan "in an establishment of moderate size," although there is apparently no disadvantage "if the employees introduce such a plan on their own initiative, or can be induced to give it active instead of passive support." The attitude of the company toward employee representation is expressed as follows:

"We are ready to re-establish Industrial Democracy or any other approved plan of representation whenever our employees are ready to enter into it and carry it out. At the same time, we see no reason for pushing such a plan on our own initiative."

Seven firms which had had representation plans of the "Industrial Democracy" type in operation, reported that the unsatisfactory results obtained had led to their discontinuance. Various reasons were given for the failure of the plans to function.

The president of one company, employing 250 workers, wrote that he made his first mistake in that

"... I appointed a man to inaugurate this system who is afflicted with a 'temperament' and a 100 H. P. idea of the Golden Rule."

The result of the "Wilsonian speeches," and the "beautiful words" posted on the bulletin board by this individual was "a number of requests for raises in wages and rather upsetting socialistic debates." At the first meeting of the House of Representatives the chief subject of discussion was whether or not it were possible "for the employees to discharge any foreman that seemed to be unpopular and did not agree with them." The first bill presented to the Cabinet was a request for a reduction of hours from fifty-six to forty-eight per week "with a corresponding increase in wages, so that the envelopes would not be any thinner."

The second mistake made, according to this correspondent, was that

> "... the constitution was prepared and presented by the House of Representatives, acted upon and approved, then sent to the Senate, and lastly, to the Cabinet. This meant that by the time it reached the Cabinet, it was loaded with dangerous ideas.... Instead of starting from the Cabinet and educating the Cabinet, we attempted to allow the House of Representatives, the most ignorant employees, to work out something the Cabinet itself had a hazy idea of."

After further consideration of the situation, the president of the company posted a notice three months after the inauguration of the Council that the "plan as developed could not be carried out." Working hours were, however, reduced from fifty-six to fifty-two per week.

It is the hope of the company to try the plan again at some time in the future, along lines set down by the correspondent as follows:

> "First, train the Cabinet. Then let the Cabinet draw the constitution, appoint the members of the Senate and House of Representatives from the employees, in its opinion, best qualified to carry out the spirit and purpose of 'Industrial Democracy'; then after they have been thoroughly trained in the purpose of the plan, gradually allow the employees to appoint their own House of Representatives. In other words, try out a model organization and educate them to stand on their own feet."

The experience of this company points out the necessity for the executives in a concern contemplating the formation of a Works Council to be thoroughly informed as to just what a plan of employee representation is, and what type of plan will best suit that concern.

An eastern furniture manufacturing concern with a working force of three hundred employees abandoned its "Industrial Democracy" plan after a year's operation because of the lack of interest on the part of the employees. The plan was installed by one of the officers of the company, who was very enthusiastic regarding the practical results to be obtained from the application of the principles of "Industrial Democracy," but there was no appreciable difference noted either in production or in the spirit of the workers. To accomplish more successfully the objects for which the plan was instituted, the services of an outside expert on industrial relations were secured, and an effort was made to obtain the enthusiastic support of the em-

27

ployees for the plan. This temporarily aroused their interest and an improvement in the operation of the plan was noted. Soon, however, the interest of the employees waned, and, as stated by one of the officials of the company, such trivial matters were discussed at the meetings that the results of the discussions did not compensate for the time taken from production. The meetings finally became so futile that the employee representatives requested that they either be given something worth while to do, or that the plan be discontinued. Although pronounced a failure, the year's test of the plan was considered to have been worth while because it brought to the front many things which the management had not known of before. The reason for the failure of the plan, as stated by one of the officials of the company, was:

> "Industrial democracy was in existence in the plant before 'Industrial Democracy' as such was introduced."

Part of the responsibility for the failure of the plan in this instance, however, would appear to be with the management. At the outset the executives of the concern were not unanimously in favor of the scheme; and it is evident from the manner in which the meetings were allowed to degenerate into mere "talk fests" that the management did not devote sufficient attention to the plan to make the meetings of interest to the representatives. It was apparently considered that the plan could work under its own steam, and without any assistance by the management. Experience proved this to be erroneous.

Another employer likewise attributed the failure of his plan of "Industrial Democracy" to the inability of the management to stimulate and maintain the interest of the employees in the plan. The plan was discontinued in this plant, which employed three hundred workers, after it had been in operation one year. The president of the company wrote:

> "We had great hope of it proving a success but the ability on our part seemed to be lacking to put it across. We believe in it thoroughly ourselves, but for some reason or other we could not seem to arouse enthusiasm enough on the part of our employees to get busy and profit by it. At the first considerable interest was shown and quite perceptible savings made, but later on it began to drag, enthusiasm waned and the savings vanished; consequently, we have given it up and gone back to the old order of things."

It is the opinion of this correspondent that "a man of exceptional training and ability must be in control of the organization to keep everything running smoothly."

One western concern found that after the leader who had developed the "Industrial Democracy" plan left its employ, the employees' enthusiasm and interest in the plan diminished so greatly "that it became necessary to eliminate the employee representation." Despite this unfavorable experience, it is the company's belief that

28

"...with proper instruction and an organization which could be depended upon to instill enthusiasm into the employees, the plan would work out most satisfactorily."

Referring to the results of a plan of representation of the "Industrial Democracy" type in an eastern company, the president of the firm wrote:

"We operated a Works Council for a period of about one year with no result that would encourage us to continue.... We do not think a Works Council in a shop of this size, 400, is of any value to anyone. We keep in touch personally with every one in our employ and they are educated to bring their troubles, if they have any, to the office."

One employer stated that as most of the representatives elected by the employees were women there was more time devoted to "petty squabbling" than to matters of importance, and this reached such an extent that the "Industrial Democracy" type of Council in that plant was abandoned after eighteen months' operation. The manager of the plant wrote:

"Personal matters seemed to have decided preference over all important issues that were brought up. The representatives failed to take hold of any of the important matters. Our experience in this matter has proven to us conclusively that the plan cannot be a success where majority of representatives are women. That is the reason we dropped it."

Another company reported that the "Industrial Democracy" plan as introduced in its plant was impractical—"it was too complicated and took up too much time." The treasurer of the company stated that this was not to be considered as a condemnation of the plan itself, but merely that it was found inapplicable to that particular concern.

The reason most commonly given by employers for the discontinuance of plans of the "committee" type, was the opposition of the labor unions or the attempts of the more radical element to utilize the Works Council for their own ends.[1]

A western packing concern employing five hundred workers said that the "violent opposition of the union element in our organization" had led to the abandonment of its plan.

It is to be noted that the company had dealt for over two years with a committee which was appointed by the local trade union and which was called into being only when the employees had something to discuss with the management. This committee, according to the secretary of the firm, had functioned satisfactorily "until the organization became controlled by radicals."

Election of representatives to the Works Council, which it was proposed should take the place of the union committee, was held, the representatives met and adopted by-laws and methods of procedure, but no further progress was made.

[1]An interesting account of the failure of a Works Council due to the opposition of organized labor is given by O. F. Carpenter in *Industrial Management*, January, 1921, in an article entitled "A Shop Committee that Failed."

> "Because of the fact that half of our plant was unionized and they positively prohibited any of their members from participating, it was impractical to try a Works Council, so we abandoned it."

It is the intention of the company to start the plan in the future, however. As the trade union element in the plant walked out in January, 1921, rather than accept a wage reduction, and as there are at present no union men employed, the correspondent stated, "we hope the plan will be more favorably received and given an opportunity to operate." The attitude of the company towards employee representation is expressed as follows:

> "We believe in collective bargaining, in employee representation, but we do not believe in outside dictation. We want to deal with our own employees, not with delegates who have nothing in common with our employees or local business interest."

Early in 1919 a middle western company employing five thousand workers introduced Works Councils into each of its four plants. Shortly after the introduction of the Councils a strike occurred in the two largest shops, and practically all of the employees quit at the call of the national trade union. The plan of employee representation continued in force in the two smaller plants, but was dropped in the other larger shops until the company was able to establish a stable force and learn more about the character and ability of its new employees.

After fourteen months, during which time past experiences had been carefully weighed, the management called a conference of foremen and employees' representatives for the purpose of drawing up new plans. The result was that a simplified plan of Works Council was decided upon. It was the general feeling of this conference that the simplified plan would be productive of good results, although but 50% of the employees were ready to approve of it. The remaining 50% were either indifferent, preferred the trade union, or did not understand the plan.

Writing in April, 1921, the president of the company reported that the employee representation plan

> "... was abandoned because of the opposition of the unions and radical agitators. There seems to be a tendency on the part of existing unions to discourage movements of this kind, because they interfere with the organization of unions."

This correspondent was of the opinion that a plan of representation would be successful "in almost every case" if there were no interference from the labor unions, but "because of this interference the chances of success are about one in one hundred—perhaps less than that." In order that "employee representation plans may succeed at all, conditions must be quite favorable."

The same opinion was expressed by the president of an eastern machinery company. A Works Council was established

30

in this plant in 1915 and, although "regular weekly meetings were held for about a year," the general result was that

"... not only the Works Council but all the employees more or less...became very independent with their employers' time and money.... Under the influence of radical labor agitators sent into the factory from outside to cause dissension, the Works Council fell into disuse, although the management kept in close touch with its help, giving them uniformly fair treatment."

With reference to the effect which the opposition of the union element has upon a plan of employee representation, this employer wrote that he did not believe

"... that any committee can withstand determined opposition from labor unions who will put in their workers and destroy the morale."

In a small eastern plant where the labor union employees were given proportional representation on the employees' committee,

"... the union end of the committee and the few union employees were continually endeavoring to introduce propaganda and friction in favor of the union, and, in our judgment, against the general interests of all of the employees."

After the committee and the management had arrived at an agreement regarding certain disputed matters, the union employees refused to adhere to the agreement and insisted that a new agreement be drawn up with the officers of the union. This the company refused to do.

After this experience with a shop committee the company stated:

"... we would recommend an employees' committee elected once each year by all of the employees, without any regard to outside influences, and with a specific schedule of what the functions of the committee were to be—what matters they were to consider and the result of their finding to be submitted to the general manager in writing; the committee, at all times to be representative of all the employees and subject to recall by the employees, and to at all times have the privilege of personal contact with the general manager."

A western company employing 550 employees, of whom only a very small proportion were union men, reported that the activities of the radical element and the efforts of that element to use the Works Council as a means of securing recognition of the trade union, led to a strike. The secretary of the company wrote:

"For some time prior to the installation of the representation plan, we had in our employ a few agitators. We always were an open shop and never gave very much encouragement to union labor, as the majority of our employees were not in favor of union organizations. We felt that through the use of the representation plan we might discourage labor agitators, but it seems that after the plan had been presented and accepted by the employees, they were successful in electing as representatives, a few of the agitators.

"Through the assistance of the plan they were in a position to get together, hold meetings, always misrepresenting the company's side of the argument, and eventually secured the following of enough men to form a labor organization. Certain demands were made of the company, through the committee, such as, requesting the company to recognize the union, wage increases, and other demands which we could not see fit to accept. Consequently, they ignored the employees' representation plan and made demands on the company as a union.

"These demands were rejected, and in turn, the men called a strike. We were successful in defeating their objects after a period of about four months, and we are now running the same as before, as an open shop."

The same correspondent stated the company did not contemplate re-establishing the plan at the time of writing (August, 1921), but that "should we at any time discover a plan that will fit into our organization," it would be given proper consideration.

In "A Works Council Manual," Research Report Number 26 of the Conference Board, it was stated:

"Experience indicates that unless a Works Council comes to participate in the adjustment of terms and conditions of employment, such as wages and hours of work, it will not possess vitality. As matters intimately concerning the employees, these must necessarily form a major subject of consideration in dealings between the representatives of management and men."[1]

The experience of a middle western plant employing two thousand workers with its Council of the committee type is a concrete illustration of the above.

At the time of the formation of the Council in January, 1919, questions of wages and hours were explicitly excluded from the consideration of the single joint committee formed under the plan, its activities being restricted to matters such as accident prevention, factory sanitation, exchange of suggestions and welfare work. In April, 1919, one of the company officials wrote regarding the effect the plan had upon the employees:

"It occupies their time and keeps them from thinking of other things to a great extent."

Writing in April, 1921, another official of the same plant stated:

"There are so many extremely important variables in the problem of safely operating a manufacturing enterprise, that we consider it quite unwise to allow any committee of employees to legislate as to hours of work, classification of men, wages, seniority rights, or promotion or shop discipline. With these eliminated, the interest of shop committees as ordinarily composed is apt to lag, and that was really our experience, as the members of the committee were not able to produce subjects of sufficient interest to warrant the continuance of the committee."

Only one firm reported that it had found it necessary to discontinue its Council because of the inability of the plan to function during a period of readjustment. This was a middle western rubber company employing eight hundred workers, none of whom are members of trades unions. The "Industrial Council" in this plant was constituted as follows:

[1] p. 3.

A Factory Council consisting of one member from each department, who in turn reported to the Executive Council, made up of three employees representing the factory, one employee representing the foremen, and two executives, the factory manager and the vice-president of the company. Problems which could not be decided by the Factory Council were taken to the Executive Council for their final decision.

The secretary of the company wrote:

> "We found this worked out very satisfactorily up to the time when the reconstruction period started. It was necessary for us, at that time, to discontinue this Council in order to bring wages back to a reasonable basis. Therefore the Council is not working at the present time, as labor is very plentiful at very low rates."

It was further stated that

> "... the readjustment period in the rubber game needed quick action. This could not be obtained through the Council; we therefore advised the Council that it would be abandoned until such a time as conditions warranted it being reorganized. This was met with approval throughout the plant."

The reasons for the abandonment of Works Councils which were originally introduced into plants by employers vary considerably. Union opposition to the plans, lack of support by management, and failure to provide the committees with work of vital interest to the employees, are among the influences that have resulted in the failure of the plans to function satisfactorily. In other cases, however, the plans have been abandoned only temporarily, due to a reduction in working force which has rendered the present operation of the committees impracticable.

PART II

Works Councils in Operation

An account of the experience which employers have had with Works Councils now in operation, is presented in the following chapters. In this connection it is interesting to note that with very few exceptions the employee representation plans functioning at the present time, were voluntarily instituted by employers. According to the Conference Board's first report on the subject of Works Councils, which dealt with 225 employee representation plans, eighty-six of these were National War Labor Board Committees; thirty-one were Shipbuilding Labor Adjustment Board Committees; three were "Government Committees"; 105 were voluntarily instituted by employers. As has already been shown, nearly all of the "shop committees" of the National War Labor Board have been abandoned, as have the larger number of the committee plans instituted by the Shipbuilding Labor Adjustment Board. This gives added significance to the number of employee representation plans— approximately 725—in existence in the United States today. It is evident that while the Works Council movement has not attained national proportions, it is receiving favorable consideration by an increasingly large number of American employers in all parts of the country.

The most noteworthy instances of the recent adoption of this method of handling industrial relations are afforded by the Pennsylvania Railroad and the leading concerns in the meat packing industry. Approval of the "industrial representation idea" was recently expressed by the National Association of Manufacturers.[1]

[1] National Association of Manufacturers. Twenty-sixth Annual Convention, New York, May, 1921. p. 21.

CHAPTER III

CHANGES MADE IN WORKS COUNCIL PLANS

The variations in Works Councils with respect to their "form, constitution, procedure, elections, meetings and various other specific features of organization" were fully described in a previous report by the National Industrial Conference Board.[1]

In general it may be said that there is little evidence that fundamental changes have been made since then, either in the manner in which Works Councils are constituted or in the manner in which they function. The greater number of changes made by employers are of the nature of minor improvements in the operating details of the plans found through practical experience to be advisable. Just as the conditions within different plants vary in so many ways, the changes made to better fit the Councils to the plant organizations must also vary. The changes outlined below are not to be taken as indicative of the attitude of employers in general toward such modifications; they are merely those changes that some employers have found it advantageous to make in order to secure a more efficient operation of their representation plans.

The nature of the changes which have been made in the great majority of Council plans is indicated in the following statements which came from two different companies:

> "We still operate along the lines originally laid down—although of course, we are constantly profiting by our experience and changing our operating details."

> "The plan is still operating along the original lines laid down but, of course, small changes have been made, in order to make the representation more uniform, and to straighten out small kinks which existed in the original plan."

INCREASE IN POWER OF COMMITTEES

Several firms have made changes in their Works Councils that are of considerable interest as showing a gradual increase of the power and responsibility of the employees.

In some cases representation plans have developed from a single committee which devoted itself to the consideration of one or more aspects of shop conditions. In the beginning this committee may have been composed of employees appointed by the foremen, election of employee representatives coming into effect at a later date.

This was the manner in which the Council of an eastern paper mill was developed. From a simple and informal begin-

[1] "Works Councils in the United States." Research Report No. 21. Boston, October, 1919, pp. 19-56.

ning, the committees have developed into an eminently satis-factory organization. The Council, installed in 1919, is even now only a "limited" plan, but its scope has so increased that it might almost be classed with plans of the "committee" type. The employer is entirely satisfied with the development of the scheme. To his mind, its working out has justified the manner of its introduction and the form of its organization. In his own words:

> "We are still of the same opinion we had when we started out with our committee, that the way to institute such a proposition is to begin with a very informal plan, especially in small mills like our own, and then allow the plan to become more formally organized as time goes on and the employees become entirely familiar with such matters."

The first committee was composed of men appointed by foremen and it concerned itself entirely with inspection of safety measures. Later the members of the committee were chosen by secret ballot, one from each department of the mill. At the same time the scope of its activities was broadened to include all matters of mutual interest. The Board's correspon-dent stated:

> "We are now using the committee for the dissemination of such information as the details of the reduced wage scale, which goes into effect May 1, (1921) and the service differential which is being estab-lished at the same time, and we feel that the idea has been very well accepted, that the committee is available for use in the submission of any questions whatever which are interesting to the employees.
> "We encourage suggestions, the airing of any grievances which cannot be settled by merely speaking to the foremen, and constructive criticisms."

It is his opinion that the limit placed upon the power of the Council is in line with the sentiment of the employees:

> "The Committee has no power of final decision or execution on any matter—being merely a body for suggestions, and we see no reason for granting any further power to them along these lines. In fact, we do not think that they desire it."

The company was "entirely satisfied" with the progress that had been made and the way the plan had worked out.

In an eastern clothing factory where a Council of the "com-mittee" type has been operating since 1918, the employer's opinion was in agreement with the one just quoted—that committees at the time of installation should be organized as simply as possible.

As originally laid out, the plan provided for departmental committees only, each one responsible for its own department. In the beginning "no special plans were made except to give the committees authority as they seemed fit to use it."

Reports within the past three months show that the plan has been considerably elaborated. In addition to the original departmental committees, a central committee, "represent-ing the body of the factory employees," has been organized.

This central committee has been given power beyond that granted the departmental committee:

> "The authority of the central committee shall be in the same province as that of the departmental committees, but the central committee shall have authority to review the decisions of the departmental committees and to recommend changes, on request of a chairman of a committee or on request of an individual through his departmental committee."

According to the Board's correspondent in this plant, the work of the various committees had been "very satisfactory." It was stated that the scope of the committees would be extended "in accordance with their ability to take responsibility." In introducing a plan of employee representation it was thought wise not to hamper the committees by many rules in the beginning.

The vice-president of a southern cotton mill expressed a similar opinion concerning the degree of responsibility which should be given the employees under a plan of representation. This official while considering that employee representation is ". . . basically right and fundamentally constructive, reflecting progress in the right direction . . ." stated that:

> "Any plan or system, however, should take into account the capabilities of the people whom it is to affect, their mental status and moral stamina; and privileges granted should be confined to such as in the opinion of competent and unbiased judges the people are qualified to use properly."

Among the changes in Works Councils which have widened their field of jurisdiction, those made in an eastern textile plant are of particular interest. In this concern, which has a scheme of profit-sharing in operation, the Board of Operatives composed of representatives of the employees had, when organized in 1918, only limited and advisory power with reference to matters of mill management. Its chief activities were connected with subjects of recreation and education. It also had full control over a number of company-owned houses. At that time representatives of the management attended the meetings of the Board of Operatives but some time later this was changed so that the employee representatives met alone. At the same time a joint committee of six members was formed, three being appointed by the Board of Operatives and three by the management. This joint body, the Board of Management, hears all complaints and grievances which the Board of Operatives brings before it and in case a majority of its members fails to agree upon any matter, a seventh member is appointed and the decision of the Board so constituted is final. In addition to this representation of the employees on the Board of Management, the Board of Operatives annually appoints one of its members to the Board of Directors of the company. Any employee may attend the meetings of the Board of Operatives.

The activities of the Board of Operatives have been widened from jurisdiction over matters of recreation, education and housing, to include wages, hours of work, and questions of shop discipline, and through the representation of the employees on the Board of Management they are given a direct voice in the management of the plant. This is evident by the fact that when a new manager was put in charge of the plant, he was chosen by the Board of Management. One of the officials of the company wrote regarding the effect which the above changes had upon the method in which the plan functioned:

". . . our plan began to be taken seriously and began truly to function when we added the more advanced features of the Board of Management and Board of Directors to the Board of Operatives and the profit-sharing."

Particularly interesting are the changes made in the Works Council of the "company union" type of a western shoe company. All the employees of the company belong to a Cooperative Association to which they pay dues. In 1915 the company provided that all employees who had been with the firm for three years should be eligible for membership in the Association. The company agreed that none of the members of the Association should be discharged without the approval and consent of the Board of Directors, the governing body of the Association, which consisted of three executives and five elected employee representatives. The Board of Directors elected from their own number a president, vice-president and secretary and selected from among the members of the Association an "Employees' Agent." The duties of the last mentioned, who attended all meetings of the Board but had no vote in them, were to take up with the Board matters which on investigation he considered required adjustment.

After a year the Association was enlarged to include all who had been with the company for two years. This was later extended to include all who had been in the company's employ one year, and finally all employees were made members of the Association.

At the same time the governing body of the Association was changed from one committee of employee and management representatives to two bodies, a Joint Council composed of four representatives of the company and four of the employees, and a Shop Committee[1] composed entirely of employee representatives.

The Joint Council elects its officers from its own membership as in the case of the original Board of Directors, but the president and vice-president must not be executives. Moreover the secretary and treasurer may be elected outside of the Joint Council.

[1] This is a special use of the term Shop Committee and is not to be confused with the "shop committees" of the National War Labor Board.

38

In addition to receiving complaints, and hearing and trying all grievances submitted to it by the Shop Committee, its approval has to be obtained by the management before any employee can be discharged, although the management may suspend any employee on full pay until the question of his or her discharge is passed on by the Joint Council. In case the members of the Joint Council are equally divided upon any question, that question is "immediately" submitted to a board of arbitration of three persons, one of whom is appointed by each of the two opposing sides, the third to be chosen by these two and to be an entirely disinterested person.

The Shop Committee appoints the four employee representatives on the Joint Council and hears and investigates all complaints of the members of the Association and, if necessary, refers them to the Joint Council. All new employees hired by the company are required to sign an application for membership in the Association. This application has to be approved within three months by the Shop Committee and the management, or the employee is discharged. The chairman of the Shop Committee, who is elected by the members of the Association from a list nominated by the Shop Committee and approved by the Joint Council, may be either a member of the Association or he may be chosen from outside the plant. No member of the management can occupy this office. The position of chairman of the Shop Committee corresponds to that of the "Employees' Agent" of the earlier plan, with the marked differences that he can be chosen from outside the plant, and that when elected from among the employees he does not remain on the company's payroll. He receives no pay from the company direct; the Shop Committee determines what the amount of his remuneration shall be, and this is paid from the funds of the Association. In the case of an employee elected chairman, that remuneration must not be less than the weekly wage he was receiving at the time of his election.

"The chairman is to have access to every part and department of the factory of said company; to be the direct representative of the employees of said company who are members of said association; to make all investigations on behalf of the Shop Committee upon the application for membership to the association; to attend all meetings of the Joint Council; to preside at all meetings of the Shop Committee; to take charge of all welfare work; . . . investigate all complaints and grievances of members of said association or the management of said company; and, after due consideration by the Shop Committee, if by it so determined, to report all grievances and complaints for determination to the Joint Council."

As described in the constitution of the plan, the chairman of the Shop Committee acts as the "business agent" for the members of the Association "in any controversy or request which shall be brought to the Joint Council for determination."

Provision is made in the present plan of this company that secret meetings of all the members of the Association may be

39

held "for the purpose of discussing matters pertaining to the welfare, wages, working conditions, grievances or any other matters connected with the work and employment of the members" of the Association. At these meetings no member of the management may be present and no minutes of the meetings are published.

An official of this plant wrote:

"Our experience with the employee representation plan in our plant the last six years has been thoroughly satisfactory."

According to the president of a middle western canning company with one hundred employees, the object of the company is "to make of its business a real 'Industrial Democracy' that is, an organization in which the employees, through their representatives, shall manage the business."

The history of the development of the Works Council in this company is of interest as showing how the employees made use of the authority given them by the company. The plan of employee representation was started in 1917, and at the same time a profit-sharing plan was set up. At that time

". . . the committee was made up of eight employees from the factory and the four officers of the firm. Majority vote ruled. The president of the company could veto any decision of the committee, but a measure could be passed over his veto by two-thirds vote. He never used his veto power. The committee could discuss anything relating to the business. There was no limit set to its activities. At first, however, it actually dealt only with factory problems."

At the end of 1917 the plan was changed to provide for the formation of two bodies—a Council and a Committee. The Council was composed of twelve members—the manager and assistant manager, superintendent, and assistant superintendent, the foremen and forewomen. The other body, called the Committee, was composed entirely of elected employees, twelve in number. The Committee "could discuss anything it wished and make any recommendations to the Council, but during 1918 its functions were purely advisory." The Council, composed of twelve representatives of the management, accomplished many important things during 1918. It reduced and increased the length of the working week several times during the year; it decided upon the hour wage rate, both for men and women; it placed all the employees of more than six months' standing on salary instead of on wage, thereby giving all such employees protection against involuntary unemployment. It classified all salaried employees, except heads of departments, into A, B, C, D for men and the same for women. A certain salary is fixed for each class. During 1918 two advances in the salary rates were made and in 1919 one advance was made. In 1920 another advance was made. Apart from their own salaries and those of the sales force, which are determined by the Board of Directors, the members of the Council decide all salaries. In 1918 and 1919 the Council filled several positions of foremen. In every case, except one, the foremen were advanced from the ranks. At the end of 1918 the Council elected the superintendent.

In 1919 the Council, "although its actual power was increased only a little over that of 1918," was "very much more alive to the problems of the business and handled them with greater firmness and skill."

Toward the end of 1919 the Council discussed the qualifications of each of its members—the general manager, the assistant general manager, the superintendent and assistant superintendent, and each foreman and forewoman.

> "The one under discussion withdrew from the Council chamber while the discussion was in progress. Later he was called back and told of his weaknesses. Time was not wasted by telling him of his strong points.
> "During 1919 the Council appointed an assistant manager.
> "At the end of 1919 the superintendent appointed the year before by the Council was demoted by it and the assistant manager was made superintendent. The former superintendent returned to his position as foreman of the mechanical department. Before his advancement to the superintendency he had been head of that department. He accepted his demotion in good spirit. Since his return to his old department he has done better work than before. The employee who had been foreman of the mechanical department during 1919 became a member of the rank and file as the former superintendent took his place. He, also, took the change in good spirit. Later he was made foreman of the shipping department."

As a last step, the position of general manager was made elective, and in 1920 the Council began to consider the sales problems of the business.

The Committee, composed of twelve elected employees, did not function during 1918 and gradually died. This was because "there were not enough members on it who had sufficient force to make it function." In 1919 another Committee was elected and during that year it accomplished many important things. It was allowed to discuss any problem and its recommendations were passed to the Council for final decision. Members of the Council and Committee received no pay for their services, and all meetings were held after working hours. During 1919 the Committee elected an assistant forewoman. "It made many recommendations for changes of employees from wage to salary and from one class to another. It made recommendations for positions in the office." The correspondent added:

> "It has become our settled policy to recruit all office positions from the factory. By action of the Council all employees work the same number of hours. The office commences and closes when the factory does. Last year we filled the position of bookkeeper with a factory employee. He was sent to school and is now in charge of our books. Our office women have all been workers in our factory and have been sent to school to prepare them for office work."

In conclusion the same correspondent wrote with reference to the plan in operation:

"It will be seen from the above brief outline that the government of the business is now in the hands of our employees. At no time during the last three years have they attempted to abuse their power. In fact they have been far more conservative than the owners. It has been the owners who have urged the employees to take more power."

As illustrating the last statement the following instance was cited:

"Last fall (1919) the president of the company and the representative of 95% of the stock, asked the Council to consider an advance in all salaries. He absented himself from the deliberation. The Council voted against an advance at the time because 'the outlook for the year was not good'."

Nothing regarding the company's business is concealed from the employees.

"The Council and likewise the Committee are informed by the president from period to period of the condition of the business and the outlook. Nothing is concealed at any time. Each employee knows the salary that all others are getting. At the end of the year, at our annual dinner, salaried employees are informed in detail of the affairs of the Company. At that dinner any matter may be discussed by the entire body."

Recently it was decided to let not more than five members of the rank and file attend Council meetings. The Committee took the same action with respect to its meetings. This was done to enable the rank and file to hear the discussions preceding the decisions of both governing bodies. A short time ago the Committee was merged with the Council, the body thus formed being called the Council. Membership in the Council at the present time is open to any regular employee who attends eight consecutive meetings. Any member of the Council who misses two meetings in succession is now dropped from the Council unless he has a very good reason for his absence.

As yet only three employees have availed themselves of the privilege of becoming members of the Council. The president of the company said:

"I am sorry that more members of the rank and file do not attend but I think it would be too much to expect, perhaps, that a large percentage of the laboring people in any business organization would attend meetings which call for as much sacrifice of time and as much brain work as our meetings call for."

The effect of this method of industrial government upon the efficiency of the plant was described by the Board's informant as follows:

"In spite of a steadily increasing wage and salary rate our unit cost of production has not increased at all. In 1919, due to the action of the government in throwing a great quantity of canned goods on the market, the canned goods trade was demoralized and our sales were much less than they had been the year before. In spite of the smaller output and the higher scale of salaries our unit cost of labor was less than in 1918."

With reference to the relations between employees and management this correspondent wrote:

> "We know that the effects, both on the spirit and on the efficiency of most of the employees, has been very helpful. We are convinced that ill will has almost disappeared and that in its place have come courage, confidence and intelligence."

Stating that the Council is not used now "for the purpose of settling grievances" but as a managerial body which "discusses almost entirely matters pertaining to the welfare of the firm," the president of the company wrote:

> "It is now clearly known to almost all members of the Council that the welfare of the employees is dependent upon the welfare of the firm."

SEPARATE MEETINGS OF EMPLOYEES' REPRESENTATIVES

In some instances changes have been made in Works Council plans whereby employee representatives have been allowed to meet separately from those of the management. Two cases have been referred to already.[1]

In the case of one firm, an eastern textile company employing six hundred workers, the original plan provided for a Plant Council composed of employee and management representatives. No separate meetings of the employee representatives were allowed, and at the joint meetings voting was done by roll call. At the end of eighteen months' operation of the plan, the management suggested that the Plant Council be divided into two bodies, a Mill Council composed of employee representatives, and a Management Council consisting of representatives of the management; and that these bodies meet separately and vote by secret ballot. Provision was also made for a joint meeting of both Councils when advisable. The object of the management in providing for separate meetings of the employee representatives, was to give them an opportunity to discuss freely and frankly among themselves all matters considered by them.

The correspondent of the Board in this plant was convinced that the change had been beneficial. Speaking after four months' experience with the new method of holding the meetings, he said:

> "Previously we had to keep 'feeding' things to the employee representatives for them to do. They didn't seem to have any initiative in bringing up matters before the Council. Now the procedure is reversed. They take much more interest in the plan and I believe will not misuse the responsibility we have placed upon them."

Employee representatives interviewed in this plant were unanimous in their approval of the change, whereby they met by themselves. The chairman of the employee representatives' body said:

See pp. 37, 39.

43

"We can talk out in meeting now. There is no one there but ourselves and you don't need to be afraid that something you say will be misunderstood or used against you. It has made a big difference in what the employees think of the plan. Before it wasn't thought much of, but now they are taking a real interest in it."

At the request of the employees in a middle western lumber company, the "committee" type of Works Council, after being in operation for over a year, was changed to a plan of the "Industrial Democracy" type. Originally two plants of the company elected representatives to the one Works Council, but with the closing of one plant the personnel of the Council suffered considerable change and the employees rather lost interest in the plan. In order to renew their interest, the company thought it well to change the plan according to the following description:

"Committees were appointed from the plant itself, and it was practically left to the employees to decide whether or not to continue some sort of a plan and if so, what sort. We are glad to state that the committee, composed entirely of employees, felt that the whole general plan had been a good one and that they would rather continue it than to drop it, but they felt that perhaps a change would be better."

In connection with the previous Works Council, a foremen's club had met monthly for several years.

"Under the new plan this foremen's club will operate as the Senate, and one representative for each fifty employees will be elected from the employees to form the House of Representatives, with the Board of Directors as the Cabinet."

At the time of the nominations the management stated that "there is much interest in the election and a good bunch of delegates will be elected."

These instances are not to be taken as indicating a general tendency on the part of employers with Works Councils of the "committee" type to make changes in their plans to provide for separate meetings of the employee representatives. Opportunity may be given the employee representatives to withdraw temporarily from a joint meeting to discuss in private some matter which has been under discussion in the joint committee, but by far the greater majority of plans of this type provide for joint meetings only.

In this connection it was the experience of a large concern manufacturing electrical appliances, that after the employee representatives had received permission to hold a meeting apart from the representatives of the management, "so little of interest developed that there seemed to be no desire to hold another."

The president of the company stated that the holding of such meetings was "at variance with the fundamental principles of our plan—that of joint conference."

44

"From time to time we have broached the subject to the Executive Committee, more as a matter of policy to impress them with the fact that we really have no objection to such meetings if there is a demand for them. We have, however, rather encouraged the elected members of the departmental committees to hold informal meetings during the lunch period for the purpose of discussing among themselves matters of a departmental nature."

SIMPLIFICATION OF WORKS COUNCILS OF THE "INDUSTRIAL DEMOCRACY" TYPE

The changes made as described above in the Works Councils of the "committee" type, are not to be taken as indicative of the general attitude of employers with such Councils toward these changes. Neither are the following changes, made in plans of the "Industrial Democracy" type, to be regarded as reflecting the attitude of the majority of employers with Works Councils of that type. Where one firm finds that the creation of separate bodies representative of management and employees improves the effectiveness of its Council, another firm finds that the combination of the two bodies into one, or the elimination of the Senate composed of the foremen of the plant, works more effectively than the maintenance of the separate bodies.

Thus an eastern concern with Works Councils in five plants, employing in the smallest plant seventy-five, and in the largest, two hundred employees, is changing its "Industrial Democracy" plan so that instead of having a Senate composed of foremen appointed by the management, and a House of Representatives composed of elected employee representatives, there will be but one body, one-half of which will be elected from the workers and the other half will be foremen appointed by the management. Under the present arrangement a great deal of time is taken up in putting a "bill" through the two bodies. It is felt that this will be remedied by the creation of the one joint body.

As the first step in effecting this change there has been formed an Executive or Congressional Committee

". . . made up of members of the House of Representatives, members of the Senate and one representative from owner or management. This change is in order that certain matters may have immediate attention and that many matters of a minor nature may be settled outside of the legislative meetings, the House of Representatives and Senate simply receiving a report of the Executive Committee for approval, these bodies passing on the basic principle rather than on the detail of individual cases. These changes are planned because of the delay entailed frequently in the past on matters which ought to have immediate attention and which eventually the House of Representatives agree to, and also because frequently matters of very minor importance are considered exhaustively by the House of Representatives, not only at one meeting but at many."

Other instances were reported of the elimination of the Senate from "Industrial Democracy" plans. A middle western

45

plant after three years' operation of a Works Council—a modified plan of the "Industrial Democracy" type—also eliminated
its "Senate." It was felt that it was necessary to eliminate
"some of the machinery" in the operation of the plan, and the
Senate was accordingly abandoned. It was stated that under
the new system the business of the Council had been expedited.

A similar reason was given by a middle western clothing
company for the elimination of the "Senate" from its Works
Council plan of the "Industrial Democracy" type. "For more
expeditious work," the functions of the Senate were eliminated,
the management now acting through a Planning Board composed of representatives of each of the major divisions of the
plant.

A further change made in the plan of this company placed
in the hands of a committee composed entirely of employees the
final decision as to whether management could discharge
an employee. The plan originally provided for a Board of
Review made up of two members of the House of Representatives and two appointed by the management, with an additional
member who acted as Chairman and was chosen by the others.
The duties of this Board were to consider all cases of discharge
which employees referred to it. Any employee who felt that
he had been unjustly discharged could appeal to the Board,
whose decision was final as to whether the employee should be
reinstated. Where it was proven that "a rule affecting the
standards of discipline or standards of production of the working force has been violated" the Board could not reinstate the
applicant, nor could it do so where the employee applying
for reinstatement had resigned from the company or "had been
dishonest."

At the present time the duties of the Board of Review have
been taken over by the Betterment Committee, which is made
up entirely of representatives of the employees—one representative from each floor of the plant. This was done at the suggestion of the House of Representatives. The procedure regarding dismissals has been reversed and now, instead of being
reviewed after the employee has been discharged, the case is
reviewed before final action is taken. The decision of the
Betterment Committee is taken as final. The reason for this
change, whereby a committee of employees is allowed to decide
as to whether employees should be discharged, was given by a
company official as follows:

"The House of Representatives considered it necessary if the union
who dominated the market outside of our house was to have some
respect for our organization, and was to believe in its validity, that
no one should be discharged without their having some voice in the
matter, particularly in a case where employees might be discharged
for activities to disrupt the organization. They felt that if the discharge would come from their own body rather than from the manage-

46

ment it would help to give their inter-organization the prestige that it deserved."

As to the experience of the company with this method of allowing a committee of employees to decide who should be discharged, the same correspondent wrote:

- "The employees did override the judgment of the management in at least one case—a young factory worker charged with indifference to his work. He was reinstated with back pay and put on trial. He lasted only a few weeks when he was again up for a hearing and discharged with the cooperation of the Betterment Committee.

"This committee has always taken this responsibility seriously and acted fairly upon the facts presented by the management in cases of contemplated dismissals or lay offs."

A southern textile mill whose plan of "Industrial Democracy" was established in October, 1919, outlined several changes which it felt would improve the effectiveness of the plan. These changes have not as yet been made, the company merely stating that it favored a modification of its plan along the following lines. The present House of Representatives is composed of twenty-five members, one representative to each thirty employees or majority thereof. The company considers that an increase in the number of constituents per representative, resulting in an attendant reduction in the size of the House, would be of value for the following reasons:

"1. It is difficult to obtain one really capable man out of every thirty workmen.

"2. By raising the number of constituents you place greater responsibility upon the representative. This would result in increasing the workman's respect for the office and would tend, further, to engender a higher sense of duty in the incumbent.

"3. By reducing the number of representatives the body is made less cumbersome, and business can be handled with greater dispatch. The greater the number of representatives, the more likelihood of dwelling at undue length upon comparatively inconsequential matters. Concomitantly, also, the proclivity on the part of some to indulge in useless tirades is encouraged by the sense of security which is always found in numbers. This, of course, is purely incidental and is not indicative of inherent fault in the system, but the cogency of the first two considerations mentioned in this paragraph is readily apparent."

Another change favored by the company would be one that "would to some extent, democratize the Senate and reduce the membership." This would be done by restricting the appointable membership to six overseers in the plant, and having a like number elected to the Senate by direct vote of the workers. The reasons given for favoring such a change in the personnel of the Senate are:

"1. To expedite the transaction of business by reducing the number of transactors.

"2. To remove the antipathy which exists between the House and the Senate. This, we believe, is due to the fact that one body is composed entirely of 'bosses,' the other solely of operatives. Further, one body is democratic, the other is not.

47

"3. To infuse greater activity into the Senate, which has inclined to lethargy and, in some cases, to reactionary resentment of the system."

A third change desired would be "the appointment of a permanant inter-body Committee on Constitutionality" composed of two members from the House, two from the Senate (one elected member and one appointed), and one member from the Cabinet.

The following are given as the reasons for this proposed change:

"1. Our system is founded upon abstract principles: Justice, Cooperation, Economy, Energy, Service, and the application of these principles—or, rather, the establishment of the relation which these principles bear to practical problems or proposed measures—requires a high order of intelligence. As men of this type are rare, we favor limiting the size of the committee to the number specified; and as proficiency will depend upon study and training, the Committee on Constitutionality should be permanent.

"2. Establishment of conflict, or agreement, with the Constitution should be arrived at through cooperative effort.

"3. When measures are declared at variance with the spirit and intent of the constitution, the responsibility will rest upon all three bodies jointly. Under the present system the entire onus of blame falls upon the body which 'kills' the measure."

These changes are of course favored by the management of this plant because of "our particular local conditions," and it is pointed out that "it might well be that identical changes would not be helpful in other organizations where conditions are certain to be widely different."

That the above changes would not be applicable to all Works Councils of the "Industrial Democracy" type is illustrated by the statement given below of the vice-president of a western company which has Councils of the "Industrial Democracy" type in a number of plants. In the larger of the company's plants the Councils are composed of a Cabinet, Senate and House of Representatives. In smaller plants a single body composed of foremen and employee representatives comprises the Council, and in other plants employing only a small number of workers, mass meetings of the employees constitute the only organized means of contact between management and men.

"We find the plan works better in the larger plants, where we have the full machinery. In the plants where we have just the one body, corresponding possibly to a shop committee, if there is a mixture of foremen and employees, we do not obtain the freedom of discussion we like and if the committee is made up entirely of employees without foremen, we do not have the cooperation of the foremen that we should have. In the plants where we operate entirely through the mass meetings, we get the poorest results of all, because of the hesitancy of the employees to discuss matters and take responsibility."

The following changes made in Works Council plans are those which experience with the operation of the plans has shown

48

to be advisable. They are not to be considered as being applicable in all concerns, as they have had their origin in conditions peculiar to the plants in which the plans were working.

Assistant Foremen Allowed to Vote for and Be Elected as Employee Representatives

In an eastern textile plant employing five hundred workers, a recent amendment to the constitution governing the Works Council provided that assistant foremen and second hands could vote for and be elected as employee representatives. This was done

> ". . . in recognition of the conclusion that their viewpoints and interests were those of the men in most of the matters which came before the mill council, such as wages, hours, working conditions and so forth . . . . Under the former rules these selected and efficient workers were not adequately represented in the management group of representatives and had no representation in the employees' group, and it is hoped that the change with regard to them will correct this condition satisfactorily."

At the first election after this amendment was made two of the sixteen representatives chosen by the employees held positions as assistants to the foremen of the departments in which they were employed. The change has not been in effect long enough to enable the management to state the results.

Deputy Representatives

Two companies reported that the constitution of their plans had been changed to permit the election by the employees, or the appointment by the duly elected departmental representatives, of deputy representatives in order to assist the employee representatives in their duties and at the same time to enlarge the circle of men who come into direct contact with the Works Council and learn more of its operation. In the case of a company with twenty-four Works Councils in operation, it was provided:

> ". . . [that] the qualifications of deputy representatives shall be the same as those of employee representatives, and the terms of office of deputy representatives shall be the same as those of employee representatives, and shall not extend beyond the terms of their respective representatives."

In this company the deputy representative may, subject to the approval of Works Council, be designated by the employee representative, or the Works Council may provide for a special election for this purpose. The same guaranty of independence of action is given the deputy representatives as the employee representatives, and their selection is revocable either upon a petition of a majority of the employees' group which they represent, upon recommendation of the employee representative if approved by the Works Council, or upon recommendation of the Works Council. Under the plan of this company

> ". . . the duties of deputy representatives shall be to assist their representative in carrying out the purposes of this plan, as directed by such representative or the Works Council; they may attend meetings of the Works Council and participate in its discussions only with the consent of the Works Council and their representative, and shall have one vote only in the absence of such representative and then only with the consent of the Works Council."

Another western firm with Works Councils in four plants wrote that, although operating along the lines originally laid down,

> ". . . we are finding that the informational value of the Council is greater than the legislative. We have found . . . that at least 90% of men desire to act rightly if they know the truth. The elected representative has great trouble, and, in fact, finds himself up against an impossible proposition in getting across to his constituents with the balanced argument as he has heard it in a meeting of the Council. Therefore, we are enlarging the size of our Council by urging councilmen to bring into the meetings deputy representatives, thus enlarging the circle of men who are on the inside and who, therefore, when an important decision emerges from a Council, are more receptive to the measure."

Formation of Small Joint Committees

Under the original constitution of the Works Council in a large eastern concern a committee of twelve members chosen by the employee representatives from their number met with an equal number of management representatives as a conference committee.

> "It was found after a trial that the size of this committee made it difficult to accomplish results. The plan was then evolved of appointing small conference committees to deal with various subjects, these committees to be composed of an equal number of members of the works committee and of the management, and never to exceed six members."

This has been found to be a much more satisfactory way of transacting the business that comes before the Council.

Addition of a "Committee of Adjustment"

In the first six months of 1920 such a large number of requests involving wage increases were brought before the Works Council of the "committee" type in an eastern plant that

> ". . . it was soon realized that the Council had not provided the necessary machinery or procedure to deal with these matters. Hence it provided for the appointment of a Committee of Adjustment. All matters of a controversial character have since been referred to this committee for adjustment."

Absorption of Employees' Organizations by a Works Council

At the time of the formation of the Works Council of the "committee" type in an eastern concern employing 500 workers, the athletic activities and the Employees' Beneficial Association were controlled by separate organizations of employees. After the Works Council was formed, it was given control of these organizations, and the solvency of the Beneficial Association was guaranteed by the firm. The Board's correspondent wrote:

"This change in management has proven satisfactory and beneficial to all parties concerned. Through the change we have been able to divert funds formerly claimed by the Athletic Association to the Beneficial Association for use in paying substantial sick and death benefits at a very low cost to the employee. In connection with this change we want to mention an interesting fact. There was apparently a great demand on the part of our employees for a baseball team to compete in a local industrial league. Since the Industrial Committee has taken over the management of athletics we have discovered that the demand for baseball was really confined to very few interested parties and that the majority of our better men were not interested in the firm having a baseball team, in fact, they rather opposed it because of the present day tendency to commercialize this particular form of sport. About one-half of the people attending the ball games did so because of a feeling of loyalty by the men towards the firm."

REGULAR MEETINGS

In a previous report of the National Industrial Conference Board it was stated:

"A Works Council which meets regularly tends ordinarily to do more constructive work than one which meets only upon special occasion. Regular meetings furnish constant opportunities for the interchange of ideas and experiences between employees and management."[1]

A concrete illustration of the above is found in an eastern concern with a working staff of 550 employees. Under the Works Council plan instituted in this company in 1919, "committee meetings were held irregularly, being called only when occasion demanded it." This system was in effect for a period of five months, when a change was made calling for a meeting of the Plant Committee once every two weeks, and for a meeting of each Group Committee every six weeks. Provision was also made for the calling of a special meeting at any time. Writing in April, 1921, one of the company officials stated that in his opinion

"whatever plan may be adopted will fail unless kept alive by holding regular meetings at the instance of the employees' representatives or by the regular plant schedule adopted by the general committee."

ELIMINATION OF "COLLECTIVE ECONOMY DIVIDEND"

The "Collective Economy Dividend" feature of certain Works Councils of the "Industrial Democracy" type is described by Mr. John Leitch in his book, "Man to Man," as follows:[2]

"I take the cost of a unit of production in the period preceding the introduction of Industrial Democracy and compare that cost with the results after democracy has gone into effect. If there is a saving, then one-half that aggregate saving is the amount of the economy dividend for the period and is paid to the men as an added percentage to wages."

[1]"A Works Council Manual." Research Report No. 26, New York, February, 1920. p. 14.
[2]p. 165.

Information was received by the Conference Board of two instances in which the economy dividend feature was abandoned by employers because they regarded it as unsatisfactory. One correspondent in a middle western clothing plant, with a Council of the "Industrial Democracy" type, wrote:

"In regard to the 'Collective Economy Dividend,' we might say that some six years ago we attempted to work it for about six months, without success. We found that it did not give us the control of the production, nor the amount of production that we desired."

A company official in an eastern shoe concern said that the economy dividend plan had been abandoned for the following reason:

"Under the plan, while one department may show a saving during a certain period, it would be wiped out by some other department. Naturally the employees in whose department the saving was made, did not relish the idea of being made to suffer on account of some other department falling behind."

These experiences are not to be taken as an evidence that employers in general who have Works Councils of the "Industrial Democracy" type have found the "Collective Economy Dividend" feature of their plan unsatisfactory. On the contrary many employers wrote the Conference Board of having distributed dividends ranging from 3% to 14% of the monthly payroll. Emphasis was placed upon the dividend plan as an incentive to the employees to increase the productive efficiency of plants.[1]

The majority of the changes made in Works Council plans are seen to be minor improvements in the operating details of the plans. They present such a wide diversity because of the great difference in the conditions existing within different plants. Each plan has to be adapted to the circumstances within the plant in which it is operating. The original plan must be so drawn up that it may be easily changed, for no plan, however well thought out at the time of its installation, can make provision for all contingencies.

Another type of change made in Works Councils is that which grants the employees a gradually increasing amount of authority and control in management. The cases cited show that where this has been done employees have not misused their authority but have seen more clearly than before the mutuality of their interests and those of their employers, with the result that they have given loyal cooperation.

[1]See pp. 75-75.

CHAPTER IV

DISPOSAL OF EMPLOYEES' COMPLAINTS AND GRIEVANCES

"Are the works committees used by the employees principally in airing their grievances, or do the employees through the committees make contributions from their practical knowledge and experience toward increasing productive efficiency and personal contentment?"

This was one of the questions which the Conference Board asked of employers, in order to learn of their experience with employee representation plans. Distinction was drawn between the airing of grievances and the contributions made by employees from their knowledge and experience toward increasing productive efficiency, in that they represent different attitudes on the part of the employees. The airing of grievances springs from a desire on the part of the employees to secure something for their own advantage alone. Contributions which they make toward increasing the productive efficiency of a plant may be said to spring, on the other hand, from a realization that it is to the mutual interest of themselves and their employer that the industry should be run as economically and efficiently as possible.

This is not to belittle the importance of that aspect of a Works Council whereby employees are given the opportunity to obtain a hearing and secure a decision in any case in which they think they are being unjustly treated. It is of paramount importance that there be kept open a channel of communication whereby the employees may present to the management matters requiring adjustment, and the management may learn of the causes of dissatisfaction among the employees. But if management profits by this knowledge and removes the causes of these troubles, and if employees, as a result of the education obtained through the Works Council, gain a deeper insight into the problems of management, there should follow a realization on the part of the employees that it is to their interest as well as to that of the employer that waste and inefficiency be lessened.

The ultimate object of employee representation may be regarded as the achievement of cooperation between management and men—the substitution of cooperation for antagonism. Cooperation cannot be achieved so long as either party regards industry as a battlefield occupied by two opposed camps, between whom there must be continuous warfare. This conception of industry has obtained among both employers and em-

53

ployees in the past because of a lack of understanding of the part that each plays in industry. A Works Council provides an opportunity, through the exchange of ideas and suggestions, for both parties to come to a closer appreciation of their respective problems and functions in industry. Suspicion and distrust can be displaced by mutual confidence and trust.

This is of necessity a matter of education, and involves in some cases a radical readjustment of ideas and attitude on the part of both employer and employee. It is not to be expected that it can be accomplished immediately following the introduction of any plan. The statements of employers furnish evidence, however, that this mutual understanding and confidence can be to some extent accomplished. To do so both parties must be interested supporters of the Works Council plan, and management in particular must be sincere in its support of the Council and must direct the interests of the employees along the proper lines.

The answers received from employers to the question at the beginning of this chapter were as varied as the plants from which they came. The majority of employers stated that the employees used the plan both for airing their grievances and for making contributions toward increasing productive efficiency. Others said that the plan had been used only as a means for the presentation of grievances and complaints. It was the experience of some that while this was the case when the plan was initiated, conditions had gradually changed, and as the causes of the grievances and complaints were removed, there was an encouraging response from the employees as regards the interest they took in the economical operation of the plant. The settlement of a grievance or a complaint formed a precedent for the consideration of other cases of a similar nature. A code of decisions on such matters was built up which was accessible to the employee representatives, and through their knowledge of the decisions rendered in previous cases they were very often able to dispose of complaints of the employees before they reached the works committees. Many employers reported that the majority of matters calling for adjustment which affected the individual employee, were settled informally between the foreman and the employee either with or without the assistance of an employee representative. In this way the works committees were left to discuss matters of a constructive nature concerning the employees as a whole, rather than individual complaints and grievances.

Statements of employers, of which the following are examples, show that whereas employees were inclined to use the Works Councils at the time of their initiation principally for airing their grievances, after the plans had been in operation for some time the airing of grievances gave place to a utilization of the Councils for the consideration of questions of efficiency and economy.

An official of a company with five Works Councils of the "committee" type in operation, wrote:

> "The first year this plan was used by the employees principally in airing their grievances, but during the second year a number of practical suggestions were made toward increasing production and improving the quality of the product."

An eastern plant with eight thousand employees reported a lessened attention paid to grievances by the committees:

> "Works committees in the beginning were used principally for airing grievances but now all subjects are discussed, so that increased efficiency and personal contentment has been the result to a marked degree."

The following came from a middle western plant manufacturing agricultural machinery:

> "The subject matter of our discussions with the committee did center about individual grievances such as wages, working conditions, promotions, etc. These cases have gradually lessened in number and importance, giving way to more general topics of discussion, such as layoff policies, promotion policies, and other policies affecting intimately the activities of the workers as a whole."

In an eastern concern manufacturing electrical appliances, the number of cases handled by the works committees had diminished since the introduction of the Works Council of the "committee" type, as follows:

First six months..................................122 cases
Second "   "   60   "
Third "   "   85   "
Fourth "   "   34   "
Fifth "   "   31   "

One of the company officials wrote with reference to the above figures:

> "Of course the number of employees in the plant has diminished within the last two and one-half years, but we feel that the drop in the number of cases is natural following the growth of confidence between management and employees."

It is interesting to note that in this plant, whenever there are no cases of claimed injustice for a Shop Committee,[1] the committee then takes up the following order of business:

1. Completion of unfinished business on docket of previous meeting
2. Output
3. Quality
4. Waste labor and scrap
5. Equipment—machine tools; small tools
6. Safety
7. Sanitation
8. Working conditions
9. Expense
10. Discipline
11. Suggestions for improvement not coming under items 2 to 10.

[1]This is a special use of the term Shop Committee and is not to be confused with the "shop committees" established by the National War Labor Board.

In this way the committee's attention has been directed not only toward the settlement of employees' complaints and grievances, but also toward shop policies and matters of general interest to the employees as a whole.

Other employers reported no such change of attitude on the part of the employees toward the committees.

It is of interest to note that in a number of the cases in which it was reported that there was no appreciable change in this respect, namely, the decreased use of the .committees by the employees for the airing of their grievances, no regular meetings were provided for in the constitutions of the plans. Meetings were held only when the employees or the management wished to bring up some subject for discussion, which usually meant that meetings were held only when employees had a grievance to bring before the management. There was apparently no effort on the part of management to direct the activities of the committees along constructive lines. Their educational value was not realized and as a result they developed into grievance committees.

The experience of one company is referred to in another chapter.[1]

Another eastern concern which introduced its plan of representation "just to be in the fashion,"[2] wrote that during the three years the committees had been in operation they had been used by the employees principally as a means of airing their grievances.

In neither of these plants were regular meetings of the committees held. Management had not sufficient interest in the committees to devote that much time to them. They were called only when the employees wanted something rectified.

In three other plants with plans of the "committee" type under which no regular meetings were provided for, the activity of the committees had drifted in the same direction.

One, an eastern shipbuilding plant, stated that the committees were used by the employees principally in bringing to the attention of the management matters affecting working conditions and wages with which they were not satisfied.

Because the employees' interests were not directed along constructive lines, the works committees in a southern iron company were used by the workers principally for presenting grievances. The vice-president wrote:

> "Practically all grievances which have not been previously settled in a routine manner are aired at these meetings. This seems to be the main function of the committee. The questions of efficiency or increasing production occupy a very small portion of their deliberations, although matters of personal contentment are often discussed."

[1]See pp. 167-168.
[2]See pp. 165-166.

It is interesting to note that the firms referred to were firms in which committees had been originally introduced either by the National War Labor Board or the Shipbuilding Labor Adjustment Board.

Where employees have used the works committees chiefly for the presentation of their complaints, the reason is usually found in the attitude of management toward the employee representation plan. An eastern steel company, for instance, reported that during the two and one-half years that their Works Council had been in operation

" . . . works committees were used mainly for airing employees' grievances and very little has been done in the way of constructive efficiency and relationship."

A visit to this plant shortly after the plan was introduced revealed that not only was the superintendent not in sympathy with the plan, but the employees regarded it with suspicion. This arose from the fact that when the employee representation plan had been introduced by the company the employees had had no voice in its formulation. Although a vote of the employees was taken at the time it was introduced and although the employees voted to accept it, only 50% of them voted.

A more recent visit to this plant revealed that the management was not dealing with the employees through their elected representatives.[1] Employee representatives, when questioned, said that the minor executives in the plant were still unsympathetic toward the plan, and were continually hampering the representatives in their attempts to carry out the provisions of the plan. Where such a condition as this exists it is evident that management, instead of endeavoring to remove the cause of grievances and complaints, is furnishing the employees additional ground for dissatisfaction.

In another eastern steel plant the plan when introduced was accepted by the employees, but by only a very small majority. The results following the introduction of the plan have not been such as to encourage the management to support it. No appreciable effect was noted on the relationship between the employees and the management. The representatives elected were described as "mediocre,"[2] and management expressed an unfavorable opinion on the subject of employee representation.[3] With reference to the use of the works committees by the employees, the superintendent of the company wrote:

"The works committees are used by the employees principally in airing their grievances with a special regard to wages. We have had, however, a few contributions that were practical to the extent of a new hour for the blowing of the whistle, etc."

Although the consideration of grievances in works committees may be taken as the secondary purpose of a plan of

[1]See p. 130.
[2]See p. 129.
[3]See p. 154.

employee representation, the primary purpose being that of enlisting the employees' aid in the economical and efficient operation of an industry following upon a realization of the mutuality of interest existing between them and their employers, this secondary purpose is none the less important. This was pointed out by several employers.

Thus the president of a large company with Councils of the "committee" type in operation in five plants, while stating that the Councils were used chiefly by the employees for presenting their grievances, emphasized the point that this tended to produce personal contentment.

To the same effect was the comment of the vice-president of an eastern silk company with Works Councils of the "Industrial Democracy" type in operation in two plants. The discussion of grievances was described by this executive as having been

> ". . . an extremely helpful thing, because unless grievances are thoroughly aired and discussed, injustices are bound to creep in."

The following was the answer given by a joint committee of employees and management representatives in a large eastern plant, to the question whether employees used the committees principally for setting forth their grievances:

> "Committees are used by the employees to obtain a hearing and decision in cases where they think they are under an injustice and this is a very important part of the plan. They are not used exclusively for this purpose and when there are no cases of claimed injustice for the committee, they have a regular order of business which gives opportunity for any member to bring up any subject connected with the efficiency and working conditions in the departments covered by that committee."

In a review of one year's operation of a Works Council of the "Industrial Democracy" type in a large middle western plant, an officer of the company drew attention to the importance of removing the causes of dissatisfaction among the employees. No matter how insignificant the matter, it should receive immediate and careful attention. This was provided for by the plan of representation.

> "Some people think that the representation plan brings men and management together to discuss only picayune things and that the plan is not worth while. It is my opinion that if men and management are brought together and there is nothing to discuss except picayune things, it shows a very healthy condition in the plant, and as long as only picayune things are brought forth, it is a sign that men and management are working together. Picayune things which are ignored grow into larger things and cause labor trouble."

The same correspondent stated that through the "just and reasonable requests" of the employee representatives "we have been able to keep our fingers on the pulse of conditions in the factory."

Examination of the manner in which grievances and complaints of the employees are dealt with under representation plans shows that the methods adopted for the treatment of such matters tend to diminish the number of such cases.

It has been the experience of several employers that matters regarding which employees may consider they are being treated unjustly, gradually come to be settled between the employees and their foremen either with or without the assistance of the employee representatives. Most plans provide that when an employee wishes to secure action on any subject which he considers requires adjustment, he shall take the question up first with his foreman. If he fails to obtain a satisfactory settlement from the foreman, he then advises his representative, who, before taking the matter up in the works committee, may endeavor to arrive at a satisfactory settlement with the foreman or department head. Only when such procedure fails to settle the matter is it brought before the Works Council. From the following reports of various employers it will be seen that a large percentage of matters calling for adjustment are settled in an informal way between the foreman and the employee bringing up the complaint. The employee representatives may also take part in the discussion and settlement of the case.

In a large manufacturing company with a modified Council of the "Industrial Democracy" type, over 90% of all cases that came up during the first year the plan was in operation were settled thus informally. In this concern about 9% of the cases covering major matters involving an entire department or plant policy, such as the introduction of permanent instead of rotating shifts, were settled without much difficulty by joint conferences in which an equal number of representatives of the men acted with an equal number of representatives of the management. Only one per cent of the disputes came before the Council itself.

During the first year that the Works Council of the "committee" type was in operation in a large eastern company employing ten thousand employees, 85% of the matters brought up by the employees for adjustment, were settled by informal conferences between the foremen and the employees either alone or assisted by their representatives. Ten per cent of the cases were settled at their first trial in joint shop committees composed of equal numbers of employee and management representatives. Failing settlement in the joint shop committees, under this plan, disputes are referred to the head of the department in which the matter arose, whereupon they are again considered by the joint shop committee. Upon a second trial, 1.7% of the cases were settled by joint shop committees. One per cent were settled by the General Joint Committee on Adjustment—a committee to which all cases are referred when no satisfactory decision has been obtained in the joint shop committees. Another 2.3% of the cases were voluntarily withdrawn by the employees at some step in the proceedings, and only one case failed of settlement by the General Joint Committee on Adjustment and was referred to the manager of the plant.

Other companies reported similar experiences. Employee representatives were able to dispose satisfactorily of a great many complaints simply through getting the foreman and the aggrieved employee together and talking things over.

An eastern paper company with Works Councils of the "committee" type in operation in four plants gave as its experience:

"Not all grievances of employees reach a hearing in the Council, not only because many of them are settled informally, but also because councilmen, as they come to see the management side of the question, refuse to bring some matters before the Council because of lack of merit."

During the three years that nine Councils of the "Industrial Democracy" type were in operation in the plants of a middle western corporation, it was found that "nothing but serious grievances get to the attention of the organized bodies." This was because grievances of the employees are "more apt to be settled by their own immediate representatives in their departments."

Of assistance to the employee representatives and the foremen in this informal settlement of disputes which may arise, are the decisions which have been made already by the works committees. These constitute precedents which act as a guide to the employee representatives and the foremen in their handling of individual cases. Consideration of decisions already rendered enables the representatives to settle similar cases without bringing them before the Council, and in this way the works committees are left free to discuss matters of general interest and to devote their time to questions of a constructive nature.

The activities of the Works Council of the "committee" type in a western company have developed in this way. Two general classes of cases have been brought to the attention of the management through the committees. At first, practically all cases concerned individual workmen, but now discussions on general policies relating to wages, hours of work, also economic problems, are the main topics. There is an increasing tendency on the part of the workers and their representatives, to handle individual cases in accord with the precedents established in previous cases of similar nature. As a result the individual cases brought through the committees are exceptional, the desire being to secure rulings or interpretations of the general policy so far as it applies to them. It is believed that a code will eventually be worked out, to be known as "Written Standard Practice for Industrial Relations," as practiced or applied in the

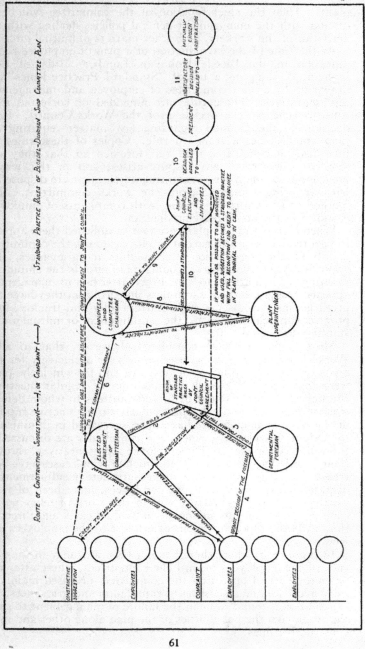

ROUTE OF CONSTRUCTIVE SUGGESTION — — — †, OR COMPLAINT ←——

STANDARD PRACTICE RULES OF BLOEDEL-DONOVAN SHOP COMMITTEE PLAN

plant. Then the chief function of the committee will be to discuss with the management general policies dealing with the activities of the workers, and other matters of mutual interest.

At the time of the introduction of a plan of employee representation in the Bloedel-Donovan Lumber Mills, of Bellingham, Washington, a list of "Standard Practice Rules" was drawn up by a joint committee of employee and management representatives. These rules are amended or corrected from time to time by the decisions of the Works Council. Each decision of the Council regarding any matter requiring adjustment becomes a standard rule. Copies of these rules are furnished all committee men and foremen so that they can refer to them when any dispute arises, and in this way a great many of the matters requiring adjustment are disposed of without being brought before the works committees. The method of procedure for dealing with complaints of employees is shown in the accompanying diagram.

When Works Council plans are first established there appears to be a tendency on the part of employees to use the committees mainly for the presentation of complaints and grievances. The opportunity which a Works Council plan affords the employees to bring such matters to the direct attention of management appeals strongly to them and unless they feel that they have this privilege and can discuss such matters fully and frankly, little progress can be made toward the establishment of mutual understanding and good will.

Most employers have considered, however, that to allow Works Council plans to be used mainly or exclusively for this purpose would be to fail to achieve the end for which the plans were instituted. Through the medium of regular meetings, through the establishment of sub-committees to whom definite work is allocated, and more particularly through active support of the plan, managements have been successful in diminishing the extent to which grievances and complaints are discussed in the works committees. The employee representatives, through their knowledge of the manner in which previous cases have been treated and their ability to make satisfactory adjustment of disputes between foremen and employees, have been of noteworthy assistance to management in this work of relieving the committees of the discussion of individual cases and directing their attention upon questions of interest to the employees as a whole.

In those cases where there has not been a change in the attitude of the employees toward the committees, where after two or more years of operation the committees are used mainly or exclusively for the discussion of complaints and grievances, the explanation is found to lie in the failure of management to show the employees the possibilities of the plan along other and more constructive lines.

CHAPTER V

SUGGESTIONS TOWARD INCREASING PRODUCTIVE EFFICIENCY AND PERSONAL CONTENTMENT

Suggestions which employees make with reference to their work may be divided into two main classes—those made with the object of improving their working conditions and those which aim at increasing production on a job. The two kinds of suggestions represent different attitudes on the part of the employees. Suggestions that a new drinking fountain be installed or that a roof be repaired are made for the purpose of adding to the comfort or increasing the safety of the employees. This is primarily a personal matter, though production may indirectly be increased thereby. Suggestions which enable the company to perform a job more economically or efficiently, on the other hand, reveal a direct interest on the part of the employees in the efficient running of the plant.

It has been shown in the preceding chapter, that where management does not devote attention to the plan in order to direct the activities of the works committees along broader lines, such organizations usually serve no other purpose than to settle complaints and grievances of employees. The investigation of the Conference Board shows that to a much greater extent, even, does the interest of the employees in improving production and making economies depend upon the attitude of management toward the Works Council.

The first essential in securing for an industry the benefit of the practical knowledge and experience of its employees, is the confidence of the employees in the fairness of the management of that industry. The second is the utilization by management of the opportunity furnished it through the works committees to direct the interests of the employees toward efficiency and economy. The employees cannot be expected to take the lead. Leadership is a function of management.

Perhaps the first thing management has to do is to make its foremen more receptive toward suggestions from employees. Foremen frequently are inclined to resent any such suggestions, regarding them as reflections upon the manner in which their duties as administrators are being carried out. This attitude has to be altered before employees may be expected to take any interest in improving the operations on which they are working. With this accomplished, and the employees convinced that they will receive due consideration from the supervisory force when they present a suggestion for increasing productive efficiency, management should institute among the employees a campaign of education in the economics of business. If through this means employees are led to appreciate that it is to their interests as well as those of the management that improved production be carried on in the most economical way possible, suggestions for the accomplishment of this object will be forthcoming from them. The experience of employers who have expended time and effort toward this end, bears this out.

This is not to say that in every case where employees have failed to contribute from their practical knowledge and experience toward increasing production, it is solely because management has not endeavored to utilize the plan as a means of showing employees the oneness of their interests with those of the employer, in having the industry run as efficiently as possible. The realization of this on the part of employees requires time. It means a readjustment of ideas and the casting out of false conceptions of industry. Not only have employees in some cases considered industry as a field of conflict between two opposing groups, but employers also have held this opinion. The need for education is common to both parties. The employees must have confidence in the management. This can come about only through management's constantly showing the workers that they have their interests at heart. If time is required for management to convince workers that it is sincere in providing employee representation, it is still more certain that time is required to educate employees to realize that their interests and those of management are one, so far as the efficient and economic operation of industry is concerned.

This point was brought out by the vice-president of a midwestern plant where a Works Council of the "committee" type was recently organized. The plan of employee representation in this plant is looked upon largely as an educational institution— educational in both directions, employer and employee. The plan was said to have clearly established ". . . the interdependability of all elements in industry—not only as between employer and employee but also with relation of those two elements to the public and to that other general branch of industry not often considered in its full relative importance, namely, the selling force." The greatest effect had been on the employee representatives; these had disseminated some of the spirit which their work had induced in them and ". . . in so far as this result has been felt by the rank and file, just that far has the true fundamental mission of employee representation been accomplished."

The Board's correspondent pointed out that only the future can show the real worth of the representation plan:

". . . The future will prove that we cannot measure fully the service of employee representation to industry if our standard of

64

measure be too minutely subdivided . . . Long time results must be looked for—and then only as fundamentals are affected.

"I care less about what an employee representation plan does at any of its meetings than about the spirit which dominates the procedure. Even the spirit is not an infallible guide to accurate judgment, but rather the spirit today as compared with six months or a year ago. Taken singly, an act, or the spirit of the assembly, may to the outsider appear blameworthy. It may appear narrow, selfish and even high-handed. To him, however, who studies the trend of the assembly's acts, that same incident may hold out most promising indications of substantial progress."

The same correspondent wrote of the education afforded the management by an employee representation plan:

". . . The employer and his representatives have on more than one occasion felt the effect on employer viewpoints of employee counsel. The intimate relationship which develops is such that without the slightest doubt the employee is enabled to mould employer sentiment quite as truly as that the employer is enabled to guide employee thought. The composite, resulting from these reciprocal relations has, and if rightly conceived and effected, must lead to mutual and highly desired advantages."

Apart from the instances described in the preceding section, in which the works committees were used principally by the employees for airing grievances and complaints—a condition for which management is largely to blame—very few cases were reported in which no suggestions, or very few, had been made by the employees for increasing productive efficiency.

An eastern concern employing three hundred workers, whose Council of the "committee" type has been in operation for three years, wrote:

"The works committees are used by the employees principally as a means of bettering personal contentment through recommendations regarding working conditions, hours of work, etc."

A visit to this plant revealed the fact that the employees had but little confidence in the plan. Management had not made use of it to keep the workers informed of business conditions. When retrenchment became necessary in this company, management, although it had promised to consult the Works Council, effected necessary economies without discussing them with the committees. This fact and others resulted in the employees' losing all interest in the Council other than as a means for improving their own conditions. In short, management had failed to direct the interest of the employees along the lines of economic production.[1]

The replies received from the great majority of employers with Councils of the "committee" type, indicated that while much had been achieved, still more remained to be accomplished. There was a realization that the development of such an attitude on the part of the employees required time.

[1]See pp. 163-165.

The president of an eastern company with three hundred and fifty employees wrote:

"It seems to me it is the duty of every industry to thoroughly inform its workers, more or less, of the problems of the management. It is a very tedious proceeding that has to be carried on with great care. When the men in the factory or any member of the organization understand the problems that have to be solved in an organization, they become more sympathetic toward the management."

He also pointed out that the nature of the suggestions and recommendations made by employees depend upon the attitude of the management.

"The suggestions that are submitted at first are for small things, and it is a question of education to lead them to suggestions of more importance. That is about all there is to it. You reap only as you sow."

A correspondent in an eastern brass works reported that although there had been a great number of suggestions, "some of them of considerable merit," received from the employees,

". . . there were none of revolutionary character, but we feel that such a thing as this would be the exception, and it is the small improvements throughout a plant that this system will really bring out. . . .

"We believe there is a feeling which is growing that the employees' interests and the employer's interests are identical to a certain degree. Of course such a movement is very slow in its growth and it is subject to violent reversal at times. In all these matters we do not look for anything extraordinary but rather slow growth by education."

A southern shoe company with a Works Council of the committee type which was installed in the summer of 1919 reported an increased interest among the employees in production methods, but it was realized that much was still to be accomplished along this line. Writing in August, 1921, a company official stated:

"During the last twelve months, we have stressed economy in every way we could, both through the shop committees and in other ways. The response has been very noticeable in cutting down damage, waste, and particularly damaged shoes, which we call "cripples."

". . . We had no definite system for suggestions, except a general invitation through the employees' handbook, to make suggestions looking toward safety, efficiency and economy. This was rather haphazard and not followed up, and consequently the response was negligible.

"Since, however, we have had the shop committee system, the representatives of the employees particularly, in the past twelve months, have shown a disposition to try to make suggestions helpful to their particular departments. We cannot say, however, that so far any revolutionary or epoch-making suggestions have been made; most of them have been of a minor though, at the same time, constructive nature.

"We will say, however, that the shop committee system did distinctly open up a channel through which the employees, through the representatives, can sit around the table informally with members of the management and suggest and criticise in a helpful way. The representatives were at first a little ill at ease and silent, but now have gotten over this and are not bashful about opening up and discussing matters. We are frank to say that so far the majority of their suggestions and requests have been of a rather pseudo-selfish nature, that is, they seem to have asked for and suggested things which would benefit the employees, rather more than the company itself. This we believe is natural and we have encouraged it, at the same time, we have tried to guide them into thinking of things from the company's standpoint."

The same correspondent wrote that while development had been slow, it had been sure. It was felt that if the same pace were kept up "the standard of intelligence and efficiency" and also the labor turnover would be greatly improved.

Apart from those concerns in which there is paid to the employees, through a "Collective Economy Dividend," one-half of the savings which they make in production, the replies from the majority of employers were of a similar strain. Considerable had been accomplished toward securing the cooperation of the employees in improving production, but this development had been slow. The extent to which the interest of the employees had been stimulated in this direction, varied in different plants. A number of employers simply said that employees, in addition to making use of the committees for airing grievances, had taken "an interest" in the efficient and economical operation of the plant. One employer said that although the employees made "constant contributions towards increasing efficiency" few of the suggestions "were of great value, although occasionally we receive one that is." Another employer said that although there had been a great increase in the number of suggestions received from the employees after the Works Council was initiated, the majority of these suggestions dealt rather with working conditions— "heat, light, ventilation, etc., all of which go to affect production indirectly, rather than suggestions dealing directly with increasing the production of a job."

A large middle western rubber firm reported that the Works Council had not resulted in any "marked increase" in the number of suggestions received from the employees, but stated that the Council had been a good influence "in having men realize that the interests of the company and the men are mutual." The company felt that there was still a great deal to do in this line, stating that "it is not possible in all cases to get men to heartily approve economies resulting from reduction in wages."

An official in a western concern with twelve hundred workers, stated that although the employees showed an interest in making suggestions toward the economical operation of the plant,

". . . generally speaking these suggestions are ones that have been thought out and worked out before and not proven successful, although I feel that suggestions received, although perhaps ones that are not applicable, are valuable because of the interest they do show."

A western shipping company, while stating that the committees were used by the employees for the airing of grievances, a process that was highly desirable "as a scientific method of sublimating the bellicose instinct," reported:

"The larger part of the discussions carried on in the committees cover such subjects as adjustments of working conditions for greater output per man hour, also clear definitions of rules covering working conditions; suggested methods for reducing fatigue; and other like subjects constructive in their nature."

This company pays its employees a bonus wage "for production efficiency exceeding a standard set by mutual agreement with them." This has had the effect of imbuing the employees with the idea

". . . that it is to their own ultimate advantage to assist the company in the efficient and economical operation of the plant."

A striking instance of the interest taken by employees in lowering production costs, came from a large western corporation which has Works Councils of the "committee" type in operation in several of its plants. One of the Councils affects the employees of a railroad owned by this company. At one of the Council meetings in February, 1921, an employee representative stated in effect that up to that time the employees seemed to have made all the requests, and that he would welcome an indication from the management of some way in which the employees might reciprocate. His suggestion was promptly met by the superintendent, who invited a committee of the employees to meet with him and discuss the matter. This was accepted by the employees, who designated Sunday afternoon for the meeting time. The result was the compilation of a report by the "Committee on the Good of the Service," which was endorsed by all the employees. The report urged employee representatives to draw the attention of the employees in their respective departments to the "extreme need of conservation of supplies of all kinds." Engineers and firemen, freight house employees, the track and car department workers, all were requested to effect every possible economy consistent with safety in the operation of the railway. The committee expressed its confidence in the management in the following terms:

"We are of the opinion and have found that the officials of the company in their dealings with the employees, wish to be fair and just, therefore each employee by following the above recommendations and in addition giving close attention to their respective duties, avoiding any waste time, can to a great extent help to overcome, the present difficulties which we now face."

At another plant belonging to this company, the employee members of the Council suggested that in order to reduce the amount of scrap losses, a regular "spoiled work" or "scrap" committee should be appointed in the Council to make investigations of methods of manufacture and to recommend changes in practice wherever they would help reduce such losses. Employees were also to be encouraged by this committee to make suggestions which might result in definite savings to the company. The Board's correspondent wrote that

> ". . . the committee functioned very actively from the time it was formed until the plant closed down, and it should be credited in large degree for the good showing made last year over previous years in the reduction of scrap losses."

A representation plan, worked out by management and employees together, was installed in a middle western plant with five hundred workers, after one year had been devoted by the management to the education of the employees in business economics. The classes, which were attended by over two hundred of the employees, dealt with such subjects as the evolution of modern business, the elements of a company balance sheet, etc. All possible phases of the company's business and industrial relations were covered by the classes. At the end of a year's time the subject of employee representation was discussed, with the outcome that the present plan— a modified Council of the "Industrial Democracy" type— was adopted.

To direct the interest of the employees along constructive lines, committees composed of employee representatives are appointed to deal with the following subjects: education and publication; wage rates and compensation; health, sanitation and safety; employment and discharge; economies, suggestions and improvements; production control; time and motion study; spoiled work; machinery and tools; attendance and tardiness; sales cooperation; pride and interest in work. A special "eight-hour committee" dealt with the request of the employees to reduce the working hours, first from ten to nine, and then to eight per day. Through the work of this committee and that on production control new quotas of production were established and the men produced as much in eight hours as they had previously produced in ten. The company reported that through these various committees productive efficiency has been greatly increased. Spoiled work has been greatly reduced; machinery and tools have been improved; absenteeism has been eliminated to a large extent, and in other ways employees have cooperated with the management to reduce inefficiency.

One of the company officials, in commenting upon the extent to which a Works Council may be successful in increasing productive efficiency, stated that this depends a great deal "upon the original committee appointments and the methods under which they operate."

> "To stimulate the employees' interest in efficient and economical operation of a plant to the extent that they will make suggestions which would assist in the accomplishing of that object, in my mind it

is very necessary that some method of stimulating and maintaining interest be initiated.

"This can be handled in various ways. Particularly I have in mind a publicity committee in the Works Council and operating in conjunction with the educational department of the firm, that is with the industrial relations department. If the firm endeavors to interpret knowledge from the 'handed down' attitude, it will fail, but if this matter is given to the Works Council for consideration, various kinds of educational work can be successfully handled.

". . . We first endeavored to interpret to the employees company policies and conditions with which the management had to cope. In the meantime the majority of the employees acquired the fundamentals of business organization, so that we were able to progress in our work. There is no question but that when you have acquired the individual's interest, you have awakened a thirst for knowledge, and such was the case here.

"To take the average worker into the problems of management was somewhat of a radical step from the usual industrial educational work. In our efforts we laid before the employees all matters of company interest, and by that I mean, matters pertaining to production, finance, distribution, etc. We worked down from the fundamentals to the practical problems and solicited suggestions from the employees when holding our representation meetings.

"Through the constructive suggestions pertaining to engineering and production improvement, we were able to establish production quotas of which we knew nothing prior to the installation of our Works Council. . . . Of course, assistance was rendered in the improvement of production control, machine improvemnet, along with engineering betterment. The value of the group suggestions made was in the ability of the firm to improve conditions pertaining to production which had not been overcome in the past."

At the present time monetary awards are paid for suggestions, but a similar system in effect before the Works Council was organized did not arouse the marked interest of the employees in improving production that has been manifest since the present plan was installed.

"The old style system of suggestions was not productive of general improvement in any sense as compared to the marked increase under the plan now in operation. In my opinion we have been able to have our workers realize that the interests of the company and themselves are mutual and that it is to their advantage to assist the company in the efficient and economical operation of our plant.

"This is best emphasized by their willingness to assist when retrenchment moves were necessary. These moves have been handled through our Works Council and we believe it has been the crucial test in the operation of such a plan."[1]

Particularly significant in this connection is the fact that the interest of the employees in lowering production costs in this plant is not associated with the payment to them of one-half the savings they may make—there is no "Collective Economy Dividend" feature in the plan.

The attitude of this company towards its educational work, which is carried on with the object of having the men "understand what they were doing and why," is described in a company pamphlet thus:

[1]See pp. 87-88.

"Our work is never done. Almost every week we have some pamphlet to pass out. We are keeping at it constantly. We believe that the more education a man gets the more he wants, and we aim to keep him supplied with all the information available on timely subjects."

Another large middle western concern employing over five thousand workers, in which the employees have taken a keen interest in production methods, stated that in order to interest the committees to this point, it was first necessary "to establish confidence on the part of the men in the committees together with an understanding of fundamental economics." A Works Council of the "committee" type has been in operation in this concern since 1915. The works committees "were originally formed for the purpose of making contacts between management and men, and for educational purposes."

"Through these committees the employees are taught to see the necessity of production and to look for the means of securing it economically. They are taken fully into the confidence of the management and given an insight into managerial problems with every opportunity to follow them up in detail and make suggestions, if the employees so desire. 'The cards are put on the table,' and the problems as they confront the management are discussed by a representative of the management at the committee meetings. Charts and tables are permanently posted in the committee rooms for study and reference."

The experience of this company in dealing with works committees leads them to believe that "increased productivity and efficiency will be brought about if employees are encouraged through their committees or Works Councils to make suggestions for increasing production and making operations more economical." The Board's correspondent wrote:

"On one occasion the men of one particular department complained as to the condition of castings coming to them to be machined. In another case, men complained of material not coming to them fast enough.

"These suggestions only came after having worked with the committees for a number of months in order to acquaint them with the underlying fundamentals of industry, the suggestions indicating that the men understood that in order for them and the industry to go ahead, efficiency must be kept up, and production continue uninterrupted, they seeming to understand that methods and processes should necessarily be changed.

"These are only two of the many suggestions that have been brought to the attention of the management.

"There is nothing provided for by the management of this company as an award for employees making suggestions, but they are encouraged to make these suggestions with the thought constantly before them that their positions and future are just as secure as they make them and that they cannot prosper if the company does not prosper, and the company cannot prosper if production is not of high standard with the greatest amount of efficiency practiced."

On another occasion management requested from the various committees of the employees, suggestions as to better methods of production in their departments.

71

"Before we had completed visiting all the committees, suggestions were so numerous and so varied in thought, that same were compiled and we now have them typewritten, and bound. The management has often stated that a person could take these suggestions secured through the shop committees and run a factory."

The excellent results so obtained in this company led one of the company officials to state:

"It is indeed encouraging and interesting to learn the keen interest displayed in production methods. The writer is very much of the opinion that much relief from our present industrial condition will be brought about by greatly lowering production costs through co-operation and suggestions of Works Councils or employees' committees."

The key to the situation as it exists in this plant is summarized in a company publication in this way, "the management and the men have the utmost confidence in each other, each having always played fair."

Suggestions made by the employees in a middle western arsenal in which there is a Works Council of the "committee" type, greatly lowered the cost of production. A list of such suggestions furnished the National Industrial Conference Board by the commanding officer of the arsenal, showed that the savings effected the Government ranged from $70 to $3,574 on the operations covered by the suggestions. The employees who made the suggestions were given a reward not exceeding ten per cent of the savings to the Government during the first year after the suggestion was used.

A company official of an eastern concern which employs seven hundred workers, said that the Works Council had been a valuable means of placing information before the employees regarding the problems of management, and that there had been a gratifying response from the employees in their endeavor to assist management in reducing costs.

"While our suggestion plan was in operation two years before the formation of the employees' Association, we did not notice any increase in the number of suggestions submitted as the result of the formation of the Association. We do know that of those submitted, a number of the ideas were the result of discussions held in the meetings of the Association.

"The employees' Association has been a valuable means of talking matters over with the employees to give them an idea of the problems of management and to explain how they might assist in solving them. Our factory superintendent has taken various occasions to show examples of high costs of manufacture and get them to join in the analysis for the reasons that made these costs excessive. The response has been very gratifying in a number of ways. Interest has been stimulated in the jobs assigned and there has been more alertness on their part to cut down waste of time and material. There have been many instances where the Council representatives have reminded their fellow employees of the desirability of staying 'on the job' and putting honest effort in the day's work. They have also responded to the advice of their associates to use greater care in the handling of company property and other expensive material, giving as arguments that if the worker were to expect high wages he must do his share to reduce the

72

cost of production and operation that the company would be in a position to maintain satisfactory wage rates."

A large eastern corporation wrote after two years' experience with its plan of representation that the plan had had the effect of stimulating the employees' interest in the efficient and economical operation of the business, and that numerous suggestions had been made by the employee representatives with a view to increasing the efficiency of their work. No system was employed by this company whereby suggestions made by employees were paid for. Through the regular joint meetings with management, employee representatives were reported to have come to realize that "the interests of the company and themselves are mutual." The result was that they had freely given to management "the benefit of their advice and counsel with respect to a number of operating problems." The plan of employee representation was described by the management as a ". . . splendid medium for emphasizing the mutuality of interests and where this idea can be inculcated in the minds of workers, the natural reaction is one of thoughtful cooperation on their part."

A middle western paint company with a Council of the "Industrial Democracy" type, found that although the number of suggestions received from the employees gradually decreased in number, they became of greater value. There is no "Collective Economy Dividend" feature in this plan.

"There is no question but that the employee representation plan is a big factor in stimulating suggestions, providing, of course, the plan is handled properly. We find that we are getting some of our best suggestions today, and while we are still using the suggestion blank, many of the members of our organization prefer bringing the suggestions in direct and not asking for any compensation. Whether this is unusual with our organization I cannot say.

"We find it necessary, of course, from time to time to post bulletins and encourage the members of our organization to contribute to the suggestion box, but this is no different than any other problem and it all depends upon how enthusiastic and sincere the executives are, for they are responsible for results. This enthusiasm is naturally reflected throughout the entire organization and has to be constantly kept up.

"When we first introduced the suggestion idea the suggestions offered were great in number, but as the years went on the numbers dropped off but the suggestions offered were of greater value, proving, of course, that the plan of Industrial Democracy was producing because the men were thinking on a higher plane, and this could only be accomplished if the men realized that the interests were mutual."

One of the officials of a western steel company wrote:

"There is no question in the mind of the writer, and those who have watched this representation plan, that it has had a marked tendency to create discussions that lead to suggestions for increasing production. In fact, the perusal of our minutes indicates that quite a considerable part of the time at each meeting is devoted to these helpful suggestions.

73

> "We did have, previous to the installation of this system, various methods for getting suggestions of this character. I do not believe on the whole that any of them have produced the same results or brought the number of suggestions that have been brought by these meetings of our Workmen's Committee."

An eastern concern with eleven hundred employees reported that its Works Council of the "committee" type had developed in many of its employees a realization that their interests and those of the company are mutual.

> "We are confident that our employee representatives after a short time of service, are convinced that it is to the mutual advantage of themselves and the company to assist the company in an efficient and economical operation of our plant."

Concerns with Councils of the "Industrial Democracy" type embracing the "Collective Economy Dividend" feature, attributed to some extent the interest of the employees in lowering production costs to the financial return they received for all savings made in production. Some employers were of the opinion that the dividends which the employees received formed the primary motive in their interest in lowering the costs of production, while others thought their interest was due rather to the greater measure of confidence and trust that the employees had in management as a result of the mutual understanding brought about by the representation plan.

An eastern film manufacturing company, whose plan has been in operation less than a year, reported "remarkably gratifying results in stimulating the interest of our employees in the efficient and economical operation of our work."

> "We are now receiving many valuable suggestions from employees, the average being at least one good idea every day. Some of these deal with big operations and some with details of a minor character, but we consider the latter fully as important as the former because nothing is too trifling, in the minds of the employees, if it promises to make our plant more efficient."

Previous to the installation of the representation plan, the company had on several occasions tried a suggestion box plan whereby rewards were paid for all suggestions used.

> "The result was always a failure. The interest, if any, died down within a few days. Today the contrary is true. Instead of dying down, the interest is growing. Only recently one of the employees disclosed an invention which he has kept under cover for several years because he was afraid someone might take it from him. Though we had always treated our people as well as we could, according to our light, we really did not have their full confidence and trust until Industrial Democracy brought us closer together. . . .

> "They are using their heads and hands where formerly they used only their hands. Knowing the details of our plant operation much more intimately than we can ever hope to know it ourselves, it is only natural that they can and do find more ways and means of improving it than we can or do find.

> "They knew these things before we installed Industrial Democracy, but they did not do anything about it. Today they are doing every-

74

thing they can to help. They not only check up on each other to eliminate waste of material and labor and improve product, but they actually check us up to make sure that we are not wasting any of our own money. For example, on a recent occasion, our work threatened to be tied up because a sewer became clogged and made it impossible to continue operations. Rather than wait for us to get a contractor and go through the ordinary routine of letting the job, they jumped into the job themselves, dug the sewer, drained away the water that was rapidly accumulating because of the clogging, and then went back to their regular jobs. On another occasion they called our attention to the fact that by installing water hydrants in one or two places not already protected we could cut down our insurance premium. Recently they showed us that we were running the risk of killing strangers and involving ourselves in heavy damage suits because of an un-protected driveway that runs through our property. A simple in-expensive fence, which they suggested, did away with this. They have shown us how to use fewer rubber gloves and other materials necessary in the work of our laboratory, even getting down to scientific exactness the number of rubber bands absolutely necessary for the proper conduct of our business.

"The great beauty back of it all is the fact that there is not the least taint of paternalism in it. Nor is there the slightest hint of speeding up or driving. We have found fine qualities in them which we never took the trouble to seek before. They, on the other hand, have found that we are simply two-legged men and not Simon Legrees. It follows, as a matter of course, that nothing but good could come from a mutual revelation of this sort."

Another company with a Council of the "Industrial Democracy" type, stated that the interest displayed among the employees with reference to the economical operation of the plant was due chiefly to the "Collective Economy Dividend" feature of the representation plan.

"The real force or influence is the prospect of a bi-weekly dividend, and there is a tendency on the part of a fairly small minority of workers—even when dividends are being paid regularly and in sub-stantial amounts—to lose whatever zeal they had and play the part of a 'passenger' on the rest of the workers, but in spite of this our production has increased very considerably and the economies effected by means of increased carefulness in handling materials have been quite large."

Another eastern company with a Council of the same type, which had a suggestion system in operation before the Works Council was installed, found the number of suggestions received from the employees increased considerably after the representation plan was set up.

"Previous to the installation of this system, we made small awards for usable suggestions but found that the increased cooperation has led to a very satisfactory increase in the number of suggestions and especially in the proportion of practical ones. At the present time, the person making a suggestion is given only a small reward, while the balance of the saving is split fifty-fifty between the company and the dividend fund paid to all employees. In some cases, this has made an appreciable increase in the dividends, which was explained to the employees and in turn offered them a further incentive for letting us have all practical ideas to use."

With reference to the number of suggestions received from employees, the experience of a western company with representation plans of the "Industrial Democracy" type in nine plants, is of particular interest. It attributes the increased number of these suggestions received since the initiation of its Works Council, not to the "Collective Economy Dividend" feature of its plan, but to the fact that the suggestions are reviewed by a joint committee of the employees and the foremen, instead of by management alone as was the case previously. According to the vice-president, the greatest difficulty experienced under the old system of giving rewards for valuable suggestions, was to convince the man who made a suggestion that it was not always a practicable idea. Under the present plan by which the suggestions are passed on by a suggestion committee of the House of Representatives and the Senate, who are not prejudiced

> ". . . in favor of the suggestion, the impossibilities of a great many of the suggestions are more quickly grasped, and the man who makes them seems to accept the judgment of the joint committee more readily than the judgment of the management, as under the previous plan."

The vice-president stated:

> "We think this has more to do with increased numbers of suggestions than the reward, because as a matter of fact, the rewards under our new plan are not anywhere near on as high a scale as they were before."

A joint committee of employee and management representatives, in an eastern plant with a plan of the "committee" type, drew attention to the same factor in its reply to the Conference Board regarding the number of suggestions received from the employees:

> "The suggestion plan functions largely through its contact with and participation in the plan of representation. Every suggestion is passed on by the shop committee, or committees, representing both the man making the suggestion and the shop affected.
> "This has the effect of inspiring the confidence of the employees in the plan, because they know that their suggestions receive the consideration of their shopmates, whom they have elected to represent them, as well as the company representatives.
> "Many of the shop committees appoint a sub-committee to personally investigate the suggestion so referred to them and their reports are sound and thorough because they deal with facts and conditions with which they are familiar."

One of the officials of this company stated that the influence which the shop committees have had on employees "to make them realize that the interests of the company are mutual with their own" has been

> ". . . one of the main benefits derived from the committee system, in that as soon as employees are given the opportunity to realize the above, one great stride has been taken towards reaching that goal toward which we all aspire, that is, cooperation between management and employees."

It is evident from the foregoing that employers consider representation plans have a stimulating effect upon the interest taken by employees in productive efficiency. The extent to which that interest is aroused and stimulated appears to be dependent in large degree upon whether management has been able to convince employees of its desire and purpose to be fair in its dealings with them. Experience further shows that valuable results are obtainable from educational work in which employees are taught business economics in which they are shown the mutuality of interest that exists between them and their employers in maintaining a high level of productive efficiency.

CLASSIFICATION OF CASES ACCORDING TO SUBJECT GROUPINGS AND SETTLEMENT HANDLED IN FIVE PLANTS OF BETHLEHEM STEEL COMPANY, OCTOBER, 1918 TO OCTOBER, 1920

SUBJECT	Affirmative (1)	Negative	Withdrawn	Compromise	Pending	Total
Wages, Piecework, Bonus, Tonnage Schedules	147	98	9	59	4	317
Employment and Working Conditions	214	55	11	16	5	301
Practice Methods and Economy	111	6	4	3		124
Safety and Prevention Accidents	97	3	1	1		102
Health and Works Sanitation	76	4		4	5	89
Employees' Transportation	57	3	1	1	1	63
Housing Domestic Economics and Living Conditions	7	4		2	2	15
Pensions and Relief	10	1		1		12
Athletics and Recreation	4	2	1			7
Education and Publication	6					6
Rules, Ways and Means	4			1		5
Continuous Employment and Conditions of Industry	4					4
Total	737	176	27	88	17	1,045

(1) In accordance with wishes of employees.

CHAPTER VI

SUBJECTS DISCUSSED AND MEETINGS HELD BY WORKS COUNCILS

The Conference Board has obtained from a number of employers a detailed statement with regard to the activities of their Works Councils over a period of from one to two years. These are of value as showing the number of meetings held by the various committees established under the representation plans, and the nature of the subjects discussed by them.

The Bethlehem Steel Company has courteously placed at the Board's disposal the chart reproduced on facing page showing the classification according to subject groupings and settlement of the various cases with which the Works Councils in its five plants dealt during the two years October, 1918, to October, 1920.

It is seen from the chart that wages and working conditions were the major subjects discussed by the Works Councils, wages constituting 30.3% and working conditions 28.7% of the total number of cases dealt with under the representation plan.

The recapitulation of the cases according to the way in which they were settled shows that 70.5% were settled in the affirmative—that is, in accordance with the wishes of the employees—while only 16.9% were settled in the negative.

RECAPITULATION

Cases settled in the affirmative	737	
Cases settled in the negative	176	
Cases withdrawn	27	
Cases compromised	88	
Cases pending	17	
Total cases	1,045	

The following list shows, by subject groupings, the percentages of the cases settled in accordance with the wishes of the employees:

Wages, piecework, bonus tonnage schedules	46.3%
Employment and working conditions	71.1%
Practice, methods and economy	89.5%
Safety and prevention accidents	95.0%

Health and works sanitation.............................. 85.4%
Employees' transportation................................. 90.5%
Housing, domestic economies and living conditions.......... 46.6%
Pensions and relief....................................... 83.5%
Athletics and recreation................................. 55.5%
Education and publication.......................... .....100.0%
Rules, ways and means................................... 80.0%
Continuous employment and conditions of industry..........100.0%

Under the plan of representation of the Bethlehem Steel Company, employees' committees are established in each plant for the consideration of the following subjects:

Rules
Ways and means
Safety and preven·ion of accident
Practice, methods and economy
Employees' transportation
Wages, piecework, bonus and tonnage schedules
Employment and working conditions
Housing, domestic economies and living conditions
Health and works sanitation
Education and publications
Pensions and relief
Athletics and recreation
Continuous employment and condi ion of industry

In addition there is a general committee which considers all matters not falling within the scope of the committees provided for above. This committee when jointly composed acts as a committee on appeals.

These committees meet regularly once a month; special meetings are held as occasion requires. All meetings are held within the plant and on company time, committee men receiving from the company "payment commensurate with their average earnings." On alternate months the committees meet as joint committees, that is, with an equal number of management representatives.

Data are not at hand regarding the number of meetings held by the various committees during the two years to which the above information applies, but during the year October, 1919, to October, 1920, there were 193 meetings of employees' standing committees separately and 136 meetings of these committees sitting with equal numbers of management representatives. During that year there were 74 meetings of all the employee representatives in each of the five plants. On four occasions the management's representatives, individuals in each plant who represent the plant management in negotiations with employees, met together.

The General Electric Company, West Lynn, Mass., gave the following analysis of the cases handled under its plan of representation for the year ending December, 1919:

Subjects of Cases

Wages.................59%		Layoff.................5%
Transfer...............17%		Discipline..............4%
Miscellaneous...........11%		Discharge..............4%

Under the General Electric Company's plan, if a Shop Committee,[1] of which there is one for each department, composed of equal numbers of employee and management representatives, renders a unanimous decision either in favor of or against an employee, that settles the matter; if the decision is a majority decision against the employee he may appeal the question to higher committees.

The above cases were decided in the following manner:

46 % Unanimous decisions favorable to employees
1.3% Majority decisions favorable to employees
52.7% Unanimous decisions adverse to employees

During the year ending December, 1920, the cases handled by the shop committees in this company were as follows:

Wages	38.9%	Discipline	5.3%
Time study	5.3%	Layoff	5.3%
Discharge	8.4%	Transfer	1.1%
Discrimination	12.6%	Miscellaneous	23.1%

The above cases were disposed of in the following manner:

37.9% settled by unanimous decision favorable to employee
2.1% settled by majority decision favorable to employee
24.2% settled by unanimous decision adverse to employee
2.1% settled by majority decision adverse to employee
15.8% referred to higher committees for action
17.9% withdrawn by employee at some step in proceedings

A summary of the matters discussed in the Works Councils of the "committee" type of an eastern corporation from April 1, 1918, to December 31, 1920, shows, as in the case of the Bethlehem Steel Company, that the discussion of wages, hours of work, and conditions constituted the greater part of the Council's activities. The classification below includes subjects discussed by seven Works Councils. Five of these are situated in industrial establishments; the other two are composed of representatives spread over a considerable area, including those employees who are engaged in the distribution of the company's products. The subjects discussed by the Councils have been classified by the company as follows:

Wages	35.0%	Sanitation	4.0%
Hours	13.0%	Housing	3.0%
Method of payment	3.0%	Social	2.0%
Promotions	4.0%	Vacations	2.0%
Discharges	2.0%	Industrial representa-	
Working conditions	10.5%	tion plan	10.5%
		General	11.0%

In each of the plants in which the plan is operating, committees of employees, elected from divisions or departments into which the plants are divided, meet with an equal number of management representatives. In certain of the plants an executive council has been formed which acts as a court of appeal from the divisional conferences. In addition, pro-

[1]This is a special use of the word Shop Committee, not to be confused with the "shop committees" installed by the National War Labor Board.

vision is made for joint conferences of all representatives, both employee and management, in each plant. In the case of the two Councils which represent the men engaged in the distribution of the company's products, provision is made for meetings of an equal number of employee and management representatives at regular intervals. On account of differences in organization, the meetings of these Councils are not classified as are the meetings of the Councils in the five plants of the company, but are included separately in the totals.

During the period to which the above information refers there were held a total of 217 meetings. These were as follows:

	Divisional Conferences	Executive Council	Works Joint Conference	Total
Plant No. 1..........	31	5	22	58
Plant No. 2..........	8	7	23	38
Plant No. 3..........	8	8	18	34
Plant No. 4..........	4	..	28	32
Plant No. 5..........	..	..	29	29
Area No. 1..........	..	..	..	16
Area No. 2..........	..	..	..	10
	51	20	120	217

A western concern manufacturing agricultural machinery and employing two hundred people, furnished the Conference Board the following summary of the work accomplished by its Works Council of the "committee" type during the year March, 1919, to March, 1920:

By Whom Brought Up	Suggestion	Action Taken
Employee	Inequality wage rates of certain moulders	Adjusted satisfactorily
Employee	Drinking fountains main shop needed	Same provided
Employee	Change in method of paying off main shop desired	Change made
Management	Exhaust fan for jointer, main plant, needed	Installed
Employee	Suggested starting foundry core oven one hour earlier	Carried out
Employee	Better tools needed in machine shop	Equipment recommended by foreman purchased
Employee	Wheel trucks for foundry bull ladles needed	Provided
Management	Cleanup on Saturday nights needed	Carried out
Council[1]	Smoking regulations needed	Provided

[1]Most of these matters were originated by the management.

82

By Whom Brought Up	Suggestion	Action Taken
Dept. 16 painters	Asked investigation why cut off from monthly bonus	Bonus awarded and improvement in handling time slips adopted
Employee	Air hoist elevator in foundry unsafe	Attempt made to safeguard same; later, belt-driven elevator installed
Employee	Men uncertain as to time allowed for washing up	Bulletin posted and practice started of blowing warning whistle
Council[1]	Wanted Saturday afternoons off with adjustment of wages to compensate	Satisfactory arrangements made
Council[1]	Advised cutting out of 10% six month bonus and adjustment of all piece rate	Carried out satisfactorily as far as possible
Employee	Surface grinder for dies in machine shop needed	Purchased and installed
Employee	Certain men in Building "E" lost bonus on account of time clock	Investigation made and bonus paid; clock sent away for repairs
Employee	Wire tops on elevators needed	Ordered and installed as fast as possible
Employee	Roof over die racks needed	All but hammer die racks covered
Council[1]	Advise discontinuance of Thrift Club	Club dropped
Council[1]	Piecework should be put on better basis	Company agreed that hereafter prices would be adjusted to satisfaction of both parties every summer; prices to be guaranteed from Aug. 1 to Aug. 1
Employee	Suggested paying off the Bldg. "E" through foremen	Carried out
Employee	Suggested change in gating feed case patterns	Carried out
Employee	Brewery floor unsafe	New timbers placed
Employee	Foundry desired to go on 6-day basis	Carried out
Council[1]	Desired going back to work Saturday afternoons	Carried out
Employee	Air pump in paint shop dangerous	New governor ordered and installed

[1]Most of these matters were originated by the management.

By Whom Brought Up	Suggestion	Action Taken
Employee	Emery stand needed for clutch assembly	Finally installed
Employee	Adjustment of wages desired by shippers	Investigation and adjustment made
Management	Potatoes ffered for sale to employees	Carried out and price in town lowered
Employee	Suggested reaming plow bushings elsewhere than in machine shop	So ordered
Employee	Suggested secretary of Aid Society post notices	Carried out
Employee	Asked for more heat in foundry wash room	Radiators installed
Employee	Improvement on drill footboard brace suggested	Investigated and will try out
Council[1]	Suggested addition of pattern shop group	Carried out
Employee	Stock room too cold	Broken radiator replaced
Employee	Wage adjustment suggested in pattern shop	Investigation and adjustment made
Employee	Platforms needed in pattern shop	Provided
Employee	Adjustable lights in pattern shop needed	Changes started and some completed
Management	Personal work on company time or company material	Proper procedure adopted
Employee	Suggested use of better coke	Poor coke all that could besecured; good grade on order
Employee	Reported men in foundry kept overtime	Investigated and report made, showing men left before five oftener than after five on the average.
Employee	Adjustment of some day and piecerates in forge shop desirable	Same carried out

During the year there were sixteen meetings of the Council. The meetings are usually held after working hours, each of the employee representatives receiving fifty cents as remuneration; hourly rates of pay are paid employees if special meetings are held during working hours.

An eastern corporation reported that during the calendar year 1920, 4520 subjects were discussed by the Councils of the "committee" type in fourteen of its plants. They were classified as follows:

[1]Most of these matters were originated by the management.

84

General Service
    Thrift, restaurant, suggestion system, salesroom, housing, smoking rooms, general service to employees.................524
Health
    Health hospital, physical examinations, first aid, lighting, ventilation, dentists, etc......................................473
Wages
    Bonuses, increases, pay, piece rates, time studies, vacations with pay, economy bonus, reduction of pay...................442
Equipment
    Buildings, time clocks, (installation of) working equipment, elevators, lasts, lockers, drinking fountains, etc...............417
Safety
    Accident, guard, safety, fire drills..........................360
Employment
    Employment, curtailment of employment, hours of work, labor disputes, transfer and promotion, factory instructions and rules, vacations and holidays (not with pay), shutdowns.............354
Production Problems
    Production waiting for stock, work incomplete, delivery of stock, economy, working conditions..........................330
Education
    Americanization, educational courses, instruction, library, service squad...238
Quality
    Quality of material poor, efforts toward improvement of quality..221
Recreational Activities
    Outings, entertainments, noon hour recreation...............203
Work Ticket
    Split tickets, poor distribution of work on ticket, illegible, etc....148
Sanitation
    Sanitation, conditions of factory (cleanliness).................136
Methods of Manufacture
    Methods of, improvement of, rack system, etc................131
Benefits and Insurance
    Benefits, subscriptions, pensions, insurance, mutual aid, etc....118
Athletics
    Baseball, basketball, bowling, etc...........................117
Publicity
    Charts for interesting worker, factory papers................115
Scrap
    Damaged goods, scrap, waste material...................... 93
Absentees.. 82
Organization Changes
    By-laws, etc... 18

                    Total...............................4520

The Conference Board has learned of one instance in which a Works Council of the "Industrial Democracy" type appointed a committee of employee representatives to deal with the problem of unemployment. This committee worked in conjunction with the labor department of the company to determine to what extent unemployment might be reduced.

CHAPTER VII

ATTITUDE OF WORKS COUNCILS TOWARD RE-DUCTIONS IN WAGES AND CHANGES IN WORK HOUR SCHEDULES

The investigation of the Conference Board shows that where employers have discussed with the employee representatives on their Works Councils the reasons for a proposed reduction in wages, a curtailment of the working force, or a change in work hour schedules, the representatives in a vast majority of cases have appreciated the cogency of the circumstances necessitating such measures of retrenchment and have concurred with the employers in the proposed changes.

In plants where employers had used their Councils as a means of keeping the representatives, and through them the employees, informed of the business outlook both for the country as a whole and for their individual concerns, the management was able to prepare the minds of the employees for acceptance of the economies in wages that would sooner or later have to be effected.

This method of procedure—the explanation to the employees of the reasons necessitating wage reductions—was stated by employers to be better than that of merely posting a notice to the effect that wages would be reduced a certain amount. It enabled them to show the employees that the need for such economies was the result of the pressure of economic forces, against which both employer and employees were helpless. When this was done, it was found that much less dissatisfaction and ill feeling were shown than would have otherwise occurred. Employers expressed themselves as being glad of the opportunity to explain directly to the representatives of the men the reasons that necessitated reductions in wages, and they also said that the representatives were of great assistance to them in placing that information before the employees through personal contact with them. The general opinion was that wage reductions and changes in work hour schedules were effected much more satisfactorily in this way than if the Works Council had not been used in informing the employees of the reasons for such measures.

The experience of a large company manufacturing agricultural machinery is of particular interest in connection with the handling of wage reductions and changes in work hour schedules, as it has Works Councils in operation in twenty-four plants. Writing in April, 1921, one of the company officials stated:

"It has been our unfortunate experience within the past thirty days to be required to reduce wages of day and piecework employees of our factories by 20 per cent, and to reduce the salaried factory employes 10 per cent. We have also been obliged to shorten the weekly hours of operation, and in some cases to curtail production to a point approximating a complete shut down of the plant. In all of these instances the management has very frankly discussed all of the conditions which necessitated such changes with the employee representatives, and they have loyally cooperated with the management in placing these reasons before the rank and file of factory employees.

"The reductions in wages and schedules were in all cases approved by the employee representatives' section of our Works Councils, in many cases after long and frank argument, and we feel that the matter has been much more satisfactorily handled as the result of the actions of the Works Councils than would otherwise have been possible."

The following method was adopted by the management of an eastern concern employing 150 workers, when it became necessary to effect a reduction in wages:

"The management called a meeting of the shop committee and all the department heads and outlined to the assembly the exact status of conditions, namely, the amount of business scheduled, the prospects (or rather lack of them) for immediate new business, the keenness of competition and the necessity for lowering selling costs a given percentage in order to meet competition.

"The various factors entering into a manufacturing business—labor, material, and overhead—were analyzed with the shop committee so that they could see the necessity for reducing the cost of production and calculate the percentage it would be necessary to decrease the rates of pay to meet the contingency.

"In short, the shop committee, and through them, the employees in general, were made to feel that the management was asking of them their help and cooperation in a matter of mutual interest, and the cut in wages decided upon was taken gracefully by all."

Another firm which has a Works Council of the "Industrial Democracy" type outlined its procedure in making a reduction in wages, as follows:

"During the month of December, 1920, the company informed its operatives through the medium of their representatives that the outlook for business resumption would probably make a wage reduction necessary. Index figures of Bradstreet's, Dun's, National Industrial Conference Board as well as United States Labor Department, were submitted to indicate that the cost of living had gone down and that we were warranted, without seriously injuring living conditions of employees, in following the downward trend, stating that we could not guarantee to obtain enough business to occupy the plant, but it was more likely that we could with wage reduction than otherwise.

"As a consequence, the Council, or as it is known with us (the House), decided to accept our recommendations and left the matter in the hands of the management. The management increased the working hours from $47\frac{1}{2}$ to 50 and decreased the wages 15%, making a net reduction in earning power of 10%. From this there was no dissent and these wages went into effect at the beginning of January."

In a middle western plant with a Council of the "Industrial Democracy" type, ". . . it became necessary to reduce the hours of work from six days a week, $44\frac{1}{2}$ hours working time, to five days a week, 40 hours working time, and to reduce the force by about 20 per cent. Each of these moves was made after a committee of the employees' Congress had gone into the matter thoroughly and concurred with the management in the course taken."

In the case of the men laid off, a joint committee of representatives of the employees and the management reviewed three lists of the employees—one list from the production records of the company, one list based on the general impressions of the foremen, and another list prepared by a committee of employee representatives. The joint committee discussed each individual name with the object of determining whether or not it should be on the layoff list. The company stated:

> "In this way we have accomplished a shrinkage and the men themselves were able to suggest just who should or should not be affected."

Further retrenchments becoming necessary, a committee from Congress was called into conference with the Cabinet and presented with facts and figures pertaining to relationship of production and sales. After a full discussion and study of the facts presented, the committee made a brief investigation of inventories of raw and process material and finished stock which was shown to be increasing to a point that was causing the company to borrow large amounts of money to finance.

The committee's report was to the effect that "in justice to the owners of the company the only recommendation they could make was a complete shutdown of the plant until such a time as the abnormal inventories might be sold."

This was approved by Congress, but the Cabinet offered the alternative of a three-day week without change of hourly rates. This was approved by Congress and put into effect. With reference to this method of handling such questions the company wrote:

> "The value of handling a matter in this way cannot be overestimated. The investigations and reports of workmen carry weight with their co-workers and stimulate confidence in the management. The men realized they were getting the best deal possible under the existing circumstances."

When it became necessary to carry out still further measures of retrenchment because of reduced output and heavy overhead the management placed before the employee representatives "all possible information regarding the operation of the company's business."

The recommendation finally made by the Cabinet to the Congress, that the company change from a three-day week to full time basis of 44½ hours per week, with an average wage reduction of 20%, was accepted by the Congress, and a joint committee was appointed to obtain all the information needed for reclassifying the men according to efficiency and length of service.

With reference to the method adopted, the company stated:

"While no one likes to have their income reduced, our men were so thoroughly informed of the conditions that made a wage reduction necessary that it was accepted in a spirit of fairness as a result of their knowledge of the facts."

Other employers stated that the representatives had been very fair in their consideration of the proposals of the management when they fully understood them. Having agreed with the management that retrenchment should be carried out, emphasis was placed on the value of their services in then explaining to the rest of the employees the necessity for management's action and the reasons for the reductions. Such a case was that of a middle western plant with two hundred employees. One of the officials of the company wrote regarding this assistance from employee representatives:

"The wage reductions which were made necessary by the revision of our selling prices, were determined by the management. The method of determination and other information pertaining to the subject was presented to the works committee and the whole matter discussed and explained to them so that they understood the reason for the reduction and the method by which we arrived at the amount of reduction. We then announced our decision and the committee gave us their full cooperation in explaining our position to the rest of the employees.

"The matter of reduction of working hours was similarly handled. Our men could see that our warehouses were being filled with surplus product and it was very evident to all that a reduction in hours must eventually be put into effect. When the time arrived when we felt that we could not afford to put any more material into stock, we called the works committee into conference and explained to them two methods of reduction which we felt would be fairest to the company in maintaining this organization and in manufacturing to the greatest efficiency, and to the men in supplying them with the greatest possible weekly wage. One of these methods was adopted and the necessary announcements made."

Another company wrote:

"We are very pleased to state that the attitude of the conference committee, when it has been necessary to call them together for the purpose of a wage reduction, has been very fair. All they wish to know is that there is a good reason for the proposed reduction or change in any work schedule. We have always found that by taking such matters up with the conference committee and they, in turn, with the men before any reduction in wages is made, the men accept any such change with very much better grace than they would otherwise."

Another western concern stated:

"We have no complaint to find with the attitude of the employees' committees relative to the reduction in wages, working schedule, etc., whenever the committees had full information upon which to base their action."

One of the company officials of an eastern plant with nine hundred workers wrote:

"The representatives have been of much assistance to us in reducing wages, and hours of work. They have carried our messages throughout the shops and have worked with us conscientiously and consistently all through our depression."

89

A correspondent of the Board in an eastern brass works wrote that, although the employees were not enthusiastic about a wage reduction, a great deal of misunderstanding had been cleared up through being able to explain to them the necessity for the reduction.

In a western coal and iron company the proposal for a 20% reduction in wages made by the management was met by the employees with a counter-proposal asking that the reduction be only 15%, with a promise on their part that if their suggestion were accepted they would make up for the difference by increased efficiency. This proposal was accepted by the management. Four months after the 15% reduction had been made, it was stated that there had been a distinct improvement in efficiency and apparently management and men were on the whole satisfied with the agreement.

A western watch company had a similar experience when the question of a change in working hours came up. The factory had been working forty-eight hours a week and as summer came on the employees began to evidence a desire to have Saturday afternoon off. This was at a time when management was urgently striving to increase production, and as it was rather anxious to keep up the full schedule of time the Advisory Council was informed accordingly. The management further suggested that if the employees felt that they must have the Saturday afternoons off, they might be willing to start working one half hour earlier in the morning, and in this way make up a good portion of the time which would be lost by the closing of the factory at noon on Saturday. With this suggestion before them the Advisory Council went into the matter, questioning a great many of the employees before making any recommendation. The final decision was to the effect that the employees desired the Saturday half holiday and did not wish to start work earlier in the morning, thus cutting down the total weekly hours from forty-eight to forty-four and a half.

The vice-president wrote:

"This, of course, was distinctly opposite to the suggestion of the executives, but we believed that the Advisory Council was acting in good faith, and we depended on their statement that the employees would put forth such effort to increase their production that the result of the change in the hours would be no loss in the total product for the week. The plan was therefore put into force and has worked very well, the employees having come up to their promise of turning out as much work in the new forty-four and a half hour week as they did in the old forty-eight hour week."

The employee representatives in a western oil company also presented a counter-proposal to the management when the latter laid before the Works Council, in February, 1921, a proposal that wages be reduced from 3% to 18%, to restore the wage scale which had been in effect in 1920. The Council proposed to the management that wages be reduced 10% straight through, basing their request upon the fact that wages had been readjusted rather than increased in 1920. The management accepted the suggestion of the employees and, although in this instance there was no promise on the part of the employees to make up by increased efficiency the difference between the two proposals, the management expressed themselves as well satisfied with the results.

In an eastern plant making printing machinery the management, while not receiving a counter-proposal from the Works Council regarding the method in which economies should be effected, laid two proposals before the employees and put into effect the one which the Council favored. The company's proposals were:

"... to continue on the 44-hour week with an actual 10% reduction in weekly wages and hourly costs, or to return to the 48-hour week, which had been in effect a year and a half ago, with the same weekly pay as on the 44-hour week, but thus making a 10% hourly reduction.

"While many of the employees were very reluctant to abandon the 44-hour week, the Council preferred to work the 48 hours with the same weekly pay as on the 44-hour week. Accordingly, the change was made."

In reducing the hours of certain departments previous to this reduction, the company had also taken into consideration the desires of the employees.

"The employees requested through the Council that the working force be kept intact and that everybody work part time rather than make a drastic reduction in the working force, and allow the remainder to work full time. The working schedule of the various departments was arranged to suit the desires of the men."

Summing up their experience with a Works Council during a period of readjustment, this company wrote:

"Although some of the employees at times have been out of sympathy with the policies which were necessarily adopted, the majority of the employees and the Council have remained steadfast in their support."

When an eastern concern with three thousand employees changed its working hours from forty-four to forty-eight per week, with a readjustment in hourly and piece work rates with the approval of the Works Council, organized labor endeavored to pull the men out on strike. The trade union workers announced that instead of quitting work at 5:30 p. m., as had been agreed to by the management and the employee representatives, they would quit at 4:45 p. m. On learning of the intended action of the trade union members in the plant, the employee members of the Works Council in secret session passed unanimously a resolution opposing any such action on the part of the employees. Copies of this resolution were posted throughout the plant, and not more than a dozen out of the three thousand employees responded to the strike call.

In order that the company might underbid other firms for a government contract, the employees of a middle western shoe company with a Works Council of the "company union" type, voted by a large majority to accept a wage reduction of 10% during the process of making the shoes, should the company be successful in securing the order. Through this expression of cooperation on the part of the employees the company was able to get the order, and the 10% reduction was put into effect.

"During the months of November and December, 1920, wage questions were naturally very much in the background, for the reason that our employees were well aware of the fact that the inevitable reaction had set in and that it was going to be a fight on the company's part to keep wages where they were, let alone make any advances.

"Just before the first of December we deemed it advisable to put in a bid for a large government contract and took the matter up frankly with our employees through the regular channels of the Association regarding the situation, which was this:

"We were practically out of orders for civilian shoes and it meant a shutdown for perhaps several months if we did not receive the government order. With this in mind, also the fact that many of our competitors were at that time shut down and undoubtedly could re-employ their employees at much less wages than heretofore, our Association took the matter under consideration and after taking a secret ballot decided very nearly unanimously to accept a 10 per cent reduction during the process of making the government shoes if the company should be successful, this proposition being made to the company in order that the company might make its bid lower than it otherwise could and, therefore, stand a better chance of getting the order.

"This action on the employees' part did in fact enable the company to get the order and this 10 per cent reduction is now in effect."

Some employers reported that from their experience they did not consider it wise to place the matter of a reduction in wages before the employee representatives in such a way that they would be put in the position of voting their approval or acceptance of the reduction. It was found that this subjected the representatives to much adverse criticism by their constituents, and that the representation plan was thereby brought into disfavor among the employees. This was the experience of an eastern electrical concern. Although the employee representatives had not agreed to the wage reduction proposed by the company, the employees were under the impression that they had done so and the result, according to the president of the concern, was very disturbing. He wrote:

"With regard to adjustment of wages downward, the committees have been of considerable help in handing down explanations as to why reductions were desirable. We have been very careful not to place committeemen in the embarrassing position of appearing to recommend reductions in wages as we believe it to be the responsibility of the management to make adjustments of this sort when necessary, and only depend on the employees to assist to the extent of explaining the need. Notwithstanding our care in this connection, the committees have received quite a considerable amount of criticism from their fellow-workers due to the fact that they thought that the committees agreed

92

to a reduction in wages, which was not the case. We have spent considerable time and energy in straightening out this misapprehension."

A southern foundry company with four hundred workers reported that, because of the criticism which was aroused by the "request" of the employee representatives for a wage reduction, in the future it would use the Works Council only as a means of explaining to the employees the necessity for measures of retrenchment. In this plant, in which there is a modified plan of the "Industrial Democracy" type, the body of the employee representatives is called the Junior Board. An official of the company wrote:

"The reduction in wages (16⅔%) was made at the request of our Junior Board after the suggestion of the company that it would be a means of continuing the employment of a larger number of men. Our experience is such that an intelligent explanation of such conditions to the employees themselves is the most logical manner to bring about readjustment of conditions through a Works Council plan."

In six plants of a western packing company the employee representatives who composed a special committee to deal with the subject, while recognizing that a wage reduction was necessary and while convinced that management's proposal was fair and equitable, did not definitely vote for a reduction, but referred the proposal back to management for final decision, with the statement that in their opinion management would give the employees every consideration possible. The report of the committee to the Works Council in one of the plants was worded thus:

"1. It is the personal opinion of the entire committee that, considering all circumstances, the proposed reduction is necessary and fair, but in so expressing themselves the members of this committee desire it to be understood that they are not definitely voting for a reduction.

"2. It is a matter of such importance to the employees as well as to the company that this committee prefers to refer it back to the Assembly for such action as may seem proper to the Assembly.

"3. It is naturally distasteful to all employees to have their wages reduced, but after a thorough review of the entire matter we feel that a reduction in operating expenses is necessary, and suggest, therefore, that the president's letter of November 15th, 1921, containing a definite proposal for a reduction, be received and filed without further action for or against the proposition by the Assembly, thereby leaving the matter in the hands of the management.

"It is thought this method of handling will be more acceptable to the representatives of the employees.

"This committee regrets that this matter had to come up so early in the life of the Assembly, but we are impressed with the possibilities of close relationship through the representation plan."

In explanation of this report the secretary of the committee made the following statement:

"I, for one, and the rest of the committee, and, I think, all the rest of us, wish to avoid being put in a position of definitely voting for a reduction of wages. We do not want to be in a position where we must answer for that. We believe that the duty of reducing wages belongs to the management. The information we have convinced me and the other members of the committee that a reduction is necessary and inevitable, but we feel that we ought not to be asked to vote for a reduction of wages of the men with whom we work every day. If the management feels that it is necessary, it should be done by an official act and the Assembly relieved."

The Assembly unanimously adopted the report. One of the employee representatives then made the following motion, which was also adopted unanimously:

"We, the members of the Assembly, in session November 18, 1921, hereby express a vote of confidence in the management as to their fair and impartial dealing with their employees and we feel that the final decision in the matter of wage adjustment will be rendered with the thought in mind that their employees are given every consideration possible."

A company official, writing with reference to the manner in which the employee representatives left the matter in the hands of management for executive action, stated:

"This was done, we are informed, because of threats of annoyance from the outside leaders of a small minority of organized employees."

In eight other plants of this company the employee representatives voted upon the merits of the reduction proposed and "in every case accepted the same by a vote well over the necessary two-thirds, the vote varying with the different plants from 72.7% up to 100%." The average vote in favor of reduction in these plants was 80.6% and out of a total of 297 votes cast in the fourteen plants, 265 were in favor of the reduction, and 32 opposed.

The Board's correspondent, commenting upon the two methods of handling reduction of wages, stated:

"It is quite natural that in the early stages of exercising their responsibilities as representatives of the employees, they should be timid about taking responsibility on a major issue in some cases; yet they have functioned fully on many important matters other than wages during the last seven months. The process is essentially an educational one and the main thing, in our opinion, is not the vote, though that was obtained beyond any doubt, but the conviction prevalent through all the thirty thousand employees that they were treated justly and that they were supplied with all the facts in the matter."

Another middle western paper company, with Works Councils of the "committee" type in four mills, reported that although the employee representatives were convinced that the proposed wage reduction of 20 per cent was fair, a number of them were afraid to vote for it in the Councils because of the reception they would receive from their fellow employees.

Individual councilmen, however, who voted unfavorably admitted later that they were personally convinced that 20 per cent was fair but they did not dare face their constituents with anything but the record of an unfavorable vote. It was the unanimous opinion of the Council, however, that some wage reduction was necessary.

Another employer who believes that the employee representatives should not be put in a position where they formally accept the proposals of the management regarding wage reductions, bases this upon his experience with a request made by the employees for a 48-hour week. At the time the request was made the employee representatives, after consultation with the management, voted against introducing a working week of forty-eight hours. This caused great dissatisfaction among the employees, and the Works Council was brought into disfavor. After this experience, the employer in this plant did not ask the employee representatives to approve of his announcement of a wage cut. The matter was simply explained before the Council, and the employee representatives then put the facts before the employees. The manager of the plant stated that the Council was "a very convenient and satisfactory medium" for this purpose.

The statement of a company official of a western rubber company with a Works Council of the "Industrial Democracy" type, is interesting in this connection. In his opinion, the success of a representation plan is dependent upon the amount of responsibility placed upon the committees organized under the plan. In this company,

" . . . the committee from the Congress on production dividends, bonuses and wages, composed of three senators, three representatives and a member of the Cabinet acting in an advisory capacity, submitted a report to the Congress recommending a reduction of 20% in the earnings of the men in the factory. They explained to the Congress that such a course was necessary in order that labor might do its share in assisting the company to meet severe competition. This report was unanimously adopted by the Congress and accepted by the entire organization with assurances on every hand . . . that every effort would be made toward increasing efficiency in order that unit labor costs might be still further lowered."

Writing with reference to the approval which the employees gave to the recommendation of this committee, the same correspondent stated:

"It has been our experience that the success of the various activities of the Industrial Congress is about in direct proportion to the amount of responsibility placed upon the committee having that particular activity in charge. With our plan a committee's recommendations, to become effective, must be ratified by the Industrial Congress, with any action of the Congress subject to veto by the president. As a matter of fact, veto by the president has in our experience never been necessary. We find that the committeemen, in their zeal to prove themselves fair-minded and free of radicalism, are most apt to err on the side of being ultra-conservative, but these committeemen are willing to accept responsibility for their recommendations and, while sometimes criticized, are in the main loyally supported by the organization at large. If freedom of action and the responsibility for that action is withheld and the committees function only as agents for the management, employee representation does not exist and Industrial Democracy is a misnomer."

A company official in a large concern with twenty-four Works Councils in operation in as many plants, discussing the subject of whether an employer should solicit the employee representatives' approval of a wage reduction, wrote that it depended

> ". . . entirely upon the attitude which the plant management and company executives have taken toward Works Council procedure, and with just what degree of frankness they are actually seeking to bring about a real intimacy of contact and how far they are willing to go in assuming a joint and mutual interest in the business between employees and management."

In this company the management had solicited the employee representatives' approval of proposed wage reductions. This correspondent stated:

> "Our own experience has been a very happy one, and the method we used in accomplishing the wage reductions has certainly very definitely strengthened the Council plan and heightened the morale of the shops."

With reference to the so-called "voluntary" voting of reduction of wages by employees themselves, an examination of such instances shows that the use of the word "voluntary" is somewhat misleading. In the sense that there was no coercion by the management to force the employees to accept the proposed reduction, the action of the employees may be termed "voluntary." But when it is remembered that the alternatives to accepting the proposals of the management (except in those cases noted above, where the employees made a counter proposal and promised to make up for the difference between their proposal and that of the management by increased efficiency and economy) were either the closing down of the plant or the loss of their jobs, the term "voluntary" cannot be correctly applied to the action of the employees.

This was well brought out by an eastern employer in whose plant a reduction in wages, made in January, 1921, was reported in the press as "voluntary" by the employees. Referring to the magazine interview, regarding which this executive stated he had "evidently been misquoted," he wrote:

> "In December, 1920, we were already experiencing very poor business. Decreases in wages had been effected by certain of our competitors which would have inevitably placed us at a serious disadvantage if we had not taken steps to meet them. Under these conditions I personally went before the joint committees of employers' and employees' representatives and explained that in order to compete, I felt that we must reduce wages. I suggested a 10% horizontal reduction and the temporary elimination of all overtime pay, as well as a revision of the differential rates paid for certain classes of both skilled and unskilled jobs.
>
> "Personally, as well as on behalf of the management, I expressed regret at the condition which seemed to require this action, and while those present agreed that it was bitter medicine, everyone showed the heartiest good feeling and one of the employees' representatives even suggested that they were perfectly willing to cooperate with the management to any extent that the latter felt necessary to get business to keep the plants going. He even suggested that the employees would be willing to take a 15% instead of a 10% reduction if that would increase the prospect of business, and concluded by a statement that the management could depend on the employees of the organization to

96

make every necessary contribution, but that the employees would in turn look to the management to get the business after the wage scale had been adjusted to what was agreed to be a fair basis."

Going on to state that the so-called "voluntary" voting of wage reductions by employees themselves is misleading, this correspondent continued:

"In the first place the average worker does not know, except upon the advice of the management, whether or not and to what extent a wage reduction is necessary. At the time of our reduction the plants were practically shut down and it was common knowledge that at least one important competitor had reduced wages. Our organization frankly stated when the proposition was put up to them that they had anticipated that some such action would be necessary and they felt rather relieved to have the matter put into concrete shape in order to get it cleared up as quickly as possible. There was no suggestion of coercion from the company to force acceptance of this reduction, but business conditions certainly indicated the necessity for it in terms that could not be mistaken by any person of ordinary intelligence."

In another company with Works Councils of the "Industrial Democracy" type in operation in two plants, where the employee representatives had unanimously accepted the wage reduction announced by the management, the president of the company stated that such action could not be described as a "voluntary" reduction on the part of the employees. He said:

"There is no such thing as a 'voluntary' wage reduction by employees. It's against human nature. Employees may, when convinced of the necessity of a wage reduction vote that they will accept it, but to state that they do so 'voluntarily' is not correct. They vote to accept the reduction because they know if they don't they will be out of a job. It is simply a case of accepting half a loaf when they can't get a whole one."

A large western rubber company, in its account of the manner in which wage reductions had been carried out through its Works Council, also drew attention to the fact that the acceptance of the reductions by the employees was not voluntary. One of the company officials wrote:

"The House and Senate did not favor wage reductions with any great enthusiasm, I may assure you. They realized, however, after listening to the management that in times like these there was little else that could be done, as economies were absolutely forced upon us.

"The subject arose in a very natural way. When the management felt it was necessary to make wage reductions, they so announced to the Assembly, answering all questions, patiently discussing all details and finally putting the wage reduction into effect. Unanimous approval of the employees does not necessarily mean hearty satisfaction. They do feel, however, I think, that we are doing our best to preserve our labor policies and to keep our wages as high as is commensurate with the business problems involving competition and refinancing, with which we have been confronted."

Another employer with Works Councils of the "committee" type in operation in five plants, commented upon the influence of economic conditions in connection with the manner in which the employees had accepted reductions in wages and changes in hours.

97

". . . We secured the acquiescence of the conference committees to the proposed changes, and we believe that their influence throughout the plants was of value in having the changes readily accepted. We, of course, believe that the pevailing conditions of unemployment had much influence in having the suggestions so readily accepted. This perhaps, however, is only another way of saying that the changes suggested were reasonable and proper."

The Conference Board has learned of three instances in which the action of the employee representatives with reference to wage reductions and changes in work hour schedules may be properly termed "voluntary." In one case, that of a film manufacturing company with a Works Council of the "Industrial Democracy" type, the employee representatives on their own initiative requested the management to reduce the working week from five and one-half to five days with a corresponding reduction in pay. They also promised they would endeavor to produce seventy thousand additional feet of film per week.

The resolution, passed at a mass meeting of the employees, follows:

WHEREAS, We, the employees of the . . . . Company realize that the industrial conditions which exist throughout the country at the present time have decreased the demand for our product, thereby necessarily decreasing our production, without a corresponding decrease in our operating cost; therefore

BE IT RESOLVED, That, in order to show in a practical way the cooperative spirit of the organization, we, the people, in Mass Meeting assembled, this Thursday, June 2, 1921, do request the company to cut off from the working schedule of the plant, until further notice from the management, one half-day each week; namely, Saturday morning for the day-shift, and a corresponding reduction for the night-shift, reducing proportionately from our pay for the time thus saved, and,

BE IT FURTHER RESOLVED, That we endeavor to produce seventy thousand additional feet per week.

Note: This is in no way to interfere with Saturday morning work whenever the management finds it necessary.

It is interesting to note that approximately 80% of the employees in this plant are members of the local trade union.

In the other instances the representatives of the employees, before any wage reductions had been made, assured their employers of the willingness of the employees to share with them whatever economies the period of readjustment should render necessary. Both of these plants, southern textile companies, have profit-sharing plans in operation. The resolutions adopted by the Board of Operatives—the representatives of the employees—in November, 1920, and presented to the management, expressed the employees' appreciation of "the Co-Partnership and Profit-Sharing Plan and its successful operation." Reference was made to "the liberal profit-sharing checks which have been distributed in the community and the spirit of harmony, cooperation and good will which has been developed thereby."

The employees expressed "grateful thanks" that the "wartime" wage scale and operations had been sustained, but realized that such favorable conditions could not continue under the depresssion in the cotton market, and stated that

". . . in the spirit of our cooperation we wish all to stand together in adversity as well as in prosperity. Therefore, we hereby express our confidence in the management and pledge our full sympathy and united support in taking whatever steps may be found necessary in serving the best interests of all parties concerned."

In only two instances, so far as the Conference Board has learned, did employers meet with opposition from either the employee members of Works Councils or the employees themselves in connection with proposed wage reductions. In the first case, that of an eastern textile plant in which there is a Council of the "Industrial Democracy" type, conditions during the summer of 1920 became such that the company could operate only three days per week. In October the company proposed that the House of Representatives should discuss a reduction in wages, which they were informed was necessary if the factory was to be kept running till the end of the year. It was explained that the company did not need to continue production, as they had sufficient in stock to take care of all orders. The only object in keeping the factory going was to provide the employees with work. The management did not present a proposal to the House of Representatives as to what amount wages should be reduced, but simply asked the employee representatives to consider the matter and let the management know what they would do about it. The representatives showed no willingness to cooperate with the management, though they reluctantly stated that they thought a reduction of 10% would be fair. A greater reduction than that, they said, would not be satisfactory to them. "Owing to this lack of willingness on the part of the employee representatives to cooperate with us, we then decided to close the plant," stated one of the executives of the company.

Accordingly the factory was closed for the months of November and December. When the employees received notice that this was to be done, they informed the management that their representatives had not truly expressed the sentiments of the mass of the employees. To this the management replied that the way to prevent the recurrence of such a condition of affairs was to see that at the next election they elected representatives who really would represent them. At the first of 1921, the plant resumed operations with new rates of pay which were 20% below the base rate of October, 1920. The new rates also involved an increase of production over that of October. It is to be noted in this instance that management did not present the Works Council with any definite plan regarding the proposed reduction in wages.

When the management of a western agricultural machinery company, with a Works Council of the "committee" type, took up the question of a wage reduction with the employee representatives, the representatives asked that a referendum vote be taken among the employees. The employees voted not to accept the reduction and stayed away from work while the matter was being discussed in the Council.

At the end of four days another vote was taken and the management's proposals were finally accepted, whereupon the employees returned to work. One of the company officials wrote that had the proposal for the reduction not been made so suddenly, and had the management not exerted undue pressure to make it effective at once, it was questionable whether there would have been any trouble.

The proposition submitted by the management and finally accepted by the men on January 15, 1921, was:

"(a) The present wage scale to continue in effect until February 16, at which time there will be a reduction of 15% in wages.
"(b) To work cooperatively to increase the collective average of production 25%.
"(c) No change in the reduced wage scale for a period of six months after February 16."

The Board's informant, writing in April, 1921, said: "Our 25% increase in production was realized." Referring to the strike this correspondent stated:

"We do not consider the strike in any way attributable to defects in the plan of representation. Instead, we think it was entirely due to the suddenness with which the proposal was brought out, for had the original plan, as laid down by our manufacturing executive, and which plan was the one finally acted on, been proposed, there is every likelihood that the announcements would have been received by the men without any disturbance to production while the terms and conditions of the proposal were being discussed by the management and the committee."

A few days after the wage reduction had been put into effect, international representatives of the pattern makers' and the moulders' unions protested to the management against the cut and endeavored to carry on separate negotiations for the members of their unions. The management in each case referred the organizers to the central committee. In the case of the pattern makers the committee convinced them they had been mistaken in their action in departing from the unanimous agreement, and after being absent for five days they returned to work on the same terms as the other employees. There was no cessation of work on the part of the moulders, the local moulders' union agreeing that because of the "harmonious relations which had so long existed between this company and its employees, they would permit their members who were employed there to work on a rate which has been reduced 15%." In the other shops in the vicinity, the moulders would not accept any reduction amounting to more than 10%.

Summing up their conclusions on the usefulness of employee representation, the same correspondent wrote:

> "I think the above experience shows that employee representation, when it is truly representative, is very useful and helpful to both parties; whereas, when special or group interest is allowed to take precedence over the mass interest, it is not satisfactory to either side. The ideal which we seek to maintain at all times is that, with regard to any proposition, 'if it is fair for one, it is fair for all—and if it is not fair for all, it is not fair for any one'."

It is interesting to note that some time after the 15% reduction in wages, this company found it necessary to reduce their working schedule to five days per week. At the time this was done management "received hearty cooperation from the committee on this proposal."

The significance of the experiences of the employers quoted above, who took up the question of wage reductions and changes in work-hour schedules with the members of their Works Councils, lies in two things. The first is the casting out of the false gods of secrecy by employers, and the second the reaction of the employees to this policy. Instead of being kept in the dark as to the reasons why economies which affected their pockets had to be made, employees were given a full explanation of the reasons necessitating such action. That this method was successful in avoiding the misunderstandings that might otherwise have arisen, is proven by the statements of employers given above. Employees appreciated the consideration of their feelings shown by employers. They appreciated being taken into the counsels of management. As an employee in an eastern mill said:

> "Being told why you have to accept a cut in wages seems to soften the blow. It shows that the management thinks it worth while to go to the trouble to explain things to us. That's a whole lot better than merely posting up a notice Saturday night saying wages will be cut so much starting Monday morning."

Employees saw that economic forces exerted a pressure upon their employer as well as upon themselves. They realized that economies had to be made if plant operations were to be maintained, and to the extent that this realization was achieved, they saw that their interests and those of the employer were mutual. Both had to work for the survival of the industry, both had to accept their share of the sacrifices necessary for this to be done. Where this realization prompted the employees in accepting necessary economies, the Works Council may be said to have made its contribution towards bringing about a realization on the part of employer and employees that their interests are fundamentally one.

CHAPTER VIII

EFFECT OF WORKS COUNCILS ON THE RELATIONS BETWEEN MANAGEMENT AND EMPLOYEES

In nearly every case covered by the present investigation by the Conference Board, the opinions of executives and workers have coincided regarding the effect of the installation of Works Councils on the relations existing in industrial plants between managements and their employees. Viewed from either angle experience has proved the organization to be an eminently satisfactory means of disposing of those difficulties which so often arise because of misunderstanding on the part of either party of the other's point of view.

Prior to the development of employee representation, the lack of any machinery for explaining contemplated changes which, through ignorance of their necessity, were often stubbornly fought by the employees, created and maintained a reciprocal attitude of "antagonism, suspicion and distrust," often developing into strikes. The fact also that the foremen's decisions in all cases of employees' grievances were final, admitting of no appeal to a higher authority, was productive of additional discontent. According to the reports of many company officials and employees, the unsatisfactory relations due to the foregoing conditions have been greatly improved by Works Councils.

Where employers have lived up to the spirit of the representation plan, they have adhered to the policy of keeping the workers informed, through their elected representatives on the committees, of the status of the business, a proceeding which has been one of the strongest factors in overcoming their erstwhile attitude of antagonism. This has been especially true, as has been seen, in times when business depression made the future uncertain in the matter of continuous employment and steady wages.

Furthermore, increased good will toward the company has been shown by employees because of the opportunity afforded them by the representation plans to come in contact with company officials other than their foremen. The knowledge that they could take their grievances to the management direct, even though they seldom availed themselves of the privilege, has been a source of satisfaction in many instances, while in other cases the mere fact of acquaintance with these representatives of the management has been sufficient to improve relations.

According to a company official in a large middle western concern operating a plan of the "Industrial Democracy" type, the primary object of their Works Council was the improvement of the relations between employer and employed. It was stated as follows:

> "The purpose of employee representation as introduced in our plant was to obtain a means of understanding our men and having our men understand the management, to quickly get problems ironed out and get each other's point of view."

Almost without exception employers who discussed the effect of the Works Council on the relations between them and their employees said that the purpose, as summarized above, had been accomplished. Where relations had been unsatisfactory previous to the installation of the Council, and had undergone no change after its organization, the reason was to be found in the failure of the management to fulfill its part of the obligation.

Various concerns operating representation plans of the "Industrial Democracy" type had almost identical experiences in this respect. Some of their reports follow:

A mid-western firm manufacturing paint wrote:

> "We have found that Congress has done a great deal towards bringing a closer cooperation and a better feeling and relationship between management and the workers."

An eastern silk mill gave a similar report:

> "There is an apparent better understanding between management and workers."

A mid-western printing concern wrote:

> "The relationship between the management and the workers is one of absolute cooperation. Each extends to the other whatever assistance can be rendered in promoting greater efficiency and contentment for both sides."

From a western rubber company came:

> "Employee representation has brought about, through the committee work where there is free discussion and interchange of ideas, closer relations between management and workers."

In discussing the effect of employee representation on the relations between management and employees, employers operating Works Councils of the "committee" type reported experience similar to that quoted under the "Industrial Democracy" plan.

From an eastern electric company, whose employees number ten thousand, came this statement:

> "We think that the plan of representation has made better relations between the management and the workers, due to better understanding of each other's difficulties and points of view. The opportunities for close understanding have, in themselves, made better relations."

From an eastern metal concern:

> "We believe the general relation between management and workers is better on account of the plan acting as a medium for both employees and management to state their positions."

From a western lumber company came:

"The relationship between management and workers . . . has been very pleasant. The tendency is for fair debate on all questions instead of threats or strikes as heretofore."

The report of a southern power company was:

"Our employees' committee plan has been instrumental in bringing about a feeling between the employees and the management of mutual good faith and fairness."

From a mid-western company manufacturing machinery:

"The effect on the relationship between the management and the workers has been to increase discipline and increase loyalty to the management. We are working 'with' each other instead of the men working 'for' us."

Of special interest are the detailed statements given by some employers regarding the beneficial effect of the Works Council on the relations between them and their workers.

An eastern paper company having a Works Council of the "committee" type employs three thousand men. One of its company officials reported that the Council had had an important influence, in that it gave to both management and employees an increased sense of responsibility.

"It is difficult to judge accurately the effect of our works committee upon the relationship of management and workers, as this is a very intangible sort of thing. We believe, however, that it has done a great deal to put across to the employees the idea that the company—its success, its policies and its reputation—belongs as much to them as it does to the management. Perhaps more important is the broadening of the point of view of the management, by making them feel that their responsibility is to the employees as well as to the directors, and that it is the welfare of the company, including its employees, its management and its customers, that is their real objective, rather than present profits."

This company has evolved, in connection with its Council, some rather striking plans which might have some bearing on the improved relationship between the management and the workers. Before the institution of the employee representation plan, the company had formed what was practically a true industrial partnership. Preferred stock owned by outside investors gave to its owners a fixed return. This stock was voting stock only when the business failed to pay this regular dividend. Each year the profits remaining after dividends on all outstanding stock had been paid, were reinvested in the business and against this investment shares of stock were issued called "Industrial Partnership Stock." Two-thirds of this was voting stock and was issued to such executives as principal foremen, chief clerks, principal salesmen, etc., in proportion to their relative salaries.

Before the installation of the works committees, the employer wished to give the workers some share in the profits, but had been able to evolve no satisfactory scheme. After its introduction at the factory the Works Council appointed a special committee which, after four months of deliberation, drew up an "Employee Industrial Partnership Plan," which was unanimously adopted. This plan provided for a fund made up of one-third of the profits remaining each year after the fixed dividends on all the preferred stock outstanding had been paid. This fund was to be distributed in the form of non-transferable, non-voting stock among the employees, the amount varying with length of service. While workers have no share in the direct control of the company,

> ". . . all non-managerial employees . . . participate with the Managerial Industrial Partners in the management of the company through their representative in the General Works Committee. . . . This committee is free to discuss any factory problem or policy and to make recommendations in regard thereto for the approval of the management. In practice it has become an active and important factor in management and through it all non-managerial employees participate in the direction of the company."

The same concern has in operation a carefully thought-out unemployment plan. This plan was worked out by the Works Council. The company has set aside certain definite sums of money to be used, as long as they last, for the relief of distress due to unemployment. Control of this fund is in the hands of a committee of four, two appointed by the management and two by the Works Committee. Employees are kept informed regarding the condition of the fund.

A company official of a mid-western concern which operates a Council of the "committee" type, believes in employee representation as a means of producing a closer relationship between management and employees and of insuring a "square deal" for all:

> "We believe where employee representation exists there is a closer understanding between employer and employee which eliminates a number of dissatisfactions. We are frank in stating that our experience with this Advisory Board has been of mutual benefit both to the employer and the employee. It paves the way for closer cooperation, avoids misunderstandings and disputes and insures for everyone a square deal."

In a western company employing thirty thousand men and operating a Council of the "committee" type in twenty-four plants, an official reported that he was especially gratified over the relations maintained between management and employees during the period of business depression. During the two years that the Councils have been in operation in this company's plants—years which have been marked by turbulence in industrial relations in the whole country—it was stated that "There has been no loss of direct contact between the men and the management at those plants where Councils have been established."

Another western concern, manufacturing machinery, found that through its "committee" plan a highly desirable contact, with important results, had been established between management and employees. On more than one occasion the employer and his representatives felt the effect on their viewpoints of employee council.. The intimate relation that developed was found to be such that the employee moulded employer sentiment quite as truly as the employer was enabled to guide employee thought.

An eastern company employing 46,000 men and having a Council of the "committee" type, found employee representation essential for securing a right relationship between management and workers. One of the company officials wrote:

> "There is no doubt but that it has, through the establishment of a better understanding of each other, improved the relationship between the management and the workers. There is no doubt in my mind but that some sort of a plan of employee representation is not only desirable but quite essential in any large industry if the relations between the management and employees are to be such as to insure the success of all parties concerned."

The commanding officer of a mid-western arsenal whose Works Council, of the "committee" type, has had an especially interesting history, gave a detailed report on the improvement in relations between management and employees effected by employee representation:

> "The effect upon the relations between the management and the workers . . . has been to produce a very much better understanding of the viewpoint of both sides."

Especially from the worker's point of view has he found the effect on relations between management and employees good:

> "If John Jones has a grievance or suggestion or idea to propose which he must get off his chest, the Works Organization as outlined here provides a place for John Jones to go. The standing committees as composed will not stand for any foolishness and a waste of time or a display of trivial matters is not tolerated by them. The fact that a means is provided to the man with an invitation so to speak, if he must make a statement, oftentimes satisfies the man because he realizes that he is not forbidden but invited to bring matters up and then, consequently, he does not desire to do it. In other words, if John Jones has the privilege of telling 'the old man' or his duly authorized representative, anything he wants to he usually doesn't want to tell him. The present procedure in the Works Council reminds me very much of the scheme embodied here and used by the Fire Department. They have red arrows located at various places around the arsenal which indicate the direction to the nearest fire alarm box, and all the man has to do is not to stop and think where the box is but to run like the dickens the way the arrows point and he is bound to run into a box. If John Jones will only go the way the arrows in the Works Council Organization point he is bound to get the matter that is in his mind given consideration and a prompt decision arrived at."

A company official in a large western rubber concern, operating a Works Council of the "Industrial Democracy" type, outlined what had been accomplished there after one year of experience with employee representation:

106

> "We have used the plan in both directions between men and management. It has benefited the men sometimes in increases in wages, and in many other ways. It has benefited the management in many particular instances where we have wanted the men's point of view. It has benefited the management in cases of labor trouble. For instance, we have had occasions where men have stopped work during the night shift. Next morning we have been able to call in the representatives and say, 'We have a grievance and expect you to get the men who stopped work together and tell them that that isn't the way the law of this company operates.' And in that way we have been able to explain how the Assembly has the power to correct wrongs and that to stop work is an old-fashioned, harmful practice."

In two instances reports stated that the employees had given material evidence of the good will which employee representation had created toward their employers. The vice-president of the first concern, an eastern silk company, operating two Works Councils of the "Industrial Democracy" type, told the following story:

> "After a wage reduction in one of our plants the company had to close down. The employees were told, on leaving, that when the plant reopened they would be taken back at the reduced rate which they were then receiving. During the time the plant was closed a new firm opened up, securing some of our employees. This concern paid them higher wages than they had been receiving from us. When we opened up again these employees were told that although they would be taken back at the rate that prevailed before the shutdown, there would have to be a reduction in a short time. Despite this fact ninety-five per cent of them came back."

The president of another concern, an eastern hosiery mill operating an "Industrial Democracy" type of Council, also was obliged on account of business depression to close some of his plants. Some of his employees showed their confidence in and good will towards their employer by offering him the use of $60,000 of their savings. Others stated that they were willing to work without being paid immediately. This employer gave the credit for the greatly improved relations which exist between him and his workers to his employee representation plan.

In several instances employee representatives were interviewed regarding their ideas of the effect of employee representation on the relations between them and their employers. It is interesting to note that in every case the workers favored the plan as a channel of communication with the management.

In an eastern paper company, where the "committee" type of Works Council is in operation, an employee representative who was also a trade-union man placed emphasis upon the opportunity afforded the employees to get in touch with the executive officers. As another representative in the same plant put it:

> "Before we had a Council we were always in the dark. Foremen delighted in telling us nothing. Now we are satisfied. We have a way of getting straight to the management."

In an eastern silver company, operating a Council of the "committee" type, the employee representatives interviewed were highly in favor of the plan because of the opportunity it afforded them to come in contact with the management. They appreciated the insight they were obtaining into the business through talks given by the company officers. The information they received in this way was passed on to the employees, who, in this present time of uncertainty, were eager to learn all they could about the company's position and the outlook for the future.

In an eastern steel company, whose Works Council also is of the "committee" type, employee representatives expressed satisfaction regarding the improved relations following the institution of employee representation, as follows:

> "We get acquainted with the officials now—can speak to them as man to man."

> "We find a much better feeling among the employees now. They are doing a day's work for a day's pay."

> "When both sides play fair this collective bargaining is the best thing yet."

> "Before the plan was in effect there wasn't a very good feeling between the company and the men. If the men wanted anything they didn't see how they could get it. The foremen stood between them and the company officials."

One of the officials of a middle western machinery company operating a Works Council of the "committee" type reported an interesting experience along this line. He found that, unless employee representatives were wisely chosen and were distinctly representative of their constituents, they prevented contact between the management and the workers by misrepresenting each to the other. Under these circumstances employee representation, as a means for improving industrial relations, would naturally be a failure. He says:

> "Whether the shop committee principle brings the workers and the management closer together or further apart is a question that we cannot answer conclusively at the present time. If it is a fact that the employees' representatives can be considered as the employees themselves, then we can say that the plan brings the two bodies together. This will be true when the representatives are truly representative. We have occasion, however, to note that the shop committee did not represent the employees directly in all questions, on some occasions, but rather prevented the management getting in direct contact with the employees' affected. In such cases the shop committee is a hindrance to the management and does not benefit employees."

This correspondents' opinion as to the advisability of introducing Works Councils into industrial plants was as follows:

> "Whether or not we would advocate a shop committee for every organization would depend to a large extent on the following circumstances: If there is no marked sentiment for such a body in an organization, we certainly would not advocate it. If there was a strong tendency for one in a shop we would advise the management to discourage it until their control functions are in good working shape. I

refer particularly to careful cost records, personnel records, etc. If these records are in first class condition so that the controlling factor of the business can be determined accurately and promptly and the employees' records are adequate to determine the status of an employee, then the organization should be in good shape to arrive at considerable benefit from a shop committee plan. Otherwise the committee men would be in a strong position to override the policies of the management because of the management's lack of facts to support their policies."

The feeling of employees in this plant with regard to the plan has been well expressed by the following article, drawn up by the chairman and the secretary of the works committee:

"It is our opinion that the success of the plan of employee representation now in practice at the plant of the . . . company, is contingent on fair and impartial understanding.

"Its failure or success depends entirely upon the attitude of fairness on the part of the management and its representatives, so as to bring about a spirit of confidence in the employees, which in turn shall pay for itself by way of hearty cooperation.

"While our viewpoint is somewhat localized, it is the consensus of opinion of the Central Committee that this plan would be a failure where organized labor is prohibited or discriminated against. Our reason for advancing this view is based upon the spirit of independence, which is born of trades union affiliation.

"We recognize that a satisfactory way to maintain harmonious relations between the employer and the employee is through committee representation. At the time of the mutual acceptance of this plan, we had neither set rules nor precedents to be governed by. And while it is not by any means perfect, we have found by our past experience that all rules of procedure must be elastic enough to absorb the various phases of the different cases presented. This has here been brought about by open discussion and thorough analysis of the causes and effects either individual or general. In our opinion it is essential to the success of this plan, that all agreements entered into or understandings reached, be accepted and lived up to, or the confidence of the entire organization cannot be maintained.

"We find that where this plan is recognized, as by the management of the . . . company, wherein all grievances of employees, individual or collective, as well as all matters pertaining to reduction or increase in working force—wherein all adjustments of wages and conditions throughout the plant are openly and generally discussed and prearranged through the representatives of the management with the committee representing the employees—and wherein all conditions and understandings of such conferences are faithfully respected and adhered to—wherein no discrimination is shown relative to affiliation of employees with labor organization—also, wherein the proper regard is given the employer by the employee in the protection of his investment and in cordial cooperation to maintain scheduled production—wherein the employee promotes the welfare of the industry at all times and realizes that the success of the industry depends largely upon the coordinated support of the workers—there the plan of representation can be carried on with much success."

In cases where firms reported that employee representation had had no effect upon the relations between management and employees, an explanation of the circumstance was usually to be found.

The correspondent of the Board in a southern foundry whose Works Council is an "Industrial Democracy," and who stated that he did not see any change in relations between management and workers, said, in a later discussion, that he had not yet succeeded in getting his workers to see the real meaning of employee representation.

Another correspondent, in an eastern steel company, operating a Council of the "committee" type, after having said that there had been no appreciable effect of their employees' committees in the relationship between management and workers, admitted that he himself was not in favor of employee representation.

Information was received from 361 plants regarding the effect which employee representation had had on the relationship between management and workers. The Works Council plans in twenty-four of the plants were of the "Industrial Democracy" type, and 337 were of the "committee" type plants.

Reports regarding 356 plants stated that the effect of the Councils on these relationships had been a beneficial one. Five firms, four having "committee" plans and one an "Industrial Democracy" plan, said that employee representation had had no effect upon the relations between employer and employee. In both groups the condition was accounted for.

In view of the figures shown it may be concluded that the effect of Works Councils on the relationship between managements and their men is, in general, a beneficial one.

CHAPTER IX

ATTITUDE OF FOREMEN TOWARD WORKS COUNCILS

In considering the attitude of foremen toward employee representation, it is well to note that a Works Council is a distinct check on his authority, in that it deprives him of the right of final decision on the grievances and complaints of employees, which has heretofore been his, and also of the exclusive privilege of defining the attitude of the management to the workers. In spite of this apparent contraction of power, however, a considerable number of foremen have signified approval of the works committees as soon as their institution was contemplated.

The restriction of the authority of foremen, however, is largely only apparent, because it lies within the power of the foremen, by the exercise of wisdom and fairness in dealing with his men under Works Councils rules, to retain his prerogatives. The Council usually makes no change in the initial procedure of settling complaints. As before, the dissatisfied employee goes first to his foreman, but at this point the Council outlines a departure from the former method. If the foreman's decision is not acceptable to the worker concerned, the latter has the right to refer the complaint, through his representative on the committee, to that committee for review and settlement. But if the foreman has, to the best of his ability, been fair in his judgment and "human" in his manner of delivering it to the employee, there is a fair chance that the dispute will end there, or, if not, that the committee will uphold the foreman's decision. This would obviously tend to be true only in plants where foremen, prior to the institution of the Councils, had, to some extent at least, held the confidence of the men under them.

In this investigation the Conference Board has recorded a large number of instances where the foremen have, for various reasons, opposed the plans at the time of installation, but have later reversed their opinions and supported them. A few objected to them simply because they knew nothing about them, but the great majority did so because they feared a lessening of their authority. The fact that, through education, so many of the foremen in this class have been converted to favor of the Works Council plans, would seem to support the theory, advanced in other chapters of this report, that the "selling" of the employee representation idea to the supervisory force and workers alike, before its introduction into the plant, is an important essential in its successful establishment.

111

The number of foremen whose aversion to the idea of works committees has persisted is negligible, and these cases, according to testimony of the employers concerned, are ascribable to the character of the men.

In view of his position in the plant, the importance of the foreman's attitude toward the Works Council, especially at its inception, cannot be too strongly stressed. His loyal support can go a long way toward making, and his determined opposition towards breaking, the organization.

In the words of one of the company officials of a western lumber concern:

> "The attitude of the foreman . . . is the most important matter in a plan of employee representation. . . . Unless they see the necessity and value of such a plan it will be seriously handicapped, and if their lack of understanding leads to opposition, a shop committee is almost certain to fail."

The various attitudes which foremen have taken towards employee representation plans are discussed below under the three classes into which they naturally fall: Those that have been in favor of the plans from their inception; those that have regarded the idea at first with disfavor, but have come later to see its effectiveness; and those that have remained indifferent to it. No case was reported in which foremen who were favorably inclined towards the Works Council at its installation, later found reason to change this attitude.

FOREMEN IN FAVOR OF COUNCILS FROM THEIR INCEPTION

In a great many instances employers have experienced no difficulty whatever in their foremen's acceptance of the Works Council. Some, of a higher intelligence than their fellows, have seen at once where the plan could support and assist them. Others have found that it lightened the burden of settling disputes. Still others have considered it wise to adopt the attitude indicated to them by the management.

Those foremen whose favor of the plan at its inception was due to an intelligent appreciation of its merits have seen in the committees a means of insuring a permanent understanding between management and employees, a way to make employees see that their interests are one with those of their employer.

Of this point of view an eastern concern employing 46,000 men, and operating its Works Council under a "committee" plan, reported:

> "The attitude of our foremen towards the plan has been one of cordial acceptance, as it is pretty generally realized that the object of the plan is to assure and further the relationship between employee and management upon a definite and durable basis of mutual understanding and confidence—an accomplishment in which the foremen have a responsibility and are keenly interested."

A company official of a large shoe concern having employee representation plans of the "committee" type in three factories, found his foremen appreciating the increased interest of the employees in general plant problems.

In two concerns of the "committee" type where foremen favored the Works Council from its inception, they felt that it relieved them of the onus of handling complaints. While all cases came to them first, they were glad to have their decisions reviewed by the committee, when they proved unsatisfactory to the workers. A fair decision would seldom be reversed, and the man who had gone back to his work disgruntled at his foreman's settlement of the case and convinced of the unfairness of his superior, was more likely to be satisfied with the decision reached by fellow workers whom he himself had been instrumental in electing. There seemed also to be a finality about these decisions. They settled the question raised for all time. They had been settled by employees and the man not satisfied got little sympathy from his comrades.

Some employers found the number of grievances brought forward by the employees decreasing under the employee representation plan. However, the fact that fewer complaints are brought to the attention of the foreman does not necessarily mean that fewer employees are finding fault. Many plans suggest that the employee discuss his trouble with one of his representatives before he makes a formal complaint regarding it to his foreman. A wise representative is often able to satisfy his fellow worker and thus relieve his foreman of the settlement of a case.

In this connection the Board's informant in a southern steel company, whose plan is of the "committee" type, said:

> "The foremen like it very much as it assumes much of their responsibilities which make for friction and discontent and also releases them to a little more time for the questions of production."

In an eastern concern manufacturing machinery, where the Works Council is of the "committee" type, a foreman who was interviewed said that employee representation had greatly lessened the number of petty disputes and grievances brought to him for settlement. He accounts for it in the following manner:

> "When a fellow comes at me with a red hot complaint, both of us are pretty sure to go off the handle. When he takes it to the representative it's different. They are both workers and the representative will take time to smooth him down and talk things over with him. A good many times they settle it up between them and I never hear of it. But if it does come on to me, by the time I get it half the punch has gone out of it."

In one or two cases where foremen have been reported as favoring the employee representation plan from the time of its installation, they have been given to understand that it was "up to them" to adopt the policy of the management on this question. This idea was made very clear by a company official

113

of a western lumber company whose Works Council is of the "committee" type:

> "Our foremen work in close harmony with the committees and with ourselves. It is clearly understood between ourselves and our foremen that foremen who do not take the same broad view of this organization as we do, are not the type of foremen which we want. The attitude of the foremen in questions of this kind is largely the attitude of the management of the plant."

In line with the same policy the manager of another western lumber concern, operating a council of the same type, found his foremen trying to adopt the attitude indicated to them by the management:

> "Our foremen as a rule have worked in line with the spirit evidenced by the management, and, so far as they could, have overcome habits formed under another system. We have had no fault to find with their attitude."

Reports regarding 352 employee representation plans show the foremen in favor of the Works Council plan from its inception. Of these, twenty-three were of the "Industrial Democracy" type, while 329 were of the "committee" type.

FOREMEN WHO AT FIRST REGARDED WORKS COUNCILS WITH DISFAVOR BUT HAVE COME LATER TO SEE THEIR EFFECTIVENESS

An interesting variety of reasons has been given for the disfavor with which the foremen in a large number of firms regarded the Works Councils when they were first installed, and for the subsequent change of this attitude to one of support.

One of those most frequently put forward was the fear of a curtailment of their authority. In a concern where foremen have been accustomed to do the right as they saw it, the ease with which this feeling could be overcome is obvious. Under most plans all individual grievances must be taken up first with the foreman, and if possible settled by him. When he is fair in his dealings with his men, he is fairly sure to make acceptable decisions. These close the cases, his prerogatives remain intact, and he sees that employee representation has not lessened his authority.

In no instance has a Works Council operating under the "Industrial Democracy" plan reported that the foremen were at first against employee representation because they feared an abridgment of their authority. This was accounted for as follows by an eastern firm whose Council was modeled after this plan:

> "Any tendency on the part of the foremen to feel their authority lessened by the Works Council is checked in an 'Industrial Democracy.' Under the 'committee' plan only a limited number are active members of the Council, but in our organization every foreman has a place. Our 'Senate' is made up of the entire foreman body."

114

Several concerns of the "committee" type, however, reported that fear lest their authority would be abridged, caused opposition among foremen at first, while the elimination of this fear brought loyal support.

From an official of an eastern steel plant came the following:

"The foremen at first were afraid the committee system might abridge their authority, but as all disputes and grievances of a personal character must first be taken up with the foremen the latter have come to regard the committees as valued assistants in smoothing out annoyances . . . I am sure that 95% of our foremen would oppose giving up the committee system."

A western lumber company expressed a similar opinion:

"Foremen as a rule do not take kindly to employee representation, and we have experienced some difficulty in getting them to work in the proper spirit to make the plan the success it should be. This is particularly a matter of education and the situation in this respect is better than when we first started the plan. In my judgment it will always be a source of more or less friction. The man who has advanced from the ranks to the position of authority is inherently more or less jealous of any machinery of influence which may curb his authority. It depends, of course, upon the breadth of the man as to how promptly he recognizes the desirability of working through committees and falling in line accordingly."

In an eastern canning factory the slightly authoritative attitude assumed by some of the employee representatives at the time of the installation of the Council, had the effect of stimulating in the foremen the feeling that their authority was being curtailed and their discipline slipping away. In the words of one of the company officials:

"When the committees were first formed some of the members showed, unconsciously perhaps, that they felt they had assumed some authority. The foremen were naturally on the lookout for such signs and made a mental note of each incident that tended to show this feeling. There was an idea also in the minds of the foremen that perhaps they were being criticized in the eyes of the committee. The foremen felt that perhaps they were missing some of their authority and for that reason were not enthusiastic about the employee representation plan. These ideas have since been dissipated, and while the foremen are not eager to see the committee plan continued, they have no objection to its existence."

Among those who reported that their foremen regarded the plan of employee representation with disfavor at the time of its inception, but later rallied to its support, a fair number of employers found that their foremen distrusted the innovation generally, fearing it as something about which they knew nothing. A little knowledge of its benefits, a little experience with its working, were all that was necessary to change their attitude from opposition to cooperation.

A western rubber company, whose Works Council is of the "Industrial Democracy" type, stated that its foremen were

" . . . skeptical at first, with a gradual awakening to the committee's possibilities in simplifying the problems of supervision. Complete cooperation at present."

115

Similarly a large western pump factory, operating under the "committee" plan:

> "At first the foremen were very skeptical about the works committees, but when the most ardent objector was elected as president he became one of the workers of the committees. The foremen themselves, after they got to know what the committees stood for, were very much in favor of them and have done everything they could to help them along."

From a western lumber company, also with a "committee" plan:

> "When this plan was first put into effect we had some trouble with our foremen working in harmony with the committees, but just as soon as they found out the beneficial effects we have found that they are only too glad to work with these committees."

In view of the fact just brought out, the question arises of having a regular plan for the education of the foremen, in connection with the works committee. Many employers already have organizations which supply this need. Foremen's clubs or conferences where instruction is given in such subjects as industrial methods, industrial relations, business administration, etc., are not uncommon in modern concerns. Others have started organizations of this sort in connection with the Works Councils. Still others have conducted informal discussions. In these meetings foremen have been given, usually by some company official, a thorough understanding of the employee representation plan, its organization, its functions, and the principles which underlie it.

In every instance where organizations of this kind were reported, employers were enthusiastic over their experience with them. The consensus of opinion was that such a method for the education of the foreman to the Works Council idea had made him a hearty supporter of the plan.

One of the company officials in a large western concern engaged in the manufacture of farm machinery, whose Works Council, operating under the "committee" plan, has had an especially interesting and successful evolution, has accomplished the desired result by means of foremen's meetings:

> "The committee men undoubtedly come between foremen and their workmen. The effect on our foremen has been that they resented the authority that the committee exercised and took steps to combat it. We have successfully overcome this difficulty by foremen's meetings. The two bodies now thoroughly understand each other's prerogatives and there is little friction between them."

An Ohio concern has reported success along this same line:

> "Through extensive training we have developed our foremen along the lines of economics and business administration so that they can see the importance and need of closer cooperation between the men and the management and committees in Congress. Foremen, in a number of cases, serve on committees and also in Congress. They were elected thereto by the employees who had faith in their judgment to protect their interests."

116

An eastern steel company, with thirty thousand employees and a representation plan of the "committee" type which has been in operation for three years, has found the attitude of its superintendents and foremen increasingly favorable as they have become accustomed to the plan. The company deemed it advisable to outline to their foremen what they regarded as the important features of employee representation, and to suggest methods for enlisting the interests of every new employee in it.

The following instructions, "Hints to Foremen in Meeting the New Employee" are placed in the hands of every foreman. The first section expresses appreciation of the importance of the foremen's position in the plant and the influence of their attitude on production and working conditions. Regarding the importance of the foremen's attitude, as a reflection of that of the management, the instructions say:

"To the employees the foreman reflects the attitude and policy of the management, and is viewed by the employees as the personal representative of the management. The reception accorded makes a marked and lasting impression on the new employee, and if the foreman is to get the necessary cooperation of his men, it is essential that they be fully cognizant of the company's labor policy from the beginning of their employment."

In order to impress on the foreman the attitude of the management towards the Works Council, and to assist him to make a supporter of that organization out of every employee, a set of suggestions follows:

"The plan of employees' representation, which is designed to bring the management and the men closer together, is one of the most important policies of the company, and in order that the foreman may have a clear idea of the best way to acquaint the new employee with the company's interest in him the following hints are offered:

"1. Hand to the new employee a copy of the plan of employees' representation.

"2. Introduce him, when possible, to the elected employees' representatives of the department in which he is to work.

"3. Explain that his representative was elected at the preceding election by the employees, by secret ballot, and that he will have an opportunity to vote at the next election (providing he is in the employ of the company 60 days).

"4. Explain that with a growing organization, the company desires to retain that close personal relationship with its employees that it had when the plants were much smaller, and in order that it may have a clear idea at all times of the employees' working conditions, has adopted the plan of employees' representation as a means of accomplishing this end.

"5. Explain that the new employee may take up with you any matter which in his opinion requires adjustment, and that if you are unable to effect a settlement, the plan of employees' representation provides a means for him to take the matter up higher, either in person or through his representatives.

"6. Impress upon the new employee the idea that the plan of representation is not merely for the purpose of handling grievances, but is rather a medium of bringing the management and employees closer

117

together and that the company will welcome suggestions from the employees for the betterment of plant and working conditions.

"7. We would suggest that you read the plan over very carefully, and we will welcome any suggestions or inquiries you may care to make regarding its provisions."

Still another phase has been noted in the attitude of foremen who at first regarded the employee representation plan with disfavor, but came later to see its effectiveness. Several cases have been reported where the attitudes of foremen in the same plant varied all the way from open opposition to hearty support of the idea.

Individuals in these cases could, in all probability, be placed in the various classes previously discussed. Those who adopted the idea at once would be the more intelligent among the foremen. Those who were slower to be converted to it could be classed as fearful of a curtailment of their authority or in need of education to its merits.

In every case of this kind reported there was a tendency on the part of those indifferent to it to become supporters of the plan. This was true of a paper concern with a Works Council of the "committee" type, whose employees number three thousand. An official of the company wrote:

"When the works committee was first established the foremen regarded it in various ways. Some were thoroughly sold, others were merely passive, and some were openly antagonistic. Little by little the last group has come over at least to the middle group, and by far the larger number of the plant to-day have come to depend upon the works committee representatives in their work in dealing with employees. This change of sentiment has been brought about not only by the splendid spirit which the works committee in general have shown, but also by the absolutely wholehearted support of the plan by the management."

An eastern electric company whose employees exceed ten thousand and whose Works Council is operating under the "committee" plan, reported a similar experience:

"Some foremen saw the possibilities and advantages of the plan at once. Others saw only difficulties and what they thought to be the curtailment of authority in their position. We think that the first group is steadily increasing and the second group steadily diminishing."

Reports concerning seventy-two employee representation plans stated that at first foremen regarded the employee representation plan with disfavor but later came to see its effectiveness. Of these, fifteen were of the "Industrial Democracy" type, while fifty-seven were of the "committee" type.

FOREMEN WHO HAVE REMAINED INDIFFERENT
TO WORKS COUNCILS

In tracing the reasons for opposition or indifference to employee representation on the part of the foremen, we naturally look first on the character of the men employed in these positions. The man who is arbitrary, and who carries this characteristic into the handling of his men, naturally does not favor an organization which is going to limit his power. If he has been in the habit of using his disciplinary power in an absolute manner, there is more than a chance that his employees are "going after" every decision he renders when the Works Council gives them their chance. It is difficult, too, to persuade a man of this kind to give the representation plan a fair trial. He is not a progressive type, and he would be able to see in the organization only an attempt to take from him his position as "boss." Unless foremen of this character can be educated to at least a tolerant attitude towards a plan of this sort, it is impossible to achieve a high type of success. The cooperation of all parties concerned is essential.

Some employers have so far failed to accomplish this result. The vice-president of a western lumber concern of the "committee" type gave this as its experience:

> "Among the men of limited vision and arbitrary disposition both among our foremen and superintendents we found opposition at first, and it still exists in one form or another in certain places."

A mid-western motor car company, operating a Works Council of the "committee" type, found the foremen resented the plan because it gave the workers a direct avenue of approach to the management. While they have not openly opposed it, their antagonism has been so apparent that the vice-president of the company feared an attempt to retaliate on the employee representatives. He has taken measures to eliminate such a condition and has succeeded in so doing. But he has failed, so far, to overcome his foremen's objections to employee representation. His statement of the case was as follows:

> "Our foremen did not see where the plan held any assistance for them and apparently they were afraid that their authority would be curtailed by the plan. This last is the fundamental reason for the resistance that they have given. . . . They have guarded very jealously against any effort on the part of the management to take part in the hiring and discharging of men, and in becoming interested in the relations of the men to the company. The foremen wanted to be the sole avenue of approach between the men and the company. . . . I am inclined to believe that the foremen will never look with favor upon the plan. . . .
>
> "For fear of retaliation by the foremen against committeemen I have kept in very close touch with the situation and when I would hear complaints and opinions expressed by the foremen antagonistic to the men's committee, I always took steps to make it very plain that any foreman would be discharged who mistreated any of the men on the committee. A number of times men on the committee reported the foremen as being antagonistic and I was always able to change the conditions before any serious consequences were brought about. . . . I made it a rule that no man was to be paid off without my O.K., also every man discharged was to have an opportunity to sign a statement as to the reasons why he was leaving. . . .

119

> "I have always found the men more than fair. . . . I am of the opinion that there would be practically no trouble at all should the managers use anything like as good judgment as is used by the men."

A few cases remain where employers have not traced the reason for the indifferent attitude of their foremen towards their Works Councils. Among these is a company official of an eastern foundry. Enthusiastic himself over his "Industrial Democracy," he has not been able to inspire his foremen with a like feeling. He reported as follows:

> "Foremen tolerate the Works Council but their action is passive rather than active. They do not seem to have got warmed up to the plan."

Attempts made by the same firm to inspire in the foremen a real interest in the organization have been so far unsuccessful. The Board's correspondent, however, is not discouraged and has planned a further campaign with this object in view.

An official of an eastern textile mill having an "Industrial Democracy" plan said that the attitude of his foremen towards the Council was "only partially satisfactory." A statement made by him in a later discussion might account, in part, for this attitude on the part of the foremen. When asked whether by reason of his experience with it, he would recommend the introduction of a Works Council plan into any plant which was under his management, he said:

> "It is doubtful whether or not I should recommend the introduction of the Works Council in an organization over which I had control."

Employers who are not wholly and sincerely in favor of employee representation will naturally find that their foremen do not support the plan. The attitude of the foremen towards any plant matter tends to be a reflection of that of the management. They are quick to detect a lack of sincerity or of enthusiasm towards the organization and to govern themselves accordingly.

Sixteen plants reported that their foremen had remained indifferent to the employee representation plan. Of these, eight were organized after the "Industrial Democracy" type, while eight were operating under the "committee" plan.

Reports regarding the attitude which foremen had adopted toward their employee representation plans were received from 440 plants. In 352 of these it was stated that their foremen had been in favor of the plan from its inception. In 72 they had regarded it at first with disfavor but had come later to see its effectiveness. Only 16 reported continued indifference to the plan.

A glance at these figures will show the trend of feeling in this quarter regarding employee representation. The majority have fallen in with the idea at once, whether from a real appreciation of its meaning to industry or from a feeling that this course was the wise one to pursue. Of those who met the plans with indifference, by far the greater number have come later to favor them. Their fears regarding its effect on their positions have been allayed by their experience with it or their education to it. The relatively small number of firms whose foremen have remained indifferent to the plan, leaves the balance well on the side of those who have favored employee representation.

CHAPTER X

EFFECT OF WORKS COUNCILS ON RELATIONS BETWEEN FOREMEN AND EMPLOYEES

One of the most satisfactory results produced by employee representation has been the improvement effected, in many cases, in the relations between the foremen and the workers. In nearly every instance covered by the present investigation of the National Industrial Conference Board, where friendly relations did not exist between the two groups prior to the institution of the Works Council, employers reported that the employee representation plan changed the feeling between them from autocratic authority on one side and unquestioned obedience on the other, to relations ranging all the way from mutual tolerance to cooperation with a common objective.

In many industrial plants the conception of the foreman's position formerly took little consideration of the human element. His attitude tended to be an absolute one; orders were orders, and as such they were not to be questioned. The complaints of the workers were often treated in an arbitrary way; decisions might be fair, but were frequently rendered in such a way as to antagonize the employees concerned. In a plant where a plan of employee representation has the sincere support of the management, it is not possible for the foremen to deal with those under them in this arbitrary manner. The works committees act as a check on the foremen, and, where necessary, effect a change in their methods of dealing with their men, with a resulting change in the workers' attitude toward them. The decisions of a foreman in matters brought to him by dissatisfied employees are subject, under the committee system, to review and possible reversal by the Works Council. It is possible for him to keep the bulk of the departmental discipline in his own hands only by the exercise of fairness and tact in the making and rendering of his decisions.

Company officials, foremen, and employees in various plants were interviewed on this phase of employee representation. In the great majority of cases the opinions of all three classes coincided. With the introduction of Works Councils foremen had, in varying degrees, seen the wisdom of adopting the method of treating their subordinates outlined above, with a resulting increase of good will on the part of the workers. A working force satisfied that it is getting a "square deal," and, therefore, more or less contented with its environment, naturally tends to do better work and to achieve more and better production than one which feels it is being treated unjustly.

Several employers reported that workers had found their foremen more approachable as a result of the employee representation plan, and a better feeling toward them had ensued.

An eastern steel company, with a Works Council of the "Industrial Democracy" type, said:

> "Our men tell us the foremen have been civilized since we started the committee."

The Board's correspondent, while characterizing this as "imaginary," stated that there was a noticeable change in the feeling of the men toward the foremen, who, as he states, were no longer regarded as "little tin gods."

The president of an eastern hardware concern having a Works Council of the "committee" type, found employee representation freeing his workers from the domination of the arbitrary foremen. Following this came an improvement in the relations between the two:

> "There is quite an advantage with this committee in the relationship between the foremen and the workers. They know that they have an influential spokesman to champion their cause, and are not subject to the will and whim of their foremen."

Statements made by employees who were interviewed as to their views on Works Councils bore out the opinions expressed on this subject by the employers. In an eastern silver company under the "committee" plan, employees said:

> "Foremen have been made more approachable by the Works Council. All employees receive better treatment from them."

In a steel company where a "committee" plan is in operation, affecting 30,000 men, employee representatives who were interviewed, thought the organization a good thing. Several favored it because of the change in their foremen. In their own words:

> "The foremen are more reasonable, none of this 'if-you-don't-like-it-get-out' business. That can't be done any more.
> "In the old days the foremen used to say 'Ich weiss; du weiss nicht.' They are more willing to be considerate with the men now because they know the company is behind the men to see that they get a square deal."

The following statement was made by a man who had been in the employ of the company for forty-two years:

> "There is a great difference in the foremen. They don't 'dog' the men any more. The representative is not ignored or slurred by the foremen."

Foremen, also, in nearly all cases said that they found a new spirit of cooperation among the workers as a result of the representation plan.

Foremen were interviewed in an eastern silk company which operates two Councils of the "Industrial Democracy" type. They had found that the "Collective Economy Dividend," which is a feature of this type of employee representation plan, had been a powerful factor in improving the employees' attitude toward their work:

123

"Their interest in their work increased by leaps and bounds. When they found that what they saved in production was split 50-50, and they got some instead of the boss all, they were constantly figuring how they could do more in less time. Any fellow who 'sojered' on the job was accountable to them because he was losing money for them, and they soon told him 'where he got off.' The plan has brought about an entirely different feeling toward their work."

The Works Council has been a means of improving the relations between the foremen and the workers in still another way. Every progressive employer welcomes suggestions from the "man on the job," who is in an excellent position to make them. Whether he makes the valuable suggestions depends on his attitude toward his job, and this is determined in large measure by his relations with his "boss." In some plants short-sighted foremen have discouraged suggestions by the workers. Instead of seeing in them a means to increase the output of the department, they have looked upon them simply as criticisms of their management.

One of the company officials of a western steamship line, whose Works Council is of the "committee" type, stated:

"Previous to the installation of our dock committee, which is the term we use for our Works Council, it was assumed that the men would make suggestions to their foremen and the foremen to the superintendents, and so on, but no such suggestions were made. They had no interest in the company; and they felt if they made any suggestions that they were intruding. Indeed, their experience taught them this because, as a rule, the foreman would resent constructive suggestions as an interference in his business. . . . I am afraid he rebuffed rather than encouraged suggestions, meeting such suggestions with the attitude that they were adverse criticisms of his administration."

A New England shoe company having an "Industrial Democracy" plan, reported the same experience. In both of these cases the introduction of the Works Council, with its machinery for making suggestions, has, perforce, overcome the hostile attitude of the foremen. The resulting increase in suggestions has been gratifying.

The steamship company's representative, in a later discussion said:

"On the installation of our committees and when we invited suggestions, a great many were received. It was shown that the men had been thinking along these lines and that they had good constructive ideas which they had long desired to express. As time goes by we find that the shop knowledge in the minds of these men is a very valuable asset to the company—a mine of information under our very streets, that of course we knew nothing about."

Information was received from 334 plants concerning the effect of Works Councils on the relations between foremen and workers. Of these, 327 found that since the installation of the Council this relation had improved, the opinions varying all the way from "slightly better," to "relations have been brought to a point that leaves little to be desired." In twenty-seven of the plants the Works Councils were of the "Industrial Democracy" type, while three hundred were operating plans of the "committee" type.

Seven firms, five having plans of the "committee" type and two of the "Industrial Democracy" type, reported that the relations between their foremen and their workers had always been pleasant and that there had been no change under the Works Council.

One plant operating a plan of the "Industrial Democracy" type and three having plans of the "committee" type, stated that there had been no change in the relations between foremen and workers.

One firm, whose Council was of the "committee" type, found it "difficult to judge" whether or not the installation of the Works Council had caused any change in the relations between foremen and workers.

CHAPTER XI

CHARACTER OF EMPLOYEE REPRESENTATIVES

The present investigation by the National Industrial Conference Board shows that in the larger proportion of cases employees have exercised good judgment in choosing their representatives. Employers almost without exception spoke in words of high commendation of the men elected to the Councils. Several employers used, without qualification, the following terms in describing the employee representatives— "the best available," "best type of men and women in respective departments," "as good as could be chosen." Two companies reported that, had they had the option of choosing the employee representatives, they would have chosen the identical men elected by the employees themselves. Several other employers stated that "with but few exceptions" or "in almost every case" they would have chosen the same representatives as did the employees.

Eleven companies with Works Councils in forty-five plants reported that the employee representatives were, for the most part, chosen from the older employees, who had had several years of service with the firms. The experience of a company manufacturing agricultural machinery is of particular interest in this connection. This company has Works Councils in operation in twenty-four plants, the majority of which were instituted in 1919.

> "From the very inception of the plan the employees have continuingly elected men and women long in the service of the company, of mature age and high standing in the community as their representatives. At its inauguration the average age of employee representatives was 38 years, the average length of service 7 years, and 85 per cent of the representatives were married. To-day, with an increased number of employee representatives, due to the establishment of new Councils and as the result of semi-annual and special elections, the personnel of the employee representatives has the same percentage of married men and women (namely, 85 per cent), the average age is 39 years, 1 month, and the average length of service 8 years, 9 months."

Another large concern reported that of a group of 314 elected representatives in fourteen plants in which Works Councils were operating, the average age was 37.9 years and the average length of service 12.6 years.

Another group of employers commented in particular upon the fact that the employees chose as their representatives men of more than average intelligence.

"The representatives chosen by the employees are undoubtedly the most intelligent people in the mill," reported the president of a silk mill with a Works Council of the "Industrial Democracy" type.

Another characteristic of the employee representatives referred to by employers, was their fairmindedness and ability to form correct and impartial judgments upon the problems discussed in the Council meetings. Thus an official of a western plant employing 750 workers, wrote:

> "The representatives chosen to our Congress are those who have proven themselves of sound judgment and who have been fair and impartial in all decisions. They have been elected for the work they can do and not on personal popularity."

Other employers wrote that the saner, more conservative type of employees had been chosen as representatives. Seven lumber companies, situated in Pacific Coast states, where the I. W. W. element was quite strong and had endeavored to disrupt the employee representation plans, were unanimous in their statements to this effect.

Similarly an eastern concern employing 8,200 employees, wrote:

> "In 85 per cent of the committeemen elected we feel that their selection was very good from the standpoint of selecting older employees, who are fairly .conservative, married, with education, etc."

On the other hand, some employers stated that the employees had in some cases elected men more for their popularity than for their ability as leaders. One plant wrote that even where representatives has been so chosen, the education which these men obtained through the Council had developed them into capable leaders. A company official of this concern, which has a Works Council of the "committee" type, and which employs 1,200 men, wrote:

> "By the elections, leaders among the men are brought to the fore. That element of leadership in the beginning may be but popularity. However, given a man who in the eyes of his comrades is trusted and admired, wonders can be worked by a little patient, careful, and unimpeachably honest education—information regarding the employer's side of the case."

Three plants reported that where men who were proven unfit had been elected to the Councils, the employees themselves took steps to remove the representatives at the earliest opportunity. This was done either by recalling them, or by not returning them to the Council when their term of office expired. An eastern plant in which a Works Council of the "Industrial Democracy" type is operating, wrote that although the representatives were on the whole "of high grade, being in many cases the ones that would have been placed in the House if the management had made the choice, there had been 'cases where popularity was the basis of choice.'" An especially glaring example of this occurred in one mill, where the workers

127

realized that they had made a mistake and recalled three of their representatives.

The following came from an eastern textile plant, employing 700 employees, in which there is a Works Council of the "Industrial Democracy" type:

> "When the plan was first introduced two or three representatives of 'Bolshevik' turn of mind were selected, but the workers later insisted upon their discharge. Since that time representatives have been chosen because of their capacity for leadership and working qualifications."

A number of employers reported that when the Works Council was initiated the employees used less discrimination in their choice of representatives than they did later, when the plan had been in operation for a longer time.

A Pacific Coast steamship company with a Works Council covering its warehousemen, longshoremen, dock clerks, coopers, etc., wrote:

> "The first representatives were radicals chosen because of their noise, and because of their promises of what they could do if given a chance to tell the management where to head in. At the first following election, workers by their votes began to indicate their desire to elect saner, more conservative men to represent them, and this indication grows more marked with each subsequent election, so that we have now in our committees elected by the men, workers who are conservative, but sanely constructive, and we are just entering an era of real constructive growth toward highly improved relations."

One of the objects of a Works Council is to enable the employees, and more particularly the representatives of the employees, to learn at first hand the reasons why management believes that certain things should be done. They are shown "the other side" of the case. What may have appeared wholly unnecessary, perhaps unjust, on the part of the management, assumes an entirely different aspect when the representatives are shown the why and the wherefore of such measures. It has been the experience of many employers that a marked change takes place in the attitude of men with radical views, after their election to the Works Council. This was explained by one employer as follows:

> "Men are sobered by responsibility. They are steadied. The new light strikes them. They carry to their constituents the new thought. They materially ameliorate viewpoints, radical and loose thinking and thereby, of course, improve conditions and add to the sum total of employee satisfaction."

One company reported that of the few radicals elected by the employees, all had become conservative except one. In the same company "one radical was defeated for re-election because he became too much of a company man."

Another eastern company with 1,700 workers, said that although a minority of the representatives were so radical "that nothing can be done with them, generally speaking these men

128

are strong characters and when faced with responsibility of decision they have somewhat receded from their ultra-radical views."

"The more radical, complaining type of representative has been converted by the saner key men who have always predominated," wrote the president of a middle western concern manufacturing heavy machinery.

On account of the opportunity which the Works Council afforded an employer to come in direct contact with the representatives and place before them facts regarding the industry, of which they had been in ignorance previously, the president of a large concern with Works Councils in four plants, stated:

"We are inclined to welcome the latter type (the radical) as we prefer to have them out in the open to present their imaginary grievances and complaints before their fellow members at the meetings where the management has an opportunity to place the subject in the proper light before the committee."

After an experience with the "worst grouches and kickers" who were elected to the Council by several departments,

" . . . partly to put them in a place where they could see for themselves what was going on and partly because no other men wanted to take the jobs and have these kickers in their department to report to,"

the vice-president of an eastern concern wrote:

"We should encourage the election of such men in the organization for the good it does them and the whole organization. The election of these malcontents proved far more wise than we dreamed of at the time. These men have got into a position where they have responsibility and where they see more of the problems than they could otherwise have seen and they are making not only good representatives, but are becoming much better men themselves."

Another plant, with a Council of the "committee" type, wrote that it found the representatives of the radical type "the most successful in presenting to their 'constituents' the views of the management."

Three firms alone out of 150 furnishing information regarding the type of employee representatives elected by the employees, reported that they had been wholly unsatisfactory. In one steel company employing 700 workers, when the plan of the "committee" type was submitted to the employees for their approval in 1919, "the majority wishing the Works Council was very small." The Board's correspondent in the plant, writing that the Works Council was not instituted as the result of labor troubles, stated:

"We have had mediocre representatives chosen by employees, and in several instances we have been unsuccessful in choosing other than the original delegates, even though the Council has been functioning approximately two years, while elections are held each six months."

A second company characterized the employee representatives as "the most radical type, or rather their leaders."

The third company, employing 2,000 men, whose Council of the "committee" type was formed in December, 1918, reported:

"Rather light-weight representatives have been chosen by employees and not the substantial backbone of the personnel of the works."

The vice-president of this company wrote that because "the elected representatives do not 'draw much water' either with the men or with the company," the management,

". . . when desiring to take up anything with the men, in a constructive manner of consultation, finds it necessary to make selection of older and more suitable employees, at the same time giving recognition to the Executive Committee of the Board of Representatives, so that they shall not be left out of it."

When the Works Council was introduced into this plan the employees were not given a voice in its formulation, and, although they voted to accept it, only 50% of the employees cast ballots. The union employees regarded it as a plan to disorganize labor organizations, and did not give their support. Employee representatives who were interviewed said the employees as a whole had lost interest in the plan because of the opposition of the superintendents toward it. They expressed confidence in the general manager of the plant, but the minor officials had put so many things in the way of the successful operation of the plan that the representatives found it almost impossible to get anything done. This was their explanation of the election in some cases of men whom the employees knew to be incapable. They had come to lose all confidence in the plan and so made a joke of the elections.

The procedure adopted by the management of the company, as outlined by the vice-president, would seem to furnish an additional stimulus to the employees for electing men of small calibre as their representatives. Apparently no effort was made by the management to educate the representatives to the responsibilities which were theirs as members of the Council. Instead of doing this, the company dealt with other employees in the plant when it wished to discuss matters requiring adjustment. This disregard for the wishes of the employees, as expressed in their selection of representatives, could not but affect them as it did. Ample evidence has been given above of the changed viewpoint which employee representatives have usually adopted after their election to the Councils. There is of course, the possibility that men of such small intelligence and biased ideas might be elected, that it would be impossible to develop them into fair-minded and capable leaders, but most employers have found that the representatives want to be fair and do the right thing. From the evidence at hand it appears that the attitude which the management in this plant adopted toward the representation plan was the determining factor with regard to the type of employees who were elected as representatives.

From the statements quoted above, it is evident that employees in the vast majority of cases have exercised good discrimination in their choice of representatives. While it is not universally true that the representatives selected have been of the highest type, it is of particular interest to learn that in many cases men who have been chosen primarily on account of their popularity have developed into leaders, through the education they have received as members of the Councils. This is especially so with regard to men whose views, radical at first, have been modified after serving on the Councils.

CHAPTER XII

THE EFFECT OF WORKS COUNCILS
ON LABOR TURNOVER

The effect of employee representation on labor turnover in industrial plants is difficult to measure because of various complicating factors which might account for the result independently. A reduction in turnover at a time of high production, when work is plentiful, wages high and labor scarce, like the war period, and that which immediately followed it, might be traceable to conditions within the plant which would offer more to employees than competing concerns could hold out, such as higher wages and superior benefits, in which a successfully operating Works Council might be included. Only conclusive evidence, however, would justify giving the credit for a reduced turnover exclusively to such an organization in a time of extreme industrial depression with resulting unemployment like that through which the country has since been passing.

Even when employees' committees are said to affect labor turnover favorably, the result is usually produced indirectly. That is, certain conditions are present in the plant because of the Works Council, and because of these conditions employees are content to remain. It may be that the organization has improved the relations between management and employees; that each has learned the other's viewpoint, with a result of greatly increased harmony and contentment. The workers' grievance can be discovered and settled by executives before it becomes serious enough to lead him to seek employment elsewhere. And often that which under other conditions would have been a grievance disappears when the worker knows his employer's side of the question.

There is frequently present also, as part of many Works Council plans, an additional incentive to remain on the job—the financial one. The "Industrial Democracy" type of council usually includes the "Collective Economy Dividend," which is a return to the workers of one-half of the savings made in the cost of production, following the formation of the Works Council. With this system in effect employees come to realize the disadvantage of a large labor turnover, because it affects their own earnings. It is also possible to make labor turnover one of the determining factors of the amount to be paid in these dividends, as in the case of an eastern silk mill:

"Reduction of labor turnover was accomplished through including this factor in the 'Collective Economy Dividend.' The employees were anxious that only employees who were likely to remain with the company should be employed. This resulted in a considerable reduction in the turnover."

Various other influences in addition to those already mentioned must be taken into consideration as bearing on labor turnover. Reports from industrial concerns describe such stabilizing features as life insurance, sick and accident benefits, pensions for retired employees, plans for stock ownership for employees, etc.

In view of these facts little information of a positive or statistical nature can be given on this subject. The statements which follow are the carefully weighed opinions of the employers interviewed. The discussions are of so varied a nature that no attempt has been made to classify them.

In a western packing company, where a Council of the "committee" type is in operation, the question of the influence of the plan on labor turnover was discussed by an employee, the chairman of the Works Council. In his opinion the value of the organization in this phase of the industrial question lay in the production of contentment among employees, by disposing of their grievances:

> "Our labor turnover is very small at this time due to the general condition of unemployment. However, considering the past, we would say that the Works Council in its work has been able to reduce the turnover considerably, settling disputes among individuals, and departments as a whole."

The report given by one of the company officials of another western concern manufacturing agricultural implements and having Works Councils of the committee type in operation in twenty-four plants, covered the effect of these organizations on labor turnover during the period of industrial depression. In his opinion the influence had been a favorable one:

> "It is difficult to state what has been the effect of Works Councils upon labor turnover as there are many different factors bearing on this figure. The Works Councils have now been established two years—years which have been marked by turbulence of industrial relations in the world and country at large, as well as in the individual communities in which our factories are operated. During this time there has been no loss of direct contact between the men and the management of the . . . company at those plants where Councils have been established.
>
> "There can be no question but that the intimate contact established through the Works Council has operated to heighten the morale of the employees as well as to increase continuity of service."

An eastern concern, where printing machinery is manufactured, employs three thousand men and operates a Council of the "committee" type. An official of this company was of the opinion that the better understanding between management and employees, created by the establishment of employees' committees in the plant, had greatly decreased the number of men quitting because of personal grievances:

133

"We cannot say that the employees' committee, as a whole, has reduced labor turnover, for the reason that the general conditions have been changed to such an extent that there is little labor turnover now as compared with a year and two years ago. We do know, however, that we have very few leaving now, so far as the relationship between the management and the workers is concerned, for the reason that grievances are taken up with the department shop committee, and are usually settled by them with the foreman, unless some principle is involved, when the department shop committee usually takes it up with the works manager, and settlement is readily obtained."

The vice-president of a western public service concern reported the successful operation of a "company union" among the employees. It was his opinion that the workers had been brought thereby to a realization of their personal interest in the business, to the extent of decreasing the number of dissatisfied workers, and so lowering the labor turnover:

"The industrial plan under which all of the labor required for this utility and its associated properties works, has exerted an important influence in reducing labor turnover and in promoting individual and group efforts to get the maximum output and accordingly, with a given scale of wages, the lowest unit costs. The plan is designed to develop and emphasize the mutuality of the interests that exist between rank and file of the workers, supervisory force and the employer."

An official of a western lumber concern where a Council of the "committee" type is in operation, believed that employee representation, with its humanizing effect on both executives and workers, had been in large measure responsible for the decrease in labor turnover noted in the plant:

"We do not give *all* the credit for the decrease in turnover to any of these committees, nor to any other one thing. The organization has brought about a better feeling between the employer and employee. Each party has become more considerate of the other; each understands the other better. In some organizations and at some times both employer and employees vie with each other to see which can be the most unselfish, and it is all these things and many others coming from better human relationship that have not only reduced the labor turnover but have had a tendency to better all conditions for both employer and employees. It seems to us it does not take figures or detailed research to establish this fact."

In a section of the country where labor turnover, due to local conditions, has always been high, an eastern glove factory believed that its Works Council, of the "committee" type had, to some extent, lowered turnover by the better relations created between executives and workers:

"The greater part of the fine gloves made in the United States are made in this county, and since there are so many firms all using the same class of labor, it is easy for labor to change employment at the slightest provocation. We feel that the percentage of such changes from our factory has been largely reduced because of the better understanding obtained, as between management and worker, through the medium of our Works Council. We believe that the clearer view of shop methods and the necessity for certain rules obtained by the worker through his representative in Council has effectually killed unnecessary dissatisfaction and, therefore, it has in many cases prevented the impulse to change jobs."

134

A southern oil company, operating a Council of the "committee" type, has felt its influence on labor turnover in a rather roundabout way. Various welfare provisions within the plant, instituted by the company, tended to stabilize the employee body. But the company was of the opinion that the employee representation plan had not only served to impress upon the workers the safeguards with which the company had surrounded them, but also to induce an appreciation of them from a monetary standpoint.

Less definite than those opinions already quoted, was the statement regarding the influence of an employee representation plan on labor turnover, submitted by the president of a southern cotton mill, whose Works Council, of the "Industrial Democracy" type, has been operating for upwards of two years. In this case also so many other elements in the plant—a flourishing industrial Y. M. C. A., new dormitories, group insurance, and special educational courses, to mention only a few—were regarded as contributing factors, that it was impossible to determine how much bearing any one of them has on the improved stability of the employee body.

The opinion given by the treasurer of a western furniture plant, whose Council is of the "Industrial Democracy" type, that "the labor turnover has been reduced since the organization of this Board," was later explained and qualified by the same official as follows:

> "We do not give our Board of Cooperation all of the credit for holding down our turnover. We are under the impression that it is as much due to the fact that there is so much unemployment, therefore more of a desire to hold their jobs. Our men are also much interested in our group life insurance, which is increased annually, as well as the fact that they are covered by health and accident insurance while in our employ."

One of the company officials of an eastern firm, operating a representation plan of the "committee" type, was unable to state what percentage of the reduction in turnover in the plant was due to the advent of the Works Council plan, and what part should be credited to other forces at work in the factory. He stated, however, the fact that this decrease was coincident with the organization of the representation plan, would seem to point to a connection between the two. One point in this connection not mentioned before was brought out by this official in his report. He had found the Works Council making a strong appeal to his skilled workmen, and, by raising their morale, increasing their length of service. In his own words:

> "Labor turnover has been reduced about 50%, the big item in this respect being that instead of half of our turnover being skilled men it is changed to such an extent that 90% of the turnover is made up of unskilled men. Through the committee we have been able to create and maintain a family spirit that holds the higher grade man after we have trained him, in other words, made him a specialist in our line of work."

135

The reduction of labor turnover following the introduction of a Council of the "Industrial Democracy" type in a western rubber concern was mainly due, according to the report of a company official, to the financial gain afforded the employees by the bonus feature of the plan.

In a chapter which follows, a detailed report received from one of the company officials in a western printing concern gives a record of a large amount of constructive work accomplished by the employees' committees.[1] Some of this work, performed by two of the sub-committees of the Council, has resulted in a reduced labor turnover. The statement of one of the company officials was:

> "The activities of our attendance and tardiness and our employment and discharge committees have had a bearing on the reduction of labor turnover.
> . . . .
>
> "Through records obtained by the attendance and tardiness committee information is at hand showing the efficiency lost by employees being absent or tardy. After pay day absenteeism has been closely checked and recommendations offered where chronic absentees were concerned. Personal investigations have been conducted by this group and great cooperation extended to department heads in establishing better conditions. Their aim is to prevent loss of time which is harmful to bigger Congressional workings. The absentee habit is not tolerated in this plant.
> . . . .
>
> "The committee on employment and discharge is charged with the responsibility of keeping up the high class of men we now have employed. If a dissatisfied employee leaves the service it is the duty of this committee to analyze the cause and decide as to the justice of the case. They have so decided in the past on matters of this kind that our employees know their positions cannot be taken away from them without due cause. But when a real cause is present the committee will be the first to suggest the dismissal of one who is not up to our standard."

The vice-president and general manager of a western motor car company having a Council of the "committee" type, was inclined to give most of the credit for the fact that "turnover has been almost eliminated" in the plant, to his representation plan. This had been accomplished, he believed, by the new spirit of cooperation which the management had been able to arouse in the workers by recognition of their importance in the efficient functioning of the plant. As a means for eliminating that friction which was caused by small grievances and often resulted in labor turnover, the Works Council had proven worth while:

> "In my opinion the reason the organization of the men's committee caused a reduction in the labor turnover is due to the fact that a large number of small matters which ordinarily cause friction in the shop were brought up by the men's committee and disposed of quickly. Another thing, when some man would begin to talk about leaving the plant and going elsewhere, the men's committee would bring the matter to my attention and I would take steps to hold the man, if possible.

[1] See p. 177.

136

"I really believe that . . . the close contact between the management and the men and the elimination of petty irritating items was the real reason for the reduction in the labor turnover. In other words, I do not consider it was the men's committee itself, nor do I consider that it was my attitude which caused this reduction, but it was due to a medium being established where all matters could be quickly handled.

"I am firmly convinced that the recognition means more to the men than anything else. In other words, in most concerns the management is firmly intrenched, of course, and inclined to be arbitrary and indifferent if conditions are such that they can be so. Furthermore, the old style idea was for both sides to be very antagonistic. My opinion is that the men are more than anxious to cooperate and also that they are wanting to take a bigger part than simply working in the shop. They know how vitally important it is for the company to have their good will and cooperation, and in return for this they want to have the satisfaction of reasonable recognition from their management."

Information was received regarding the effect which 349 employee representation plans had had on labor turnover. In the foregoing chapter the opinions quoted are representative of those employers who believed that employee representation had had a favorable influence on labor turnover.

In twenty-five concerns employers stated their inability to determine whether or to what extent their Councils had been instrumental in decreasing turnover. While their committees were functioning successfully and their turnover had, in nearly every case, been cut, there seemed to be so many other causal factors that an opinion on the subject could not be risked.

In fourteen plants executives have not been able to trace any decrease in labor turnover for which employee representation might be responsible. In a few of these cases the turnover had always been negligible, therefore eliminating the necessity for the Council to function along this line.

CHAPTER XIII

ATTITUDE OF ORGANIZED LABOR TOWARD WORKS COUNCILS

Organized labor is officially against all plans of industrial government that do not provide for union recognition, though it does not object to a system of employees' committees elected within a shop if those committees are supplemental to a trade union agreement. At the Atlantic City convention of the American Federation of Labor in 1919, "company unions," as Works Councils were termed, were condemned as "a delusion and a snare,"[1] set up by employers "for the express purpose of deluding the workers into the belief that they have some protection and thus have no need for trade union organization." The trade union was stated to be the "only kind of organization" fitted for the purpose of collective bargaining, and all trade unionists were advised "to have nothing to do" with "company unions."

This attitude toward employee representation plans still characterizes the speeches and writings of the leaders of the American Federation of Labor, and a general propaganda against Works Councils has been constantly conducted by the Federation.

In the discussion of the cases that follow, it will be noted that in spite of this fact, individual trade unionists in many instances have taken part in Works Council activities, and have not followed their leaders in the latter's opposition toward "company unions."

Most representation plans make no discrimination against employees because of membership in a labor organization. Trade union employees are eligible for election as representatives —not as representatives of an outside labor organization, but as representatives of the employees in the plant. In some instances trade unions have been successful in creating committees composed entirely of union employees, and this has often been followed by an endeavor to secure benefits for the unions irrespective of the effect upon the industry. In some cases plans have had to be abandoned because of the determination of trade unions to utilize the committees for their own ends.[2]

This has not been true, however, in the majority of plants. Employers have reported that members of trade unions as employee representatives have been quite as satisfactory as

[1] American Federation of Labor. Report of the Proceedings of the Thirty-ninth Annual Convention, June, 1919, pp. 249, 250. The other quotations in this and the following paragraphs are from the same source.

[2] See pp. 29-31.

non-union employees. They have appreciated the benefits that accrue from a Works Council animated by a spirit of fairness on both sides, and have not attempted to convert the Councils into organs for the propagation of trade union principles.

The experience of a large company with Works Councils in twenty-four plants, is of particular interest in this connection. No direct attempts have been made by organized labor to undermine or overthrow the Works Councils at any of the plants. The only direct influence exerted by organized labor has been "the general propaganda of the American Federation of Labor on the subject." One of the company officials stated that probably "fully 50% of our employee representatives are union men."

> "There has never been any indication from their attitude or acts in Council that they were not as fully in accord with the principle underlying the plan as have been those employee representatives who are not members of trades unions."

A western coal and iron mining company reported a varied experience with regard to the attitude of the employee representatives who were members of trade unions. The Councils in the five plants of this company were first formed in 1915, following a serious strike. Both the United Mine Workers and trade unions connected with the steel industry have endeavored to induce the employees to ignore the representation plan, and in some instances these attempts have met with a temporary success. At the time of the steel strike in 1919, the employee representatives at one of the company's plants were largely union men and "apparently interested in promoting union policies." This condition has not prevailed since the steel strike, although, wrote a company official, "probably some of the representatives are members of unions."

Despite the action of the National Machinists' Union, who decided to oppose the Works Council of the "committee" type in a mid-western arsenal, the individual machinists have taken an active part in the Council's activities. The chairman and vice-chairman and one other member of the joint conference committee are machinists. It is noteworthy that the other trade unions represented in the arsenal have "lent their support, interest and cooperation to all moves in connection with the Council."

In an eastern plant in which a number of local unions are represented, the union employees have taken the lead in securing representatives on the works committees. The Works Council was introduced into this plant under exceptionally trying circumstances following a strike. The National War Labor Board, under whose jurisdiction the case came, ordered the formation of "shop committees." A carefully prepared plan of representation drawn up between representatives of the employees and the management, was agreed to by both parties and has been working successfully since its inception in 1919. Some of the employees who led the strike which precipitated the intervention of the War Labor Board, are now ardent supporters of the Works Council. These men are trade unionists and occupy prominent positions in the local trade union movement. The company reported itself as well satisfied with the type of employees elected as representatives, 90% of whom are trade unionists. Management characterized them as "the recognized leaders in each department." One of the employee representatives, who is also an official in the local Trades and Labor Council, gave his opinion of the relation between the Council and the union as follows:

> "In a plant where the employer won't recognize the unions and won't deal with them, I think the unions should make all the use they can of a Works Council. It's the only way we have of getting in touch with the management and why shouldn't we use it? There is nothing to be gained by standing off and refusing to take part in the Council.
> "We see to it that union men are elected to the committees. We can bring up before the management in that way the things we want them to do. If we didn't make use of the Council plan our point of view wouldn't receive any consideration at all."

A different attitude was found to characterize the business agent of one of the local trade unions. The plan was assailed by this union official as being simply a means of getting union employees to drop their memberships in the unions. Those representatives who were trade unionists were accused of having "sold out" to the company; they were getting in well with "the boss," so as to get a "white-collared" job. An international officer of the same union attacked the plan on the ground that it broke down the workers' solidarity, leaving them powerless and at the mercy of the employer. In the eyes of this official the workers would sooner or later see through the employers' "little game" and then there would be an immense rush to join the trade unions again. In August, 1919, the plant was said to be 90% unionized. Since that time, however, a large number of the employees have dropped their union memberships, till at the present time it is believed that not more than 60% of the employees belong to trade unions.

In another plant with a plan of the "Industrial Democracy" type, the president of the company, writing with regard to the relations between the trade unions and the Works Council, stated there was a constant tendency

> ". . . for questions which might come under union action to be referred directly to the union by the House of Representatives previous to discussion by the House on the matter."

Investigation at this plant revealed that a certain group of the employees was well organized into a local union. This union did not pay for the services of a business agent, the members selecting their officers from among their own number. At the time of elections for the House of Representatives in this plant, these employees nominated certain of their numbers in different departments and from those who were elected were chosen the officials of the union. In this way the union always had some of its members in the House of Representatives. At the regular union meetings, those who were members in the House of Representatives reported to the rest of the union employees the proceedings of the House.

The union employee representatives interviewed at this plant spoke highly of the plan. They did not believe that it had been introduced in order to do away with the union. On more than one occasion the president of the plant had urged employees to take a real interest in the union if they were members, to attend the union meetings, and to give it their support.

In one company where it was stated that there had been no noticeable opposition on the part of the union employees to the representation plan, trade unionists are allowed to choose representatives equal in number to those chosen by the non-union employees.

A western company, on the other hand, reported that there was a desire among the union men in the plant, to "convert the shop through its union representatives on the shop committee[1] into a closed union shop." One of the company officials wrote:

> "There has been no well-organized attempt to do this, but the desire exists. Organized labor is not opposed to our shop committee and, in fact, the strong union men in our shop are the ones who first proposed it and served as charter members. I believe that union members understand thoroughly that there will be no recognition of the union in our shop and therefore we expect their activities along this line to gradually lessen, as they have already done."

A serious crisis in the history of this Council occurred shortly after it was formed, when nearly all of the local industries were tied up with a general strike. Although a large percentage of the employees belonged to trade unions and pressure was brought on them from outside the plant to join the strike, the employee representatives unanimously refused to take part in it. In addition the Works Council members appeared before the local trades and labor council, and their statement of the issues involved was so convincing that the strike was soon called off. Recently, when a wage reduction was made in this company, the efforts of local unions to call their members out on strike was unsuccessful.[2]

In some plants trade unionists have been unwilling to act as employee representatives. Whole departments of employees, the majority of whom belonged to unions, have sometimes

---

[1] This is a special use of the term Shop Committee and is not to be confused with the "shop committees" established by the National War Labor Board.
[2] See p. 100.

refused to take any part in the activities of the Council. This has been changed in some instances, after the plan has been in operation for some time, and the employees came to realize they were depriving themselves of benefits which were theirs for the asking. This was the case in an eastern silk mill where, when the plan was introduced, a certain group of highly organized workers refused to take any part in the Council. The representation plan in this concern is of the "Industrial Democracy" type, and the "Collective Economy Dividend". is included in it. After three months' operation of the plan, during which time the other employees had received dividends amounting to 5% of their weekly wages, the trade unionists who had refused to take part in the Council requested the management to allow them to share in the dividends, expressing a desire to take their place along with the rest of the employees under the representation plan.

In a western motor concern, one department which consisted almost entirely of union employees refused to elect any representatives, and maintained this attitude for over two years. Recently, when a wage reduction was necessary in that plant, those employees refused to accept it and were accordingly discharged. The employees hired to take their places have manifested an interest in the Council and have joined the rest of the employees in supporting it.

An eastern tanning company, which introduced its representation plan at the time the local union was endeavoring to enforce the closed shop, reported that union men who were elected representatives refused to serve as such. Shortly after the plan was put into operation a union agitator caused trouble in the plant, and, on his refusal to have the matter referred to the Works Council, was discharged. The union demanded his reinstatement, but the company refused to do so unless the case was submitted to the Works Council. This the discharged employee refused to have done, and a strike was called against the plant. After one week's time the strike was called off by the union. Since that time,

". . . several officials of the union have worked for us in various departments and expressed satisfaction with the relationship existing between employer and employees here."

In an eastern plant the introduction of a Works Council of the "committee" type was followed by an energetic campaign to organize the machinists in the plant, and 90% of these employees joined the union. Although they had elected a representative on the Council, they also set up a separate committee and asked for an increase in wages, along with recognition of the trade union. The company placed the matter before the Works Council, who appointed a special committee to investigate and report. The employee representatives took the stand that the machinists, who comprised one electoral division, were unfair to the representative they had elected. The special committee recommended that all the machinists should be paid up in full, and that they should not be rehired, "until they were willing to pledge themselves that they would give the committee system a fair trial before calling on the union for help." The committee stated that in their minds

". . . the firm had no ulterior motive in introducing the committee system and that so long as the management was 'on the level' there was no need of a business agent to speak for the men and create dissatisfaction."

Regarding this, an official of the company stated:

"It will be noted that the action of our committee was not because our men were opposed to labor unions, but rather because the action of the unionized men in the machine shop did not line up with the committee's idea of a square deal all around. As one of our old employees told the writer at the time: 'Quarreling and striking is old stuff. It may be necessary in some plants, but none of it for me, so long as the boss shows himself willing to meet me half way. Reasonable men should be able to compose their differences without a strike that nearly always ends in a compromise. Why not compromise at the start'?"

Other instances have been furnished the Conference Board, in which the efforts of trades unions to induce employees to abandon Works Councils have failed, because of the spirit of loyalty among the workers toward their representation plan.

An eastern steel company reported:

"Efforts were made from time to time by labor organizations to get a foothold here, but the men gave very little heed to them, our plant committee saying that 'if we can't get along together amongst ourselves there would be little use for any outsiders to come in to try to accomplish anything.' At the time of the steel strike in 1919 the plant committee stood loyal to the company and refused to affiliate with the outside labor organization."

The vice-president of a middle western textile company wrote:

"Organized labor has talked against our plan, but our people are so well sold on the system that 'unionism' as at present constituted, is not at all in favor, especially since the committee system has been attacked. Awhile ago I took up a vote of our men and found that only 5 out of 175 favored a closed shop with no committee. Our women are almost all opposed to unionism. We employ 550 women."

A middle western machinery company wrote that the efforts of the local union to organize its foundry failed because the men preferred the Works Council organization to the trade union. The president of the company stated:

"We have really done some remarkable things in this small town community in the way of staving off unionization of the foundry. This was done in the face of determined efforts by the union to organize the entire town. We have at least one union man on our committee of six or eight, but the union gave up in despair when they found they had not only the management of the organization to fight, but also the men."

One company with representation plans of the "Industrial Democracy" type in four plants, whose committee system has

143

been the object of continual opposition on the part of organized labor, said that it considered the failure of either employees or management to live up to the requirements of the plan was much more dangerous than opposition directed against the plan from outside.

"There has been constant knocking of our plan by representatives of organized labor, but we cannot see that it has had any material effect up to the present time. We feel that such opposition is not a bad thing as it keeps us studying all the while to make our plan more potent. We feel that the dangers from within, the hazards which arise from arbitrary measures, lack of consideration, etc., are more to be feared than the hazards from without."

A middle western rubber company with a plan of the "Industrial Democracy" type, related the following experience in connection with an attempt of the local machinists' union to call a city-wide strike. The machinists employed in this company presented their demands to the management, who in turn referred them to the "Industrial Assembly." The latter agreed to deal with the machinists after they had stated they came as "company employees, and that they were not being guided by outside influences." The grievance committee of the Assembly recommended that rates be increased, and that overtime be paid on the basic eight-hour day instead of on the forty-eight hour week. This recommendation was accepted by the management, who immediately put a large force of men at work reviewing the rates with a view to giving a higher rate to all men deserving it.

The Industrial Assembly then called a mass meeting of machinists and explained what had been done. In addition, each machinist was visited personally by a member of the Assembly and informed what his new rating was, or was given a reason why he did not receive a new rating. When the city-wide machinists' strike was called, 60% of the company machinists upheld the action of the representatives whom they had elected to the Industrial Assembly, and remained at work.

One firm reported that at the time of a city-wide strike which affected the union employees working in two departments of the plant, not only did its union men remain at work, but they denounced the wage demands of the union as being "excessive."[1]

In another plant the action of the Works Council in condemning a general strike was said to be responsible for the failure of the strike.

"About a year ago, when a general strike was ordered by the Millworkers' Union of this city, our House of Representatives, composed largely of union men, went on record against it, giving their reasons, and sent a copy of the resolutions to both of our daily papers, and their action killed the general strike in the city. At the time of this action of our House of Representatives, I think at least 95% of our men belonged to this union, although we run an open shop."

[1]Cf. p. 91.

Distinct from these cases in which trade unions directed strikes against plants where Works Councils were operating, are the experiences of another group of employers who reported organized labor as confining itself to an attempt to ridicule the plans. This was often done only when the plan was introduced. After it was seen that the plans were satisfactory to the employees, no further action was taken by the trade unions. A western construction company stated that while there had been no direct and open attempt made by organized labor to discredit the Works Council, there had been, for over six months after the plan was initiated, "a whispering campaign" which was "rather annoying and difficult to overcome." This had been successfully met, however, with the result that the great majority of the workers had accepted the Works Council "as an entirely satisfactory substitute for the labor union organization."

Organized labor, while opposed to the formation of "company unions," does not object to a system of employees' committees elected within the shop if those committees are supplemental to a trade union agreement. This was the subject of the resolutions of the Executive Council of the American Federation of Labor at the annual convention of the Federation in 1918. The Executive Council placed itself on record as being in favor of a "regular arrangement" in all "large, permanent shops" whereby:

"First, a committee of the workers would regularly meet with the shop management to confer over matters of production; and whereby:

"Second, such committee could carry, beyond the foreman and the superintendent, to the general manager or to the president, any important grievance which the workers may have with references to wages, hours and conditions."

These demands were predicated upon "the basic principle of the right and opportunity of workers to organize and make collective agreements."

Three instances have come to the attention of the Conference Board, of Works Councils in firms which have agreements with labor unions covering wages and working hours.

At the time the "Industrial Democracy" type of Council was introduced into an eastern shoe company, the company had an agreement covering wages and working hours with the United Shoe Workers of America. The original constitution of the Council provided for the discussion of wages and working hours. This provision was not looked upon favorably by the employees, nearly all of whom belonged to the trade union. Consequently the subjects of wages and working hours were removed from the jurisdiction of the Works Council.[1] With this change made, the company reported that the employees took much more interest in the committee system.

[1] Contrast this with the case cited on p. 46, in which union influence had a directly opposite effect upon the jurisdiction of the Works Council in cases of discharge.

In the case of another company, an eastern fishery, the "committee" type of plan works in conjunction with a union agreement covering wages and working hours. The company reported the elected representatives were "a very fair type of men." With regard to the attitude of the employees towards the committees which discuss neither rates of pay nor hours of work, a company official stated:

> "The employees who are union members do not look to the committees to secure changes or to protect them against cuts, but rather continue to look to the unions. The non-union men are content to let their fellow union workers make arrangements with the unions and accept any changes made. The non-union workers do not . . . take any more interest in the representation plan than do the union men."

No attempt has been made by organized labor to induce the employees to abandon the plan, "principally because our method does not come in contact with the union." The company feels, however, that if a firm is obliged to deal with the union,

> ". . . the employees' conference will not have as much importance in the eyes of the workers as it would if the company dealt directly with the employees."

In another plant, an eastern printing company, agreements as to hours of work and conditions are made with a trades council made up of representatives of the several trade unions working in the plant, and wage agreements are made with each one of the local unions. The employees' committees

> ". . . do not discuss union matters such as base rates or hours of labor, but frequently do take up matters such as a particular job, where a special element enters not common to other jobs."

The committees are not permanent, "but are appointed when a matter comes up for discussion." Each committee is composed as follows: A representative of each department affected (this representative being chosen by the members in that department), the representative of the particular union involved, the works manager representing the firm, and the employment manager, who is a neutral member. The "representative of the union involved" is usually the president of the local trade union. These committees have been functioning since 1915. One of the company officials wrote that they had functioned satisfactorily and had been helpful "in establishing a co-operative feeling between management and workers."

In view of the reluctance of employers to furnish information regarding the attitude adopted by trades unions towards Works Councils, it has been difficult to form an accurate judgment as to the relative number of cases in which organized labor has opposed Councils and those in which it has made no attempt to discredit the plans. The Conference Board has found that a large number of employers either disregarded the question, or simply stated that if any steps to oppose the plans had been

146

taken by labor organizations, such steps had not been obvious or had been unsuccessful.

Field investigation, moreover, showed that in some cases the accounts given by employers of the attitude of local unions towards Works Councils were at variance with the statements of union officials themselves. Although the local unions may not have endeavored to disrupt the Councils by any organized assault upon them, it was found that they regarded the Councils very unfavorably and were doing much to induce employees to put no faith in them. The common belief among union officials was that, under a Works Council system, the work of organizing the employees was made more difficult; employees tended to drop their union membership because they could gain advantages through the Works Council that cost them nothing, whereas there was a fee demanded of them from the unions.

In view of this reluctance on the part of employers to furnish information and of the discrepancies found between the information furnished the Board and that gained by investigation in the field, no reliable statement can be made as to the extent to which trades unions have combated Works Councils.

PART III

Employers' Opinions as to the Value of Works Councils in Industry

The testimony of employers regarding their Works Councils indicates the various factors which are important influences in determining the success or failure of any plan of employee representation.

First, there is the manner of its introduction. It has been found in many plants that employees have a tendency to oppose new ideas of which they have no previous knowledge. This tendency may be overcome in various ways. Employers may institute a regular educational campaign in which, by instruction in industrial methods, economics, etc., they may convince the workers of the need for the proposed plan, and also of the sincerity and fair-mindedness of the management in offering it. Or the Works Council idea may be submitted to the employees, their decision to be the final one as to whether or not it shall be introduced, and theirs to be the responsibility of organizing it. By this method the plan originates with them and is, therefore, fairly sure of their support. This manner of installing committee systems has been tried out with a high degree of success in some instances. There are plants where the understanding between management and employees is such that an elaborate "selling" of the plan is unnecessary. But even in these the wise executive will give his men a vote on its introduction, and a hand in its organization. Various methods for introducing employee representation, successfully tried out by as many concerns, are outlined in the chapter which follows.

A second important factor in the success of a Works Council plan is the attitude toward it of both the parties concerned. Its activity, especially at the outset, is dependent on the amount of interest displayed in it by the management. If it is not used by them for the dissemination of information concerning business conditions, whether these conditions be good or bad, for the encouragement of practical suggestions by workers in the shops, for getting the collective opinion of the employee body on matters where this opinion counts, the Council tends to be dormant, or at least to degenerate into a grievance committee. If, on the other hand, the executives display an active interest in the organization, the resulting reaction on the part of the employees is practically certain to be a favorable one. With this foundation a satisfactory channel of communication between management and employees is assured.

With regard to what has been accomplished by employees' committees, some employers have been content with the degree of usefulness just outlined. The improved understanding of each other's viewpoint, the increased sense of a common interest in business, has justified the organization in their minds. But in other cases the possibility has been demonstrated of developing that sense of common interest in the worker to a point where committees will do valuable constructive work. It lies, to a large extent, within the power of the management to extend the committees' usefulness in this direction. It is they who must prove to the workers that what is done to improve efficiency or increase production redounds to the ultimate good of employed as well as employer. And when this point has been reached, encouragement must come from every executive to those working under them, stimulating new ideas for inducing either more productive efficiency or more personal contentment within the plant.

All these points, and various others which do not fall within these classifications, have been illustrated by the concrete examples which follow.

CHAPTER XIV

INTRODUCING THE PLAN

One of the points most frequently stressed by employers in their reports was that of "selling" the idea of employee representation to the employees before attempting to install it in the plant. It has been found that the worker is inclined to be suspicious of any innovation suggested by the management. Even though it seems to be greatly to his benefit he is constantly looking for the "joker in the pack." In the words of one of the company officials of a machinery concern:

> "Instituting a Works Council or any form of employee representation is bound to cause a great deal of suspicion and distrust in the early stages of its growth."

A similar comment was made by the head of an eastern hosiery firm:

> "Employees are never keen for benefits offered by the management. They distrust them. They are constantly on the alert to discover what the company is getting out of it."

Various employers, whose Works Councils are operating successfully, strongly favored the plan, but were emphatic in their statements that no degree of success could be attained unless the workers wanted the plan.

The vice-president of an eastern watch company employing 3,500 men, whose Works Council is of the "committee" type, said:

> "In view of our experience we would most certainly advocate the establishment of some sort of Works Council or advisory committee in every large factory, if the organization is worked out by the employees themselves so that they will have a real interest in it."

A company official of an eastern silk concern, having in operation two Councils of the "Industrial Democracy" type, voiced a similar opinion:

> "From our experience we believe that the proper way to institute a Works Council plan in an establishment is to present the plan to the employees and leave it for them to decide whether or not they wish to take up the work. It is a well established fact that any organization superimposed by the management would surely prove a failure."

In a western coal company, employing twelve thousand men and having a Works Council which has been operating for seven years under the "committee" plan, experience has dictated the wisdom of "selling" employee representation to superintendents, foremen and employees.

> "I would favor the introduction of a Works Council plan, preferably after preparing the foremen and superintendents for it in advance, and after having had the employees elect representatives to help draw up the plan."

150

Some employers, who place considerable stress on this idea, have gone so far as to suggest methods by which the representation plan may be "sold" to the employees. Some of these are merely general suggestions as to the method of approach, but in one or two instances, elaborate schemes have been planned and executed, usually with a good measure of success.

A company official of a New England textile plant, operating a Council of the "Industrial Democracy" type, gave from his experience the following opinion of how a Works Council should be launched:

> "We would first endeavor to build a foundation of good will between ourselves and the workers, then gradually disclose a scheme of "Industrial Democracy", and if there was any response we would call for a meeting of workers' representatives and outline the plan to them so that they could report at a later date whether a large majority of workers were receptive to the idea; if so, then a meeting of all employees would be called and after further explanations of the system, a ballot would be taken."

One of the company officials in an eastern concern which employs 46,000 men and operates a Council of the "committee" type, was of the opinion that "some sort of a plan of employee representation is not only desirable, but quite essential in any large industry," for the maintenance of right industrial relations. He gave also his idea of the ideal introduction of such a plan:

> "It seems to me that the ideal way of introducing any such plan in an establishment is to merely convey the idea to the workers and then let them work out the details of the plan, presenting it to the management for acceptance or rejection when they have finally decided what they want. If this is done in the proper manner, in nine cases out of ten the management will be able to accept the plan developed by the workers without fundamental change."

An eastern paper company having three thousand employees, operates a Works Council of the "committee" type. The organization has a partnership plan and an unemployment fund which must be considered as important factors in the pleasant relations existing between the company and the employees. These have been fully outlined in a previous chapter.[1]

A company official stated that the danger in establishing a representation plan is that of handing it down ready-made to the employees, rather than letting it be developed by the employees themselves. In this particular company the construction of the works committee plan and the development of all its details was the work of the employees; the management's only part was to approve the work of the committee. That the committee did its work well can be judged by the fact that but few changes have been found necessary in the plan as originally adopted.

[1] See p. 104.

It is believed that it is due to the spirit of partnership growing up in the company that dealings between the management and the employees, as represented in the "works committee," rarely show the characteristics of competitive negotiations. The Board's informant stated:

> "In a large majority of cases the works committee and the management have sat down together in a spirit of confidence and understanding and tried to work their problems out together from the point of view of the company as a whole."

The president of the company said:

> "The works committee plan by providing for the adjustment of grievances, has made them rare; by providing a committee of representatives it has made possible government with the consent of the governed; and by providing joint committees for the thorough and thoughtful investigation of specific subjects it has secured to us the opportunity to create continuously those new plans for efficiency and contentment which will make sure our steady progress in the future."

In an eastern hardware manufacturing plant where the Council is of the "committee" type, a company official found that the value of the plan lay in the means which it provided for creating confidence between management and employees. It is interesting to note that this firm has entrusted to its committee the right of final decision on the matters which come within its province, and that the committee has proven itself entirely worthy of this trust:

> "We allow the vote of our employees' representative committee to be final instead of being merely recommendations, as in so many of the other establishments. We put this in purposely, as we felt that it gave the committee more punch, and showed the committee that the firm had confidence in it.
>
> "Our employees had been educated two years on the 'square deal' before an employees' representative committee was formed. It would be very inadvisable for a firm starting out on welfare and personnel work with a dash, thinking that by putting in all these things in a few weeks, they would cure all their ills. If such a firm gives the employees full power, especially if the men have been ill treated before the change of policy, in all probability the employees will use the committee to the detriment of the firm.
>
> "Our people realized the power they had and never abused it. As a matter of fact, I think I can safely say their tendency was to make sure that the firm was treated right."

The same correspondent emphasized the necessity of starting wisely. He found his method for installing the Council eminently satisfactory:

> 'In any plant where the number of employees is too large to make it possible to have an intimate acquaintanceship with each and every employee, we would certainly advocate an employees' representative committee. Before starting this, however, we would take several months to educate the employees to the idea. We would then appoint the first committee to serve six months. At the end of that time we would hold a general election and have the members elected by the employees. This is the way we started our Employees' Representative Committee, and found it to be successful."

The commanding officer of a mid-western arsenal has been very successful with a Works Council of the "committee" type. His experience has made him strongly in favor of employee representation. He has laid down two rules, the rigid adherence to which he has found necessary to the success of such a plan. The first, which concerns the support and interest which the employer himself must give to the organization, is discussed in another chapter.[1] The second relates to the method in which the Works Council is introduced. This officer was at such great pains to get the employee representation idea to his men, that up to the present time they believe that the whole scheme was originated by them. He states:

"The one thing in connection with the Council which I cannot bring out too strongly is this—the establishment of it must not be at the suggestion of the management. In other words, it must not be forced on the men. The management can accept any proposed scheme and then let the men have it through representatives that can be trusted, but in no sense must the scheme be presented to the men with an ultimatum telling them that this is what must be put in. American working men, especially those in government employ, have minds of their own. They think and carefully consider the problems that interest them personally and they can no more be forced to take a constructive part in a works organization than a horse can be forced to drink when you bring him up to the drinking trough."

One of the company officials of an eastern firm operating a Works Council of the "committee" type, furnished an interesting example of a plan in which

". . . the request for representation came from the men in the factory, and the scheme was worked out independently from company influence even to the calling of preliminary meetings of all the employees to consider the matter and the formation of the constitution, which was framed entirely by them and adopted intact by the company's management."

An attempt by the management to install a Council proved a failure. Just prior to the time when the subject of employee representation was broached, certain unions were especially active in the shop, and although the management did its part towards the maintenance of friendly relations with these organizations, an unfavorable situation developed. Despite this, however, the company fostered the idea of employee representation, and after several meetings had been held in which the scheme was explained to the employees, the company called for a vote on a plan that had been drawn up. The result was three to one against the plan. In view of this it was decided that the company would take no further action in the matter until the general sentiment of the employees should be in favor of the idea, and until they should take the initiative.

Later the employees themselves began to feel the need of some channel of communication with the management. Their views came to the company through a request made to the

[1] See p. 162.

personnel superintendent that the company permit some form of employee representation.

"The committee appointed by the employees, when asked concerning their object, made the statement to the effect that it was their opinion that the only way to insure industrial harmony was to have some definite channel of communication between the men and the management, that the men might secure a better idea of the plans and policies of the company, and that the management might secure the viewpoint of the employees."

The management neither granted nor refused this request at once, but "put up" to the committee the formation of a definite plan of organization to be submitted, on its completion, to the company for a decision. The committee undertook the promotion of an organization on this basis. Assistance was rendered by management in providing the committee with outlines of representation plans and advice was given whenever requested, but the decision was left to the committee. One of the company officials stated that the committee acted in "a very fair-minded manner to both employees and management." The outcome was considered "a great success," and although there are small factions that display only a slight interest in the organization this is evidenced by only a few, mainly clerical workers.

In the opinion of the superintendent, the Works Council has more than justified itself. From his experience two conditions must accompany the successful development of an employee representation plan:

"1. An attitude of sincerity on the part of the management for square dealing in everything.

"2. An appreciation of the benefits to be derived from such a plan on the part of the employees."

The executive's conclusion with regard to employee representation was:

"We believe that there is no one plan that can fit all conditions, that the machinery for organization is not so important as honesty of purpose and frankness in dealing with situations pertaining to both the management and employees. We do not believe that the management should give up the right of final decision on points affecting the control and the administration of the company's affairs, but we do believe that valuable cooperation and assistance can be secured from the workmen when they are given the opportunity of a fuller understanding of conditions that affect them directly."

Failure to create a desire for representation among the employees in his plant before attempting to install a plan might account, in part, for the unqualified disapproval of the Works Council expressed by an official in an eastern iron and steel company, operating a representation plan of the "committee" type. The workers were allowed to vote on the introduction of a Council, but the management failed to profit by the indifference expressed in the vote. They proceeded to install the council without attempting to "sell" the idea to the lukewarm and opposing members of the employee body:

"Our Works Council was instituted voluntarily on the part of the management after allowing the employees to voice their opinion with a ballot. The majority wishing the Works Council was very small. There was no demand for the Works Council due to any labor troubles whatsoever."

The use of the committees mainly for the airing of complaints and grievances,[1] and the poor type of worker chosen to represent the employers on the committees[2] have been fully described in other chapters of this report.

A representation plan of the "committee" type has functioned for more than two years, to the satisfaction of the management, in the Union Construction Company, a shipyard located at Oakland, California.

An interesting aspect of this particular case is the method by which the Council was installed. No step in its institution was taken without the knowledge of the employee body. A carefully planned attempt was made to "sell" the idea thoroughly to every worker in the company's employ.

The concern, from the time of its organization in 1918, had been provided with a personnel department, the functions of which were hiring and discharge, the taking of precautions for safety, the running of the restaurant, etc. The Board's correspondent was of the opinion that this department had been an influencing factor of value in the development of the works committee system.

In January, 1919, the management reached the decision that it was desirable to install in the plant a plan for employee representation. The first step in this direction was the posting in various parts of the yard, of charts, illustrating a simple Works Council plan, announcing the management's wish for the system, and outlining the method by which the employees might elect representatives and work out the details of organization. (See Chart 1.)

The twenty-five journeymen mechanics (Chart 1 (a)) were nominated by the management. To each of these a letter, drawn up by the executives, was sent. This letter expressed the dissatisfaction which the company had experienced in dealing with representatives of the unions; it stated the need for an organization that should be truly representative of the shipyard employees, and it outlined the following three duties for the successful candidates for the committee:

"*First*: Prepare a plan for a permanent representative organization, and supervise the putting of it into effect.

"*Second*: Adjust grievances which the workmen have been unable to adjust through their foreman in the regular way.

"*Third*: Assist the management in such other ways as experience shows to be possible and advisable."

Five foremen were selected by the management and appointed to the committee (Chart 1 (c)). A letter to each of these gave

[1] See p. 57.
[2] See p. 29.

155

reasons for the installation of the employee representation plan
and explained the machinery by which any workman could get
his grievance or suggestion to the management (Chart 2.)
The theory upon which the works committee was organized
was stated as follows:

"(a) The service manager—who is the chairman of the works committee—is the personal representative of the general manager, from
whom he gets his instructions. He therefore represents the interest
of the management.

"(b) The five foremen are to be selected from among the group of
yard executives, which is responsible for production and for the practical administration of the yard.

"(c) The five workmen represent the workers in the yard."

This arrangement provided a committee which, except for
the service manager—who ordinarily has no vote—was divided
equally between the yard management and the workmen. It
was expected that this would lead to decisions based on justice
both to the men and to the company.

After the nomination of the twenty-five journeymen mechanics (Chart 1 (a)), the company posted a notice bearing
the names of the nominees and instructions for voting on them.
The vote was taken by secret ballot as the men came to work in
the morning. The assistant manager made the following comment on this first election:

"Approximately one-half of the men in the plant voted at this first
election, which we considered very satisfactory in view of the suspicion
with which the men looked upon the whole movement."

With the announcement of the election, a letter expressing
the company's hope that through this organization the cooperation of the workers might be secured, and impressing upon
the representative the responsibility of his position in helping
to bring this about, was signed by the president and sent to
each of the five candidates elected.

In order that they might feel that their interest had been appreciated, another letter, also signed by the president of the
concern, was sent to each of the twenty unsuccessful candidates
for the committee.

The names of the ten members of the temporary works committee (five workers elected, five management representatives
appointed) were posted, together with the following outline of
their duties.

"(1) To appoint craft representatives. (Chart 1 (d).)

"(2) To adjust grievances which the workmen have been unable
to adjust through their foreman in the regular way.

"(3) To prepare a plan for a permanent representative organization and supervise the putting of it into effect in about ninety days.

"(4) To assist the management in such other ways as experience
shows to be possible and advisable."

The first act of this temporary works committee was the
appointment of the craft representatives. (Chart 1 (d).)
This representation was provided for in the management's

156

(Chart 1)

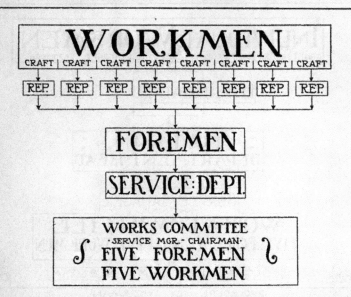

~ WORKS COUNCIL ~

WORKMEN

| CRAFT | CRAFT | CRAFT | CRAFT | CRAFT | CRAFT | CRAFT | CRAFT |

| REP. | REP. | REP. | REP. | REP. | REP. | REP. | REP. |

FOREMEN

SERVICE·DEPT.

WORKS COMMITTEE
·SERVICE MGR.·-CHAIRMAN·
FIVE FOREMEN
FIVE WORKMEN

━ · · NOTICE · · ━

In accordance with the labor policy of this Company (as posted in this Yard), we desire to set up a simple plan of representation for our workmen, to serve as a medium of adjustment between ourselves and our workers, and to act upon matters of mutual interest.

The plan proposed and presented in the diagram is simple, and is to be considered the starting point from which the Company and its employees may develop as extensive a plan as may be mutually acceptable.

In order to create an organizing committee (to serve for ninety days), the following program is announced:

(a) On January 15th, the Company will nominate twenty-five journey men mechanics in groups of five, representing five main departments of the Plant, and will also appoint an election committee of three mechanics.

(b) On January 17th, the Company will call for the election, by secret ballot under the direction of the election committee, of five journey men-one from each group.

(c) On January 19th, the Company will announce the result of the election, and appoint five foremen or quartermen to serve with the five elected representatives, thus forming the temporary Works Committee.

(d) The Company will then turn over to the temporary Works Committee the responsibility for the appointment of temporary craft representatives, for the development of by-laws, etc., and the arrangements for putting the final plan into operation, in accordance with the by-laws as finally adopted.

UNION·CONSTRUCTION·CO.
By
President

(Chart 2)

WORKS COUNCIL
UNION CONSTRUCTION CO.

INDIVIDUAL WORKMEN
CRAFT | CRAFT | CRAFT | CRAFT | CRAFT | CRAFT | CRAFT | CRAFT | CRAFT

REPRESENTATIVE

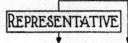

: • FOREMAN • : DEPARTMENT HEAD

SERVICE MANAGER
(CHAIRMAN)

WORKS COMMITTEE
FIVE FOREMEN & FIVE WORKMEN

| SPEC. COMM. | SPEC. COMM. | SPEC. COMM. |

PROCEDURE BY WORKMAN

ANY COMPLAINT OR OTHER MATTER UPON WHICH AN EMPLOYEE WISHES TO GET ACTION, CAN BE HANDLED AS FOLLOWS:

(1) Take up the question (either in person or with the help of your representative) with your foreman, & then if necessary with your Department Head

(2) If you are still unable to get satisfaction place your case before the Service Manager who will either make an acceptable settlement or else refer you to the Works Committee whose Decision is final.

For complete information concerning the Works Council refer to the Constitution & By laws, a copy of which can be obtained from the Service Manager.

WORKS COMMITTEE

NAME OF WORKMAN · NAME OF WORKMAN · NAME OF WORKMAN · NAME OF WORKMAN · NAME OF WORKMAN · NAME OF WORKMAN

CRAFT REPRESENTATIVES

~ CLERICAL DEPARTMENT ~
NAME OF WORKMAN · NAME OF WORKMAN

~ ENGINEERING DEPARTMENT ~
NAME OF WORKMAN

SHIPFITTING DEPARTMENT	NAME OF WORKMAN	MACHINERY DEPARTMENT	NAME OF WORKMAN
MATERIAL YARD		MARINE MACHINIST	
MOLD LOFT		BLACKSMITH	
PLATE SHOP		MACHINE SHOP	
ANGLE SHOP (INCL. SLABMEN. ETC.)		BOILERMAKER	
CRANE OPERATORS, PLATE HANGERS			
ERECTORS			
SHIPFITTERS		WOOD WORKING DEPARTMENT	
MATERIAL CHECKERS		JOINERS	
ANGLESMITHS ON BOATS		MILLMEN	
BURNERS AND WELDERS		STAGE-BUILDERS	
TOOL ROOM, FOREGMEN, HOSEMEN, ETC.		SHIPWRIGHT & CAULKERS	
RIVETING & DRILLING DEPARTMENT		MISC. MECHANICAL DEPARTMENT	
PIECE COUNTERS & TIMEKEEPERS		LABORERS	
BOLT RECOVERY & CLEANUP		STOREROOM	
BOLTERS & PACKERS		RIGGERS	
HEATER & PASSERS		PAINTERS	
CHIPPER, CAULKERS & TESTERS		ELECTRICIANS	
RIVETERS & HOLDERS ON		COPPERSMITHS	
DRILLERS		PIPEFITTERS	

plan "for the purpose of securing a representative on the job in each department." Appointment was made by a letter to each, signed by the chairman of the temporary works committee and containing, together with such sections of a constitution and by-laws as the committee had been able to get into shape, an outline of the duties of the craft representative.

At the first meeting of the works committee it was decided that one alternate member of the committee should be appointed by the management, and one should be chosen from among the unsuccessful candidates of the last election. Letters were accordingly sent, one to the defeated employee candidate who had received the highest vote, and one to the chosen alternate foreman. Their standing on the committee was defined as follows:

> "These two members are to have all the rights and privileges of full membership in the works committee, except that they do not vote except in the absence of any foreman or a workman, as the case may be."

With the completion of this organization the company posted a chart which explained to the workman with a grievance how to get it settled (Chart 2). To this chart was later appended the lower section showing the names and working numbers of members of the works committee and the various craft representatives.

This chart, with minor changes, was later painted on bulletin boards which carried the permanent works committee organization notices. The Board's correspondent remarked the following as worthy of note, as an indication of the feeling of the men towards the organization:

> "These permanent notices are still up in the yard and have only received a moderate amount of defacement. To anyone who is familiar with the shipyard workers the fact that these notices have received only a moderate amount of defacement is an indication that they have been looked upon by a great majority of the men with reasonable respect and that the men as a whole approve of the thing that these signs explain."

Since craft representatives did not meet with the works committee, but had as their duties the handling of grievances in their departments and the reporting of business transacted by the committee to their co-workers, the need was felt for a means by which the action taken by the works committee could be communicated to the craft representatives, in order that they, in turn, might be in a position to keep their constituents informed. Accordingly a weekly letter was issued, a copy of which was sent to each craft representative. After the organization was completed, the constitution adopted, etc., this weekly letter was replaced by a weekly paper called *Works and Ways*, also published by the works committee.

A company official's endorsement of the employee representation plan, which has been so carefully built up in his plant, was strong. He made enthusiastic comparison of the first election held and the last one:

> "At the time the first election was held the average attendance was 2,500 and the total number of ballots cast was 1,200, giving a 48% of the men voting. The elections come every six months and at the last election nearly 70% of the men in attendance on the voting day deposited legal ballots. At the time of the first election there was naturally a suspicion on the part of many of the men that the whole performance was more or less a joke or fad, and many of them who were perhaps in sympathy with the idea refrained from voting for fear of being made fun of by the other men. At the last election, however, the situation was entirely different. Campaign signs were placed up all over the yard, election cards were printed and handed out in a true American fashion, and speeches were made by some of the candidates. We were particularly pleased at the spirit of the last election because it made us feel that the men as a body had accepted the works committee and had entered into the spirit of the thing."

The Council is now on a good financial basis. On two occasions it hired the local theatre and sold the house to the employees, making in each instance about $350. An arrangement made with a local hospital association whereby that association has the exclusive right to solicit in the yard, and whereby the men can insure at reduced rates, nets the Council a commission of 5% on all premiums collected. In addition the company pays fifty cents against every dollar spent by the Council out of money raised by the men in the yard. The bank balance of the works committee now varies from $750 to $1000.

Monthly joint meetings of the craft representatives and the works committee are held which are also open to any workman from the yard who wishes to attend. The discussions are free to anyone with an opinion which he wishes to express. The interest taken in these meetings is shown by the fact that from 150 to 175 men attend them.

The foregoing statements of employers' experience with Works Council plans for periods varying from two to seven years are unanimous with respect to the manner in which a representation plan should be introduced into a plant. Before establishing a plan management should determine whether the employees favor it. A plan formulated by management alone and submitted to the workers as an established organization will have the result of arousing the employees' distrust and suspicion. This will have a serious effect upon the functioning of the plan. Opinion differs as to whether the employees should work out the plan alone and submit it to the management for review, whether the plan should be the joint work of employees and management, or whether the employees should be allowed to vote to accept or reject the plan. There is no deviation from the opinion, however, that management should in one of these ways learn before the plan is set up whether the employees are in favor of working under it.

160

CHAPTER XV

IMPORTANCE OF EMPLOYERS' INTEREST

Many employers who gave favorable opinions of employee representation, based on personal experience with it, found that it was necessary for the management, if not the head of the concern himself, among other things to keep in close touch with the Council. They have discovered that if the scheme is to function with any degree of success, it must hold the interest and confidence of the workers, and that this requires the constant and conscientious attention of the executives. In this connection, the Conference Board has obtained not only the stories of Councils in concerns where the close interest of the management has been attended by the successful functioning of the plans, but also a record of experiences where the failure of the executives to convince the workers of the sincerity of their intentions has been followed by an absolute loss of confidence in the scheme on the part of the employees.

A mid-western paint company has a Works Council of the "Industrial Democracy" type. Employee representation has functioned successfully in this plant for eleven years, with never a record of an unsatisfactory decision rendered. The vice-president emphasized the necessity for close contact and fair dealing between management and employees:

> "If we were to do the work over again we would start using the same plan, as we find it enables us to bring up any question, regardless of what its nature is, through the Congress, and in no time during the eleven years have we had any reason to complain of the final decision or vote on serious questions brought up, such as wages, working hours and differences that affected everybody in the organization. Of course it is necessary for the management to keep active and in close touch with the Congress, and above all to be absolutely frank, playing the cards open and above board."

An interesting opinion of similar purport was given by a company official in an eastern concern employing three thousand men. A Works Council of the "committee" type is in operation there. Emphasis was laid not only on the importance of the management's keeping in close touch with the committee, but also on the wise choice of the officials who were to maintain this contact:

> "In so far as the Works Council plan in our establishment is concerned, our attitude is that we would continue, in view of the good results obtained. The writer personally feels that it is the only plan, regardless of conditions. It is necessary to be a success that the attitude of the management be right toward the shop committee, also the personality of the individual who is in direct contact with the employees. Tact and confidence must be established between the

161

management and the shop committee if any good results are to be obtained. If this is not used, the committee is of no value.

"The entire proposition is simply one of human engineering, and regardless of shop committee plan, the direction must be on the basis of confidence, and the understanding of human nature. Arbitrary, careless, and inconsiderate decisions not giving the employees a fair deal, make for trouble. On the other hand, discipline and strict enforcement of rules, is necessary to establish firmly in the minds of the worker the proper requirement, or needs, in operating any business, and this is not difficult when properly organized."

The vice-president and general manager of a western motor car company, whose Council is of the "committee" type, went so far as to say that an employee representation plan could not function successfully without the close personal attention of the chief executive of the firm:

"We are well pleased with the operation of the present plan in our shops. Wish to say that the writer expresses the opinion that the plan cannot be worked as in operation here without the active cooperation and participation of the executive head of the company. There is so much petty opposition to the plan that when handled by a minor official it would have poor chance for success. The writer has given the matter a great deal of attention and feels well repaid for all the effort the plan has required."

In a large, eastern electric company where a Council of the "committee" type is in operation, employee representation has proved of material value to the executive end of the concern. The management realizes that the worker, through his practical experience, is in a position to see places where time or labor, and thus, money, may be saved. The Works Council, functioning successfully, has furnished him with both the incentive and the machinery for getting his ideas to the management. In this plant:

"An important outcome of the plan has been the disclosure of weak points in the management, which has resulted in many improvements in organization."

One of the company officials was of the opinion that without the support of the head of the plant the plan must be a failure:

"Any plan of representation must have the conscientious support of the higher executive of the plant in order to be successful. It is, of course, obvious that the executive must show patience and must expect that any plan of representation which is founded on a square deal will show up weak points in his organization which must be accepted, and afterwards rectified.

"If the executive takes the stand at the beginning that nothing can be wrong in his part of the organization, he might better refrain from installing any plan of representation. If a foreman is right, he should receive the utmost support. If, however, he is wrong, it should be acknowledged and the matter rectified. The plan merely calls for firmness with justice."

The commanding officer of a mid-western arsenal, whose Council is of the "committee" type, believes his success with his employee representation plan, as a solution of the problem of industrial relations, to be due, in large measure, to two things.

162

One of these, discussed in another chapter,[1] was to the effect that the establishment "must not be at the suggestion of the management—must not be forced on the men." The other was in line with the opinions just quoted—that a Works Council requires the painstaking attention of the management. The latter was expressed by the officer as follows:

"The other point about the Works Council is that it must have the unquestioned support and interest of the management if it is adopted. It can be killed quicker by indifference, lack of support and obstruction to its workings on the part of the management than in any other way, and my sincere advice to any concern contemplating the installation is to ask the question of themselves—'Are you willing loyally to give the Works Council your support, interest and aid?' If this can be answered in the affirmative, then put it in. If it cannot be answered in the affirmative without reservation, leave the Works Council idea alone.

"The Council here is a success. It has produced contentment among the employees to a very marked degree and I feel that with the proper support of the management it will continue a success."

The opinion of a company official of an eastern chemical concern, where a Council of the "committee" type is in operation, coincided with those just cited, but went one step farther. It was his belief that the management, in order to hold the workers' interest in the plan, must not only give it attention and support, but must also grant the committees the right of final decision on matters handled by them:

"From the experience which we have had with employee representation we would not hesitate to recommend the adoption of some sort of a plan, providing the management actually believed in it and was willing to show the sincerity of that belief by authorizing the committees a sufficient degree of power to make final decisions. If there are strings tied to the power which is invested in the committees, the members will eventually lose interest."

How this system would work out in the case of reductions in wages or working hours has not yet been demonstrated in this concern, as

". . . both committees have so far avoided the consideration of questions concerning wages, changes in hourly schedules, etc., although the plan contains no limitation which would prevent them from doing so."

Like various other employers, this official has felt the necessity for a watchful avoidance of any prejudice against employee representatives because of any stand taken by them in the performance of their duties as such.

A general statement of his opinion of the plan showed hope for its further development:

"While we are not exactly satisfied that our plan is showing the best possible results, we would not care to abandon it, but rather to experiment with certain changes in the plan with a view to improving it."

The story of the Works Council, a "committee" type, of an eastern concern, forms an interesting antithesis to those just

1 See p. 153.

163

related. The case is one where, according to foremen and other employees interviewed, the Council is gradually degenerating because the management has failed to fulfill its obligation to the organization.

The method of introducing the plan was favorable to its success. To quote one of the officials of the company:

> "I believe that the method of introducing a Works Council which was used by this company was excellent. It consisted in discussing the matter first with the foremen, then with all employees who had been in the company more than five years, and finally with the entire personnel of the plant at a mass meeting."

Three Councils have been elected since the plan was started. The first, composed almost entirely of foremen and minor executives, was fairly successful. The second, with fewer foremen on it, accomplished less. The present one, made up almost entirely of the rank and file, is accomplishing very little. The employees placed the blame for this on the unwillingness of the management to meet them half-way. They put it this way:

> "We bring up a proposition to the management and in order to test us to see how much we really want anything, the management puts up all sorts of arguments as to whether or not it should be granted."

In other words, the management, instead of cooperating with the employee representatives, makes it as difficult as possible for them to "sell" their ideas. Two foremen who were on the first Council attributed their success to their "nerve." "We had to hammer it into the heads of the management," was their statement. The present Council, composed of rank and file workers, lacks this "nerve," and so the workers feel that the plan has become more or less futile.

Employees of the company who were interviewed, were specific in their statements regarding the failure of the management to live up to their part of the bargain. One representative cited the cases of two reductions in staff and working hours:

> "The company told the Council that business was falling off and that although in all probability some change in hours or staff would be necessary, immediate action was not considered likely. Ten days after these announcements the company reduced the staff and reduced the working hours. The first time this happened the Council complained, saying that the company had not kept faith with them. The president of the company, in addressing the Council, admitted a mistake had been made but assured them if changes should be necessary again, they would receive the consideration they wanted. The second time the same thing was repeated. That was the last straw."

According to another employee representative, recommendations made and questions asked by the Council do not receive any reply from the Executive Committee.

> "When business was good and production was wanted, the Council was used by the company to tell us how business was going and how it was up to us to produce. Just now we are very anxious to know how business conditions are and we can't find out. Eight months

ago an official, in explaining the reduction in staff that was sprung on us, said it had to be done because of the large inventory on hand and the smaller number of orders. He showed that they would have to make a large number of shipments to bring things nearer normal."

In the plant cafeteria there has been for some time a chart, placed there at the request of the Council, showing the total number of orders received and the total number of shipments made over given periods. To this was later added, also at the request of the committee, postings as to the orders remaining on the books at the end of each month. A careful examination of these figures showed that for some time shipments had exceeded orders; that month by month orders were falling off. This state of affairs made employees anxious to know what the business outlook was. From what they saw they concluded: "Orders aren't coming in; shipments are away high. We better go slow on the job." Accordingly they did slow up, with the idea that this would make their jobs last longer. The Works Council might have been used to explain that any slowing up on their part, instead of lengthening their jobs, would shorten them. It might have been pointed out to them that a slowing-up process increases the cost of production, affects the selling price of the commodities manufactured, and thus precludes competition with firms not similarly situated, still further cutting down orders.

The failure of the management to use the Council to take the employees into their confidence at this time has caused both representatives and employees at large to lose faith in the company sincerity toward the Council and in the value of the Council. Representatives believe that the management has no confidence in them and does not think them intelligent enough to understand business conditions if explained to them.

The president of the company refused to see that the management was at fault, but stated his belief in the Council. Employees, however, showed no faith in the Council and have gone so far as to suggest that the employee representation plan is not worth keeping up.

A like experience was reported by a New England machinery concern. Opinions gathered from both executives and employees agreed that there was no demand for the plan at its installation, from either party. Thus, at the very beginning, there was a lack of interest. According to one of the company officials the plan was put in "just to be in the fashion," and one of the employee representatives corroborated this statement:

"When the plan was being talked of in the first place a meeting of the men was called in a building not in the industrial district of the city, but fully two miles from the section where the men lived and worked. This showed that there was no great interest on the part of the management. Only a few men went to the meeting, and from this beginning it was concluded that neither men nor management cared a great deal about it."

In addition, the Council was modeled after a plan which called for no regular meetings of the committee; it being called together only when the necessity arose. With these two characteristics of the plan in mind, it is not difficult to explain what followed. In reply to a request by the Conference Board in January, 1921, for information as to what the committee had accomplished over a certain given period, a company official made the following significant statement, showing only three Council meetings in one entire year:

> "We find that in that period nothing was brought up for consideration by the shop committee. As a matter of fact, we have had but three conferences with our shop committee since last February. One was in connection with the revision of by-laws, increasing the executive committee from five to seven. Another was a conference in regard to increase in wages, and the last one was in connection with a request that the company see what it could do to purchase coal at a saving to the employees."

Even though not used by either executives or employees, the management thought the plan worth while—a good thing to have "because it provides a channel whereby the management can keep in touch with the employees and vice versa,"—and would not discontinue it.

The employee representatives interviewed showed an entirely different attitude towards the organization. Several of them said that "the men regarded it as a joke." Some showed by their comments a lack of faith in the management's sincerity in installing the plan. They said:

> "Grievances can be redressed, but after that a foreman can make it so uncomfortable for a man that all he can do is to leave. You can't always prove discrimination."
>
> "Manufacturers have put representation plans in to ward off unionism. That's all right, but they've got to convince the employees that it's worth while. If not, the employees will see through it."
>
> "Interest in it may be renewed when times become normal. Then we can come back at the boss without fear of being out of a job. You can't say anything now. It's 'take it or leave it.'"
>
> "On the recent wage reduction the management said they were going to reduce wages anyway, so what was the use of the shop committee? We didn't feel that the cost of living had decreased as much as the management stated, but what was the use in kicking?"

In reviewing the cases previously reported, where managements have given painstaking attention to their Councils; have provided for regular meetings and a meeting place; have kept the workers fully informed as to business conditions, and as to the likelihood of changes to come on account of these conditions; in short, have convinced the employees of the sincerity of their intentions in installing a Council, the reason for the non-activity of this particular committee becomes apparent.

The vice-president of an eastern wire company, where a Council of a "limited" type was organized in 1918, gave as his opinion of employee representation that

" . . . the committee has two distinct advantages:

"First, it serves as a representative organization which either spontaneously or through direct questioning supplies the management in good season with anything which may be disturbing the minds of an appreciable number of our organization.

"Second, like the safety valve of a low pressure boiler, although it may probably never be used, it is there for the use of anyone who cares to make use of it; . . . an individual in dealing with me as the management's representative in the shop can either obtain the sympathy of his fellow workers or approach some other official of the company if he feels that my view of his case is unsatisfactory."

Expanding further his idea, the same executive said:

"Our whole theory of the shop committee is very simply expressed, since it seems quite stupid to attempt to handle any problem without consideration of the factors which clearly enter into the problem. Therefore an attempt to handle the labor problem without considering the point of view of the workmen, not as the management thinks it is or ought to be, but as the workmen themselves express it, is a waste of time.

"The shop committee offers a means by which the collective opinion of the workmen may be obtained by the management at any time, or may be expressed to the management by its men in an orderly and recognized way. Beyond this point we do not go, and what the committee may be in any organization in the future is something which we deliberately avoid forecasting as we wish it to take its own course of development under whatever circumstances may arise."

Firms mentioned elsewhere have sent in records of functions assigned and activities suggested to the committees by the management. These efforts on the part of the executives have produced far-reaching results. Suggestions for increasing efficiency have been the result sometimes of more personal contentment among the workers, and sometimes of the advent of a feeling of a common interest with the company. To the Works Council was given the credit for the new attitude of the workers.

In the present instance, where value has been claimed for the plan only as a handy machine to be used by either party should the occasion arise, the committee has been reported for three successive years as "dormant." No record has been received that would point toward use of the committees by the management, and, in the words of the vice-president: "The employees do not seem disposed to use our shop committee."

A similar attitude on the part of the management of another eastern concern was found to have had the same effect upon the employees' estimation of the representation plan. The management's attitude toward the plan was admittedly "passive, not active." Although the employee representatives interviewed were convinced that the plan had been of value during the time that wage increases were obtained, during the recent period of business depression, the plan was in their opinion "lifeless." The management found that the employees' committees had resolved themselves into practically nothing but a means for the adjustment of wages:

167

"At the start, when things were booming, and the chances seemed good to get increases in wages, the committees were quite active and we received requests for increases from nearly all the committees. In every case, conditions were looked into and adjustment made where necessary. After business fell off and wages started to come down, practically nothing was heard from the committees at all. Our records show that there were very few matters brought up by any of the members, with the exception of the question of wages. As the committees were formed to take care of the subjects affecting the welfare of both employer and employees, we do not like to see it resolve itself into a plan for the adjustment of wages."

The management of this concern is divided in its opinion as to whether the plan as it operates at present may be termed a success. The employee representatives interviewed spoke in terms that left no doubts as to their estimation of it. They said there would be no regret on their part if the whole scheme were dropped.

This situation is directly attributable to the neglect of the management to make the plan of vital interest to the employees. Employees naturally would not use the plan for the presentation of minor grievances or complaints at a time when the country was suffering from widespread business depression. They no doubt felt that at such a time they were fortunate to have a job at all, and complaints which at another time they might bring before the Works Council would not be brought to the attention of the employee representatives. The plan accordingly became to them a scheme that would work all right when wages were going up, but was of no benefit when wages were coming down.

Management did not utilize the committees to present to the employees information regarding business conditions as they affected the company. It has been clearly shown that this is one of the great advantages of a Works Council during a period of business depression, and that the employees appreciate the action of employers who do inform them as to how business is going.

No regular meetings for constructive work were held in the plant just referred to. There was no opportunity for the interchange of ideas and experiences between employees and management that such meetings afford. The management's idea seemed to be that the introduction of the plan was sufficient. It could then run itself. That it could not is proven by the doubt in the minds of the management as to whether the plan was a success, and by the attitude of the employee representatives, in whose minds there was no doubt as to its being a failure.

The viewpoints of employee representatives in an eastern steel plant, regarding the value of their representation plan during a period of business depression, is in striking contrast to these just quoted. In this plant a representative of the management devotes the whole of his time to the administration of the representation plan.

168

Regular meetings of the committees are held monthly. The management has taken a live interest in the plan, which was initiated "to establish a closer relationship with the employees in order that the greatest degree of cooperation might be obtained." At the time of the visit of a field investigator, the employees' wages had been considerably reduced and the plant was working only part time.

Employee representatives questioned, were unanimous in their approval of the plan. They said the management had shown themselves willing to play the game according to the rules laid down in the plan. Management was "on the square." The recent wage reduction and curtailment of workhour schedules were believed by the employee representatives to have been necessary. They had come to realize this through the monthly talks by the higher executives of the company, telling how the company was standing the strain of business adversity. This was one thing on which the representatives laid particular stress—the opportunity of finding out what the prospects were. Through the information they received from the president of the firm and other high officials, they were able to answer the questions of the employees. Interest in the Council, instead of waning, had increased. A company official stated that the attendance at the meetings was greater when wages were coming down and the business of the company was falling off than in times of business prosperity. An employee representative speaking of this said:

> "Employee representation is all right if it is worked the way it is here. We get in direct touch with the executives. We get to know them and we can talk to them as man to man. We believe they are honest and want to be fair to us. They have got to be that way or the plan would be a failure.
>
> "We go to the meetings and get inside dope on the business situation. We know how many orders are coming in. We know if there is going to be another blast furnace opened up soon. We aren't in the dark any more and we appreciate it."

The foregoing experiences are evidence of the importance of a sincere and constant interest in and attention to an employee representation plan on the part of the management. In general, plans carefully fostered by employers, used to disseminate information of interest to employees, and to assure the latter of a direct channel whereby their grievances might reach the executives, have operated successfully. But where employers have not first convinced the workers of their own sincerity in inaugurating the plan, or have failed to take advantage of the machinery provided by the Councils for keeping the employees informed about business conditions, especially when those conditions were adverse, employees have lost confidence in both the management and the Council, and the organization has either become dormant or has gone out of existence altogether.

CHAPTER XVI

IMPORTANCE OF WORKERS' INTEREST

In the chapter preceding, employers were quoted who emphasized the idea that unless the management gave the Works Council constant and sincere attention it was more than likely to fail. Other officials have gone further than this in their discussions of the success of employee representation plans, and have pointed out the necessity for a corresponding interest and cooperation on the part of the workers. Given these two factors to start with, many employers have found that the Works Council is a highly satisfactory channel of communication between the management and the employees, and that it furnishes a means for discussing and often for settling to the satisfaction of both parties concerned, those questions which especially interest and affect the worker.

It is the expressed opinion of still other officials that employee representation should not stop here. It may be made to function far more broadly than as a mere point of contact between management and employees. It has not attained its maximum of usefulness until the interest of the employees has been enlisted to the extent that they have at least some realization of the oneness of their interests with those of the company, and manifest this interest and realization by attempting work of a constructive nature for the furtherance of production. This work may take the form of suggestions for improvements in production processes brought to the attention of the workers by their practical experience,[1] or it may relate to safety and sanitation, education, studies of wage rates, etc.

Some plants have merely stated that interest on the part of the executives, and a response to this from the workers, had evolved a Council that was a complete success as a means of communication between the two. But a few employers have given histories which began with earnest endeavor on the part of the management to make the scheme a living thing, which recorded a hearty cooperative spirit among the employees, and which followed this with a record of truly valuable constructive work.

A company official of an eastern steel plant, where a plan of the "committee" type is in existence, gave detailed comment on the necessity for creating a true appreciation of the other's viewpoint in the case of both management and employees. With this as a foundation, he was of the opinion that almost any

[1] A full discussion of this point will be found in Chapter V.

type of representation plan could meet with success. This conclusion was reached after the plan had stood the test of a carefully planned but unsuccessful attack by organized labor:[1]

"Each organization has problems peculiar to itself which must be understood before any workable plan can be mapped out. Probably the biggest task confronting a person contemplating introducing a shop committee is first to convince the management that human nature is pretty much the same in the shop as in the office, and that there is little difference in the aspirations of the humblest worker and those of the president of the company. Both want what they term a good living, although their ideas of what constitutes a good living may differ greatly. The next difficult problem is to convince the working men that the manager is just as human as they, and that instead of being a slave driver, whose main interest is profits, he is an intelligent man, of necessity vitally interested in the well-being of his employees, and that the question of wages is of minor importance as compared with the volume of production and the total cost of production. A complete understanding of this can be followed by the introduction of almost any form of committee representation and meet with success, both in making for a contented working force and a greater volume of production, so long as both parties are fair and open, and the management realizes that the duty of the management is to lead and direct."

In a southern shoe factory where the Council is of the "committee" type, the management, by a wise handling of the scheme, has been able gradually to develop in the workers an interest and confidence in the plan. Executives have planned for regular meeting times and topics to be discussed. They have themselves encouraged the workers to discuss the subjects which affected them. With regard to the necessity for retrenchment in the plant, one of the company officials said:

"This phase has been taken up in our meetings incessantly for the last few months, and our employee representatives in the main have grasped the spirit of the retrenchment and the economy program and have helped pass it along in their respective rooms."

The meetings were held under circumstances which encouraged employees to frank discussion:

"The meetings take place once a month in a sort of informal round-table discussion; the atmosphere is easy and the general manager of the works usually acts as chairman and leads the discussion. It has been nearly two years since this plan was adopted and at first the employee representatives were rather inclined to be silent and diffident about expressing themselves. At this time, though, they have thawed out to a great extent and enter freely into discussions."

The management expressed distinct approval of the effect which the plan had had on the spirit of the employees, and was optimistic over the outlook for the future:

"The judgment of the management with respect to shop committees is that it has distinctly shown good results in breaking the vague suspicion and distrust which exists in all wage earning groups. It has brought about a much more cordial feeling, the employees feeling that they know the company much more intelligently and understand their problems better, and vice versa.

"We approve of the shop committee plan and expect it to improve. We feel that while we have gone slowly we have certainly gone some-

[1] See p. 142.

171

where and that if we keep up the present pace, in five more years or so, the standard of intelligence and efficiency in our plants . . . will be vastly improved."

An eastern oil company employing eleven thousand men and operating a Works Council of the "committee" type has had three years of successful experience with its plan. It has been described as a "great method for educating the workers." The men have proven that "if you take them into your confidence they will repay you by deserving it." Fairness and sincerity on the part of the management have created a similar feeling among the employees. And this feeling has formed the basis for the successful working out of the employee representation plan:

"Industrial representation . . . is based on the fundmental principle that the purpose of the joint conference is 'to discuss and settle, subject to final review by the Board of Directors, all matters of general interest, such as hours, wages and working conditions, adjusting of grievances.' In the three years since the inauguration of our first joint conference all such matters have come before the joint conferences and as yet there has not been a single instance in which a fair and amicable conclusion has not been reached. As a satisfactory means of direct contact for the elimination of unsatisfactory conditions and for the development of better relations, the plan has the confidence of both employees and management."

In a western rubber company, where the Works Council operating is of the "Industrial Democracy" type, one of the company officials laid down a definite set of rules covering the part which the management must play in developing a successful representation plan. It had been the executive's experience that a sense of fair play on the part of the employees followed the perfect frankness and sincerity evinced by the management in the plan; that while final decisions had not been placed in the hands of the workers, it had been possible in every case to let their rulings stand. The following he stipulated as essential:

"1. There must be no secrets, no forbidden ground in the organization adopting the plan. All the cards must be on the table. This company issues regular quarterly financial statements to its employees just as to its stockholders.

"2. There must be complete freedom in the expression of opinion.

"3. The form of the plan is not important except that the machinery must make it impossible for the free action of the workers to be stifled by plant officialdom. It is the spirit which is important. The presence or absence of sincerity and the desire for fair play will determine success or failure."

The same official made the statement that if, with the experience with his own Works Council plan, he had to decide whether or not he would introduce a representation plan in an establishment controlled by him, he

". . . would immediately develop such a plan with complete power of the representative body to initiate and adopt legislation which must always be subject to the management's veto, though experience proves that with wise leadership the workers themselves are ultra conservative and the veto power is never used."

In an eastern plant where a council of the "committee" type is in operation, both executives and employee representatives were highly in favor of employee representation as a point of contact. The management felt that it "created a better understanding; was a means of getting closer to the operatives," while the workers

"... appreciated the insight they were obtaining into the business through talks of the company officers."

This feeling of a common interest was the natural outgrowth of the manner in which the organization had been handled. After securing the approval of the employee body to the introduction of the plan, the management proceeded to keep their interest in it alive by suggesting, at the earlier meetings, subjects for discussion such as "savings plans, safety work, English classes, etc." Later, when business conditions became uncertain and employees were anxious about future prospects, the company used the committees to keep them fully informed regarding plant conditions:

"This information was passed on to the employees who, at the present time of uncertainty, were very eager to learn all they could about the company's position and the outlook for the future."

In this connection, a point not heretofore mentioned was brought up by the Board's correspondent. This was the difficulty of getting information transmitted from management to employees and from employees to management, correctly reported by employee representatives. Any representative unable to explain clearly to his constituents the import of a message from the executives tended to forfeit the latter's confidence. The workers, in their turn, distrusted his ability to make a clear statement of their views. The remedy recommended by this official was education for representatives by frank discussion in frequent meetings.

This writer's opinion on the value of employee representation in general, with special reference to his own experience with it, was as follows:

"We feel that some form of employee representation is necessary, that there must be some well regulated means of communication between employee and management and between management and employee.

"The great problem, as we see it in the representation plan, is the establishment of confidence of the employees in their representatives on the committees. It is a matter of education which can only be brought out by holding frequent regular meetings at which matters are frankly discussed. The employees will have faith in their representative and in the committee plan only after they have continually seen and have experienced the results of discussions and matters which have been taken up at committee meetings. The employee representation plan will fail, with those concerns who consider such a plan and such committees simply in the light of grievance committees."

Both executives and workers have appreciated the value of the educational opportunities afforded those who were fortunate enough to be elected to the committees. It was remarked by another official in the plant that "the committee was a great place for a man to receive training to become an assistant foreman."

In a large eastern rubber concern operating fourteen Councils of the "committee" type, the report of one of the company officials indicated a high degree of satisfaction with the progress of the plans. The management has kept in touch with them; the employees have supported them. The committees have discussed and satisfactorily settled problems in which a wide range of subjects was involved. As a means of keeping the viewpoint of each party before the other, and of eliminating small disputes before they assumed importance, employee representation has proven of great value.

> "It provides a means of contact which cannot otherwise be obtained and gives opportunity for the management of a plant to inform their employees of their viewpoint, and likewise gives opportunity for the employees to present their viewpoint.
>
> "Misunderstandings in regard to small things quite frequently grow to large difficulties if permitted to go on. Employee representation provides means whereby the smaller difficulties are settled as they arise, and if we can settle all our small difficulties as they come up, we may never have to face the big ones so far as our dealings with employees go."

A mid-western steel company has operated Works Councils of the "committee" type in four plants for upwards of two years. The organizations have been unusually successful as a means of communication between management and employees. This success has been attained, according to statements made by one of the company officials, by the constantly demonstrated interest in the Council by the executives, attended by the active cooperation of the workers.

In the beginning the plan was not even suggested by the management; it was requested entirely by the employee body.

A favorable answer to this request was returned by the management and plans laid for an election. Aside from advising the workers to exercise judgment in their choice of the men they elected to represent them on the committee, the management took no part in installing the system. For two years the Council operated without even a constitution, and when that was finally drawn up and adopted, it too was at the suggestion of the workers.

But, though the officials of the company showed no tendency to interfere in the installation or work of the Council, they were at great pains to keep the employees ever conscious of their interest in the plan and their support of it. In this way they developed more and more the workers' confidence in them and in the Councils.

The scope of the committees' activities has been wide. They have "discussed every conceivable question... wages, hours, working conditions, sanitation, safety and comforts," and always with results satisfactory to both management and men:

"While at times the progress would be quite stormy, there never has been an occasion where our men did not show good judgment and exceeding fairness with the company in their final conclusions."

An additional factor to be considered in these results is the education of employee representatives afforded by the management:

"The representatives themselves must be taught as you go along some fundamental thinking in regard to business economics, but after they have obtained ideas about production and costs, we have found no instance where they have been unfair."

While the management does not consider its plan a perfect one, it finds it increasingly satisfactory in its functioning.

Another example of keen interest in and right use of the Works Council on the part of the management, a response in kind from the employee body, and the subsequent functioning of the organization as a highly satisfactory channel of communication between the two parties concerned, was furnished by an eastern concern whose representation plan, of the "committee" type, has operated since 1919.

The president of this concern has used the Council constantly since its installation to keep his workers informed on every phase of business conditions. Especially has he made use of it during the time of business depression. In every case of a change made necessary by economic pressure, the reason has been explained to the men. And it has not been the employee representatives alone who have had opportunities to learn how things were going. In addition to meeting the employee representatives at Council meetings, the president has made it a policy to hold mass meetings of all the men in several departments, at which he placed before them subjects of common interest.

The response of the workers to the efforts of the management has been satisfactory. While there has been no enthusiasm manifested over necessary reductions in wages and hours, at least they have been understood and accepted in good spirit. A keen appreciation of the frankness of the executives, as well as a recognition of the Council as a means of getting their grievances to the management, has been expressed by the majority of the men.

Employee representatives interviewed by a field investigator of the National Industrial Conference Board, spoke well of the Council:

"We like it because when anything goes wrong we can get it right to the 'boss.'"

175

Some of the men had been inclined to get all they could out of the plan and give nothing in return. But, under the influence of the fair-minded attitude of the management, that feeling was gradually disappearing. Employees in general were realizing that the Council was intended for the benefit of both parties. A statement made by one of the executives indicated that the period of business depression had in no way interfered with the successful functioning of the plan.

A company official of a large eastern firm, whose Works Council, of the "committee" type, has been operating successfully for nearly three years, stated his belief, as drawn from his own experience, that the success of any plan of employee representation was entirely dependent on the attitude toward it of the two parties concerned. Each must be convinced of the sincerity and fair intentions of the other. Special reference was made to the satisfactory functioning of the Council during the period of business depression:

> "The Works Council has weathered the stress of the last few months of industrial depression, which has entailed an increase in the hours of labor and thereby a decrease in hourly earnings, although weekly pay remains the same. During this period the number of hours worked were cut from one-half to one-third for a considerable number of employees, although part continued to work full time."

This company has a firm belief in employee representation, not as a cure for all industrial ills, not as a weapon to be used against unionism, but as a means, to be universally employed in industry in the future, of inducing a clear understanding between employer and employed:

> "The attitude of this firm toward the establishment of a Works Council and the spread of any plan of representation would be highly favorable. This attitude is determined by the firm belief that some plan of representation will ultimately be adopted throughout industry as a matter of fairness and value, both to employer and employee. If any plan of representation is installed with the idea of combating the unions, *per se*, or of dominating the employees, the plan is bound to fail ultimately.
>
> "It will take a long time for each firm to work out the plan to its logical and best conclusion, to be of value to both employer and employee. It will never be a panacea for all the ills of any company."

Various employers quoted in the preceding pages have discovered, by experience with the organization, that a sincere interest and an honest intent for fair play on the part of the management make for a like interest and cooperation from the employees, resulting in a Council which forms an ideal channel of communication between management and workers.

A few of the manufacturers interviewed by the National Industrial Conference Board have found that the spirit of cooperation between executives and workers created by the Council may develop to the point where employees will feel that the company's interests are theirs. The natural result—a

176

desire to do something constructive—follows. A striking illustration of the extent to which this may be carried was afforded by a mid-western printing concern. The representation plan there is of the "Industrial Democracy" type, and has been in operation for more than two years.

A statement made by the company shows an intent to "practice as well as preach the 'Square Deal'" toward their men. The work that the Council has accomplished is ample proof of the interest and cooperation with which the employee body has responded to the management's policy towards them. The committees have not been content to function merely as a channel through which information regarding economic conditions might flow from executives to workers, and workers might get their grievances to the management direct. It has gone farther than that. Constructive work has been done without a money incentive, for the "Collective Economy Dividend," usually a feature of the "Industrial Democracy" type of Council, has been left out of this organization.

Employers' opinions quoted in another chapter have emphasized the importance of the method in which a representation plan is introduced. The necessity for educating the employees to it, for thoroughly "selling" it to them, has been demonstrated. This was the method adopted in the installation of this particular Council. And the efficiency developed by the committee in one year's time has more than compensated the company for the time and pains spent in preparing the employees for the introduction of the plan. It was accomplished as follows:

"In our case our campaign of education was running for more than a year before we said anything about any system of employee representation. Our plan came as a factor in a whole campaign to have men understand what they were doing and why. Never has it dominated the situation—and we hope it never will."

An outline of what was achieved by this works committee during the first year of its existence is of interest here, as a concrete illustration of what the organization is capable of accomplishing, given the sincere cooperation of both the parties concerned. A sub-committee has, after a careful survey of the subject, established an elaborate educational course which includes a wide range of subjects; regular academic subjects for those who have not had the opportunity for them; technical courses for those who wished to train for better positions and cultural courses for those interested in them. Through this committee also, the plant has obtained a branch of the public library. Another branch of the Council, after careful investigation of the methods used by other firms in job analysis and specification, has classified and rated every individual in the plant, basing this on quality and quantity of the work produced. By this system it is possible to progress from one class to another. "As soon as a man shows himself worth more, he gets it."

177

Great strides have been made toward health sanitation and safety. A committee on economies, suggestions and improvements has collected and passed judgment on hundreds of suggestions by employees, after having established a new suggestion system. Another committee has been of great assistance in the attempt to increase efficiency and thereby earnings to both employees and management. Spoiled work has been investigated and improvements in machinery and tools suggested. Attendance has been carefully followed up and greatly improved and tardiness reduced.

At the end of its first year, a vote was taken to learn the sentiment of the employees on the representation plan. Five hundred and ninety-five men voted to continue it and nine went on record against it. The management, wishing to find out the objections of the latter group, requested that they send in unsigned letters stating reasons for their attitude. Not one such letter was received. This would seem a fairly conclusive proof of employee sentiment on the subject.

The attitude of the company toward employee representation is as follows:

"We are for shop representation, as we believe that men are fair. We need them. They need us. Their actions in 'Congress' and the things they have accomplished prove to us that the solution of industrial misunderstandings is possible through giving the employees an opportunity to express their personal opinions regarding their working hours, working wages, and working conditions."

A report of constructive work accomplished by its committees was received by the Board from an eastern steel company, where a Works Council of the "committee" type is in operation. The interest and satisfaction of both management and employees in the plan, and their extensive use of it, have been discussed in another chapter.[1] In the eyes of the management, the Council has been a distinct success as a means for giving each of the parties concerned an increased appreciation of the problems of the other:

"We feel that the employees, through their representatives, are becoming more familiar with the problems of the management, and management, by personal contact with the representatives of the employees, are getting a better understanding of the workers' point of view. We feel that many misunderstandings can be avoided when the employer and the employee really understand the reasons for the attitude of the other. By establishing this point of contact we feel an *esprit de corps* has been created among the employees which is bound to produce better team work."

The cooperative spirit induced by the Council has been instrumental in producing a highly satisfactory record of constructive work. In confirmation of this conclusion is a statement from the management:

"The following are some of the general accomplishments which can be credited to the plan:

[1] See pp. 168-169.

178

"(1) Originated and recommended set of rules governing suspension and discharge of employees which was adopted by the management.

"(2) Studied and recommended a Savings Plan through wage deductions which resulted in the adoption of a plan for the purchase of Victory Notes.

"(3) Recommended institution of Plant Schools during working hours for non-English speaking employees.

"(4) Suggested and secured many improvements resulting in greater safety to employees.

"(5) Recommended that provision be made for classroom as well as shop training for apprentices.

"(6) Suggested better methods of paying off.

"(7) Production of bolt and nut department increased by following suggestion of representative regarding quality and distribution of stock.

"(8) Representatives of very material assistance in adjusting wage reductions equitably."

The foregoing discussion emphasizes the idea that a Works Council cannot function successfully without the sincere interest and painstaking attention of the management and the cooperation of the workers. Nearly every employer from whom an opinion on this subject was received laid stress on the necessity for these two prerequisites to the operation of a representation plan as a means for smoothing out the misunderstandings which so often exist between employers and their workers, and for establishing a satisfactory channel of communication between the two, a means by which each may comprehend the other's point of view. A fair number of employers, with this background of experience, have cited results which go far beyond the establishment of a clearer understanding between executives and workers. With an appreciation of the business from the company's point of view the workers have been found ambitious to undertake constructive work and, in several instances, have accomplished highly desirable results.

CHAPTER XVII

IMPORTANCE IN LARGE ORGANIZATIONS

A few employers, when asked for a statement of their opinions on the subject of employee representation, have made a special point of their value in large organizations—plants where the number of workers employed precluded any degree of personal contact between management and employees.

A western lumber concern, employing upwards of eight hundred men and operating three Councils of the "committee" type, reported that employee representation is a necessity in any plant where the number of employees made it impossible for an employer to know all of his men. The Board's correspondent was "convinced that employee representation is necessary in plants of this size and larger."

The management made a special point of the manner in which these Councils, organized in 1919, have stood up under the business depression and have facilitated the changes made necessary by business conditions during that period:

> "Our shop committee[1] was organized during times of business prosperity, and during that period met with no test as critical as the one to which it has been subjected during the recent period of wage reductions. We had anticipated serious objection on the part of the men to the wage cut that we have been forced to make, since the extremely rapid decline in the lumber market necessitated a reduction in wages seemingly out of proportion to the reduction in the cost of living. However, the objections were not so strong as we had feared and the men are now working on a wage schedule that represents an approximate decline of 30% from the high wages of 1919 and 1920, and at the shop committee elections held last week the vote for committeemen compared favorably with that of previous elections."

With regard to the establishment of a Council in another concern, after experience with this one, a company official said:

> "I would not hesitate to establish a shop committee plan like ours if the decision were left to me."

This executive's further recommendations as to rules to be observed in installing a works committee were in line with one of the essentials laid down in a previous report of the Conference Board,[2] discussing the scope of the Works Council. It was his opinion that the company should be honest and definite with the employees concerning the amount of power to be really theirs; that workers should not be permitted to hope for authority which the employer had no intention of giving them.

The next prerequisite to success for a representation plan, in the opinion of the same official, was:

[1] This is a special use of the term Shop Committee and should not be confused with the "shop committees" established by the National War Labor Board.
[2] "A Works Council Manual." Research Report No. 26, February, 1920, p. 2.

"The foremen should be thoroughly sold to the idea and trained in modern industrial methods before the plan is entered upon."

The necessity for this has been borne in upon him by his own experience. Another chapter of this report contains a detailed discussion of the necessity for a favorable attitude towards employee representation on the part of foremen, if the plan is to function with any degree of success. Through opinions quoted from employers, it suggests methods of educating foremen to see that a Works Council, by producing greater contentment and good will among the workers, may be made to influence them to increase production either by more conscientious labor or by making constructive suggestions out of their practical experience, for greater efficiency in the plant. The need for such education for the foremen has been keenly felt in this plant, as it was found that

". . . suggestions for improving the efficiency of various departments have not, on the whole, been kindly received by the foremen and superintendents, and their attitude has served to discourage the men in making these suggestions."

The Board's correspondent stated that it seemed "almost impossible" to convince foremen that

". . . the acceptance of such suggestions is not a reflection upon their skill in the management of their various departments."

Emphasis was placed, in conclusion, on a point already discussed in several cases: that of the importance of sincere interest, intelligent guidance, and the assurance of a square deal on the part of the management:

"It is my conviction that there is very little danger that the shop committee would become a body difficult to handle if it were intelligently guided, since it has been our experience that the men are much more interested in securing the assurance of being fairly dealt with and treated humanly, than in using their organization to force greater monetary returns for their labor."

An eastern dye concern where, in normal times, 4,400 men were employed, organized a Works Council, a "committee" type, because the greatly increased size of the plant made it impossible for the executives to come in contact with more than a small fraction of the rank and file workers. A desire to preserve the cooperation between management and employees and to keep alive among the workers the interest heretofore manifested in the company's welfare led to the presentation of a plan of employee representation; this plan to be a point of contact for executives and workers; for avoiding misunderstandings or for eliminating them in their initial stages.

The plan, as outlined, was offered to the employee body, their vote on its installation to be final.

The Council as proposed by the management was accepted by the employees and has been in operation for two years.

181

From the report received by the Board it is evident that the plan has justified, to some extent at least, its installation:

> "In curtailing the weekly working period, retrenching in industrial betterment plans, etc., we have received excellent cooperation from the committees."

The organization has also—

> "... improved the relationship between the management and the workers by causing men to feel that the management is easily approachable on all matters of mutual interest."

To some extent the management has felt itself handicapped by the necessity for using in every case the machinery provided by the Works Council. Executives have found much valuable time lost because even minor changes desired by them had to be submitted to the Council before they were made. This was best explained by a company official:

> "Frequently a desirable change is contemplated, investigated and determined upon, but in order to prevent the slightest suspicion from arising in the minds of the workmen that we are not playing fair with them, such items are submitted to the conference.
>
> "Some of the kind of items referred to are, changes in train schedules, changes in working rules, changes in personnel, elimination of certain classes of work, assignment of houses, etc., etc.
>
> "In practically all cases, the conference agrees as to the desirability of such changes, and therefore the time lost in submitting such items to the conference is a handicap, frequently not justified by the results obtained."

The same official was asked whether his experience with this Council would influence him to organize another, should the occasion arise. His opinion was as follows:

> "This depends on the size of the establishment. Where small, we feel that proper direct contact with employees, and especially with the foremen, is preferable and will secure the desired results fully as effectively, and even where the establishment is large, we feel that no decision should be made on introducing a conference plan until a careful analysis has been made and the necessity for providing a plan is made evident. Local conditions and nature of industry are probably of even more importance in arriving at a decision than size of works."

In contrast to the opinion expressed above regarding the loss of valuable time through having to obtain the consent of the employees' committees to any proposed changes that management may determine upon, is the statement of the vice-president of a textile plant in which there is a plan of the "Industrial Democracy" type. This executive was of the opinion that, although such a method took more time than would be otherwise necessary, it was productive of better results:

> "Real accomplishment comes slowly. Although things were done quicker under the old line management than under the Works Council method, we received only a half-hearted compliance then. It is better to take three weeks and secure the backing of your employees, gained through their thoroughly understanding the situation, than to take one week and be without it."

Executives quoted in this chapter have brought out various points already discussed in favor of the Works Council, such as its value as a means for keeping the worker informed and satisfied when depressed business conditions made changes necessary, its use as a means for improving the relations between management and men, etc. But the fact which most recommends the organization to these officials is its value in large organizations where the personal touch between management and men is sure to be lost unless it is retained by some such method as the one under discussion. As plants increased in size it became impossible for executives to come in contact with more than a small fraction of the rank and file workers, but, in the instances cited, the machinery furnished by the Works Council has preserved the friendly contact which existed between officials and employees.

APPENDIX

Industrial Concerns Having a Form of Employee Representation

Note.—This list contains the names of companies that are known to have a form of employee representation in operation at the present time. Firms in which the representation plans have been abandoned are omitted from the list though considered in the report; those whose experience forms the basis of the body of this report are printed in italics.

Key.—The types of plans are designated as follows:

N. W. L. Bd.—"National War Labor Board Committee."
Br. P.　　　—"Bridgeport Plan."
S. L. A. Bd. —"Shipbuilding Labor Adjustment Board Committee."
Ltd.　　　　—"Limited" Plan.
C. U.　　　—Plan based on "Company Union."
I. D.　　　—"Industrial Democracy" Plan.
E. P.　　　—Other plans introduced voluntarily by employers.

Name of Company	Location	Date of Introduction of Plan	Type of Plan
Abbeville Cotton Mills	Abbeville, S. C.	1919	E. P.
*Aberdeen Coal Company	Elkins, W. Va.	1920	
*Abrams Creek Coal & Coke Company	Fairmont, W. Va.	1920	
Acme Wire Company	New Haven, Conn.	1918	Ltd.
*Adams Coal Company	Westernport, Md.	1920	
Admiral Line	Seattle, Wash.	1920	E. P.
*Allegheny Coal Company	Westernport, Md.	1920	
American Brass Company	Waterbury, Conn.	1919	E. P.
American LaFrance Fire Engine Company	Elmira, N. Y.		E. P.
American Multigraph Co.	Cleveland, Ohio	1919	I. D.
American Pulley Co.	Philadelphia, Pa.	1919	E. P.
American Rolling Mill Co.	Middletown, Ohio	1918	E. P.
American Woolen Co.	Lawrence, Mass.	1921	Ltd.
*Annan & Jeffries	Frostburg, Md.	1920	
Arco Company	Cleveland, Ohio	1919	I. D.
Armour & Company	Chicago, Ill.	1921	E. P.
Art in Buttons	Rochester, N. Y.		
Ascher, Simon, & Company, Inc.	New York, N. Y.	1918	I. D.
Bath Iron Works, Ltd.	Bath, Maine	1918	S. L. A. Bd.
Beacon Falls Rubber Shoe Company	Beacon Falls, Conn.	1919	I. D.
Berkey & Gay Furniture Company	Grand Rapids, Mich.	1919	I. D.
Bethlehem Steel Company	Bethlehem, Pa.	1918	E. P.
*Blackwater Coal Co.	Davis, W. Va.	1920	
Bloedel Donovan Lumber Mills	Bellingham, Wash.	1919	E. P.

Name of Company	Location	Date of Introduction of Plan	Type of Plan
Blumenthal, Sidney & Company, Inc.	Shelton, Conn.	1917	I. D.
Boone Fork Lumber Co.	Shull's Mills, N. C.		I. D.
Borden's Farm Products Company, Inc.	New York, N. Y.	1922	E. P.
Bowser, S. F., & Company, Inc.	Fort Wayne, Ind.	1919	E. P.
*Brailer Mining Company	Mt. Savage, Md.	1920	
Bridgeport Brass Co.	Bridgeport, Conn.	1918	E. P.
Bridgeport Malleable Iron Works	Bridgeport, Conn.	1918	E. P.
Brooklyn Rapid Transit Company	Brooklyn, N. Y.	1920	E. P.
*Brophy Hitchins Coal Co.	Frostburg, Md.	1920	
Brown, Thos. E. & Sons.	Philadelphia, Pa.		E. P.
Browning Company	Cleveland, Ohio	1917	E. P.
*Carroll Cross Coal Co.	Piedmont, W. Va.	1920	
Champlain Silk Mills	New York, N. Y.	1919	I. D.
*Chapman Coal Mining Company	Baltimore, Md.	1920	
Chicago Bridge & Iron Works	Chicago, Ill.	1919	E. P.
Cincinnati Coffin Co.	Cincinnati, Ohio		I. D.
*Clise Brothers Coal Co.	Emeryville, W. Va.	1920	
Collins, A. M. Company	Philadelphia, Pa.	1919	E. P.
Colorado Fuel & Iron Company	Denver, Colo.	1915	E. P.
Columbia Conserve Co.	Indianapolis, Ind.	1917	E. P.
Columbia Graphophone Company	Bridgeport, Conn.	1919	E. P.
Commonwealth Edison Company	Chicago, Ill.	1921	E. P.
Commonwealth Steel Co.	Granite City, Ill.	1921	E. P.
*Consolidation Coal Co.	Baltimore, Md.	1920	
Continental Mills.	Philadelphia, Pa.	1919	E. P.
Courier Journal Job Printing Company	Louisville, Ky.		I. D.
Craddock Terry Co.	Lynchburg, Va.	1919	E. P.
Crocker McElwain Co.	Holyoke, Mass.	1919	Ltd.
Cudahy Brothers Co.	Cudahy, Wis.	1920	E. P.
*Cumberland Big Vein Coal Company	Cumberland, Md.	1920	
*Cumberland Coal Co.	Baltimore, Md.	1920	
Curtis Companies.	Clinton, Iowa	1919	I. D.
Darlington Manufacturing Company	Darlington, S. C.	1919	E. P.
David B. Edmund, Inc.	Paterson, N. J.	1919	I. D.
Davis Coal & Coke Co.	Cumberland, Md.	1920	
Day & Zimmerman, Inc.	Philadelphia, Pa.	1921	E. P.
*Dean Coal Company.	Elk Garden, W. Va.	1920	
Demuth, William, & Co.	New York, N. Y.	1917	I. D.
Dennison Manufacturing Company	Framingham, Mass.	1919	E. P.
Derby, P., & Company.	Gardner, Mass.		E. P.
Dexter Folder Company.	New York, N. Y.	1920	I. D.
Dodge, Nathan D., Shoe Company.	Newburyport, Mass.	1919	I. D.

186

Name of Company	Location	Date of Introduction of Plan	Type of Plan
Dold, Jacob, Packing Co.	Buffalo, N. Y.		C. U.
Dorris Motor Car Co.	St. Louis, Mo.	1919	E. P.
DuPont de Nemours & Company	Wilmington, Del.	1919	E. P.
Durham Hosiery Mills	Durham, N. C.	1919	I. D.
Dutchess Bleachery, Inc.	Wappingers Falls, N. Y.	1919	E. P.
Dutchess Manufacturing Company	Poughkeepsie, N. Y.	1918	E. P.
Eastern Manufacturing Company	Bangor, Me.	1918	E. P.
Eastman Kodak Co.	Rochester, N. Y.	1921	E. P.
Easton Furniture Co.	Easton, Md.	1920	E. P.
Elgin National Watch Co.	Elgin, Ill.	1918	E. P.
Emerson Electric Manufacturing Company	St. Louis, Mo.	1919	E. P.
*Emmons Coal Mining Co.	Philadelphia, Pa.	1920	
Erie City Iron Works	Erie, Pa.	1919	E. P.
Farquhar, A. B. Co., Ltd.	York, Pa.	1919	E. P.
Forbes Lithograph Mfg. Company	Boston, Mass.		I. D.
Fownes Brothers & Co.	Gloversville, N. Y.	1919	E. P.
Frick Company, Inc.	Waynesboro, Pa.	1920	N.W.L. Bd. & E. P.
*Frostburg Big Vein Coal Company	Frostburg, Md.	1920	
*Garrett Coal & Mining Company	Bethlehem, Pa.	1920	
Gates Rubber Company	Denver, Colo.	1919	I. D.
General Chemical Company	New York, N. Y.	1914	C. U.
General Electric Company	Lynn, Mass.	1918	N.W.L.Bd.
General Electric Company	Taunton, Mass.	1918	E. P.
General Necessities Corporation	Detroit, Mich.	1919	E. P.
*Georges Creek Coal Co.	Cumberland, Md.	1920	
Gilbert & Barker Manufacturing Company	Springfield, Mass.	1918	E. P.
*Gleason Coal & Coke Co.	Frostburg, Md.	1920	
Globe-Wernicke Co.	Cincinnati, Ohio.	1921	Ltd.
Goodyear Tire & Rubber Company	Akron, Ohio.	1919	I. D.
Gorton-Pew Fisheries Co.	Gloucester, Mass.	1921	E. P.
Graton & Knight Mfg. Co.	Worcester, Mass.	1919	E. P.
Greenfield Tap & Die Corporation.	Greenfield, Mass.	1919	I. D.
*Hamill Coal & Coke Co.	Blaine, W. Va.	1920	
Hard Manufacturing Co.	Buffalo, N. Y.	1920	I. D.
Hardwick & Magee Co.	Philadelphia, Pa.	1921	E. P.
Hartsville Cotton Mills	Hartsville, S. C.	1919	E. P.
Hamilton Watch Co.	Lancaster, Pa.		E. P.
Hill Pump & Valve Co.	Chicago, Ill.	1919	E. P.
Holt Manufacturing Co.	Peoria, Ill.	1919	E. P.
Holtzer-Cabot Electric Co.	Boston, Mass.		E. P.
Hood, H. P., & Sons.	Boston, Mass.		E. P.
Hooker Electro Chemical Company	Niagara Falls, N. Y.	1919	E. P.
*Hubbard Coal Mining Co.	Hubbard, W. Va.	1920	

Name of Company	Location	Date of Introduction of Plan	Type of Plan
Hydraulic Pressed Steel Company	Cleveland, Ohio	1919	E. P.
†Inland Steel Company	Indiana Harbor, Ind	1919	E. P.
Interborough Rapid Transit Company	New York, N. Y	1919	C. U.
International Harvester Company	Chicago, Ill	1919	E. P.
International Silver Company	Meriden, Conn	1919	E. P.
Intertype Corporation	Brooklyn, N. Y	1919	E. P.
Irving-Pitt Mfg. Co	Kansas City, Mo	1917	C. U.
Joseph & Feiss Company	Cleveland, Ohio	1915	C. U.
*Kalbaugh Coal Company	Cumberland, Md	1920	
Kansas City Railways	Kansas City, Mo	1920	E. P.
Kimberly Clark Co	Neenah, Wis	1920	E. P.
Knox Hat Company	Brooklyn, N. Y	1919	E. P.
LaCrosse Plow Company	LaCrosse, Wis	1919	E. P.
Lake Torpedo Boat Co	Bridgeport, Conn	1918	S. L. A. Bd.
Landis Tool & Machine Company	Waynesboro, Pa	1918	N.W.L.Bd. & E. P.
Leeds & Northrup Co	Philadelphia, Pa	1918	C. U.
Lewis I. Cigar Mfg. Co	Newark, N. J		I. D.
†Louisiana Shipbuilding Corporation	Slidell, La	1918	S. L. A. Bd.
Louisville Railway Co	Louisville, Ky	1920	C. U.
Loyal Legion of Loggers & Lumbermen	Portland, Oregon	1917	C. U.
Lukens Steel Company	Coatesville, Pa	1918	E. P.
Lupton's David Sons Co	Philadelphia, Pa	1919	E. P.
Lynchburg Foundry Co	Lynchburg, Va	1920	I. D.
Macullar Parker Co	Boston, Mass	1921	E. P.
McCallum Hosiery Co	Northampton, Mass	1919	I. D.
McElwain, W. H. Co	Manchester, N. H	1921	E. P.
*Manor Coal Company	Johnstown, Pa	1920	
*Mapleville Coal Co	Elk Garden, W. Va	1920	
Maryland Coal Company	New York, N. Y	1920	
*Mastellar Coal Company	Keyser, W. Va	1920	
Max, Ams Machine Co	Bridgeport, Conn	1919	Br. P.
Mergenthaler Linotype Company	Brooklyn, N. Y	1919	E. P.
Miami Copper Company	Miami, Ariz	1919	E. P.
Midvale Steel & Ordnance Company	Midvale, Pa	1918	E. P.
Midwest Refining Co	Denver, Colo	1919	E. P.
Miller Lock Company	Philadelphia, Pa	1918	E. P.
*Miller & Green Coal Co	Westernport, Md	1920	
Milwaukee Coke & Gas Company	Milwaukee, Wis		E. P.
Milwaukee Electric Railway & Light Company	Milwaukee, Wis	1918	C. U.
Monarch Mfg. Company	Milwaukee, Wis		E. P.
Moore Shipbuilding Co	Oakland, Calif	1920	E. P.
Morse Chain Company	Ithaca, N. Y	1917	E. P.
Morse Dry Dock & Repair Company	New York, N. Y	1917	C. U.

Name of Company	Location	Date of Introduction of Plan	Type of Plan
*Moscoe Georges Creek Coal Company	Frostburg, Md	1920	
Mueller Metals Company	Port Huron, Mich	1919	E. P.
National Cash Register Company	Dayton, Ohio	1920	E. P.
Neptune Meter Company	New York, N. Y	1919	I. D.
†Newburgh Shipyards, Inc	Newburgh, N. Y	1918	S. L. A. Bd.
New York Railways Co	New York, N. Y	1919	E. P.
New York Shipbuilding Corporation	Camden, N. J	1918	S. L. A. Bd.
New York Telephone Co	New York, N. Y	1919	E. P.
*North Maryland Coal Mining Company	Johnstown, Pa	1920	
Nunn Bush & Weldon Shoe Company	Milwaukee, Wis	1915	C. U.
Oliver Iron Mining Co	Duluth, Minn	1918	E. P.
Oliver Mfg. Company	Oakland, Calif	1920	E. P.
Pacific Coast Coal Co	Seattle, Wash	1922	E. P.
†Packard Piano Company	Fort Wayne, Ind	1913	I. D.
†Passaic Metal Ware Co	Passaic, N. J	1919	I. D.
Penberthy Injector Co	Detroit, Mich	1919	Ltd.
Pennsylvania Railroad	Philadelphia, Pa	1921	E. P.
People's Gas Light & Coke Company	Chicago, Ill	1921	E. P.
Phelps Dodge Corporation	Bisbee, Ariz	1921	I. D.
Philadelphia Rapid Transit Company	Philadelphia, Pa	1918	
*Piedmont & Georges Coal Company	Frostburg, Md	1920	
Phoenix Silk Mfg. Co	Allentown, Pa	1920	I. D.
Plankington Packing Co	Milwaukee, Wis	1921	E. P.
Plant, Thomas G. & Co	Boston, Mass		E. P.
Plimpton Press	Norwood, Mass	1915	Ltd.
Plumb, Fayette R., Inc	Philadelphia, Pa	1918	E. P.
*Potomac & Cumberland Coal Company	Philadelphia, Pa	1920	
*Potomac Valley Coal Co	Philadelphia, Pa	1920	
Power Specialty Co	Dansville, N. Y	1919	E. P.
Printz-Biederman Co	Cleveland, Ohio	1914	I. D.
Procter & Gamble Co	Cincinnati, Ohio	1918	E. P.
Public Service Company of Northern Ill	Chicago, Ill	1920	E. P.
Pullman Company	Pullman, Ill	1920	E. P.
Quaker City Rubber Co	Philadelphia, Pa	1919	I. D.
Reed & Prince Mfg. Co	Worcester, Mass		Ltd.
Remington U. M. C. Works	Bridgeport, Conn	1919	Br. P.
Renfrew Mfg. Company	Adams, Mass	1920	I. D.
Riverside & Dan River Cotton Mills	Danville, Va	1919	I. D.
‡Rock Island Arsenal	Rock Island, Ill	1919	
Rockland Finishing Co	Garnerville, N. Y	1918	E. P.
Rome Brass & Copper Co	Rome, N. Y	1920	E. P.
Roots, P. H. & F. M. Co	Connersville, Ind	1918	N.W.L.Bd. & E. P.
*Rowe, C. J. & Brother	Meyersdale, Pa	1920	

Name of Company	Location	Date of Introduction of Plan	Type of Plan
Seng Company.............	Chicago, Ill..............	1919....	I. D.
*Silver Coal Company......	Luke, Md................	1920....	....
Singer Manufacturing Co....	Bridgeport, Conn.........	1919....	Br. P.
Smith & Kaufman, Inc......	Paterson, N. J.,........	1921....	E. P.
Sperry Gyroscope Co.........	Brooklyn, N. Y..........	1920....	E. P.
Sprague Electric Works of General Electric Co........	Bloomfield, N. J.........	1918....	E. P.
*St. Cloud Coal Mining Co....	Cumberland, Md.........	1920....	
Standard Gas Engine Co.....	Oakland, Calif...........	1920....	I. D.
Standard Oil Company of New Jersey............	New York, N. Y.........	1918....	E. P.
Standard Oil Company of Indiana.................	Chicago, Ill.............	1919....	E. P.
Stetson, John B. Co..........	Philadelphia, Pa.........	1919....	E. P.
*Sullivan Brothers Coal Company	Frostburg, Md.........	1920....	
Susquehanna Silk Mills.....	Sunbury, Pa............	1919....	I. D.
Swift & Company..........	Chicago, Ill.............	1921....	E. P.
Taunton-New Bedford Copper Company...........	Taunton, Mass..........		E. P.
Taylor-Wharton Iron & Steel Company...........	High Bridge, N. J.......	1919....	E. P.
Temtor Corn & Fruit Products Company..........	St. Louis, Mo...........	1918....	N.W.L.Bd. & E. P.
Tennessee Copper Co......	Copper Hill, Tenn......	1920....	E. P.
†Troutwine Sons Company...	Gloversville, N. Y......	1919....	E. P.
Tweedy Silk Mills Co.......	Danbury, Conn.........	1920....	I. D.
Union Buffalo Mills Company, Inc...............	Union, S. C...........	1919....	I. D.
Union Construction Co......	Oakland, Calif.........	1919....	E. P.
United Brethren..........	Dayton, Ohio..........	1920....	I. D.
†United Railways & Electric Co. of Baltimore......	Baltimore, Md..........	1918....	C. U.
United States' Rubber Company.................	New York, N. Y........	1919....	E. P.
Universal Film Mfg. Co.......	New York, N. Y........	1920....	I. D.
Van Tassel Tanning Co.......	Stoneham, Mass........	1919....	I. D.
Virginia Bridge & Iron Company.................	Roanoke, Va...........	1918...	N.W. L.Bd. & E. P.
Vulcan Iron Works, Inc......	Jersey City, N. J........	1920....	E. P.
Walworth Mfg. Co..........	Boston, Mass...........	1919....	N.W.L.Bd. & E. P.
Warner Bros..............	Bridgeport, Conn.......		Ltd.
Waterfront Employers' Union of Seattle.........	Seattle, Wash..........	1921....	E. P.
Western Union Telegraph Company.................	New York, N. Y........	1918....	C. U.
*Westernport Coal Co.......	Westernport, Md........	1920....	
Westinghouse Air Brake Company	Pittsburgh, Pa..........	1919....	E. P.
Westinghouse Electric & Manufacturing Co..........	Pittsburgh, Pa..........	1919....	E. P.
White Motor Company.......	Cleveland, Ohio.........	1914....	E. P.

Name of Company	Location	Date of Introduction of Plan	Type of Plan
White Sewing Machine Company	Cleveland, Ohio	1919	E. P.
Williams, A. C., & Co	Ravenna, Ohio		E. P.
Willys-Overland Co	Toledo, Ohio	1919	E. P.
Wilson & Company	Chicago, Ill	1921	E. P.
Windsor Print Works	North Adams, Mass	1919	I. D.
Wright's Underwear Company	Troy, N. Y	1922	I. D.
Yale & Towne Mfg. Co	Stamford, Conn	1919	E. P.
Youngstown Sheet & Tube Company	Youngstown, Ohio	1918	E. P.

*Party to the Maryland Agreement.
†Representation plan in operation at date of last correspondence with company, 1918-19.
‡Instituted by the U. S. War Department.

Trieste

Trieste Publishing has a massive catalogue of classic book titles. Our aim is to provide readers with the highest quality reproductions of fiction and non-fiction literature that has stood the test of time. The many thousands of books in our collection have been sourced from libraries and private collections around the world.

The titles that Trieste Publishing has chosen to be part of the collection have been scanned to simulate the original. Our readers see the books the same way that their first readers did decades or a hundred or more years ago. Books from that period are often spoiled by imperfections that did not exist in the original. Imperfections could be in the form of blurred text, photographs, or missing pages. It is highly unlikely that this would occur with one of our books. Our extensive quality control ensures that the readers of Trieste Publishing's books will be delighted with their purchase. Our staff has thoroughly reviewed every page of all the books in the collection, repairing, or if necessary, rejecting titles that are not of the highest quality. This process ensures that the reader of one of Trieste Publishing's titles receives a volume that faithfully reproduces the original, and to the maximum degree possible, gives them the experience of owning the original work.

We pride ourselves on not only creating a pathway to an extensive reservoir of books of the finest quality, but also providing value to every one of our readers. Generally, Trieste books are purchased singly - on demand, however they may also be purchased in bulk. Readers interested in bulk purchases are invited to contact us directly to enquire about our tailored bulk rates. Email: customerservice@triestepublishing.com

You May Also Like

ISBN: 9780649738618
Paperback: 144 pages
Dimensions: 6.14 x 0.31 x 9.21 inches
Language: eng

Zoe: An Athenian Tale

J. C. Colquhoun

ISBN: 9780649057054
Paperback: 140 pages
Dimensions: 6.14 x 0.30 x 9.21 inches
Language: eng

The University of Minnesota. The Calendar for the Year 1883-84

University Minneapolis

www.triestepublishing.com

You May Also Like

ISBN: 9780649565733
Paperback: 170 pages
Dimensions: 6.14 x 0.36 x 9.21 inches
Language: eng

Longmans' English Classics; Dryden's Palamon and Arcite

William Tenney Brewster

ISBN: 9780649663057
Paperback: 188 pages
Dimensions: 6.14 x 0.40 x 9.21 inches
Language: eng

On Spermatorrhœa: Its Pathology, Results, and Complications

J. L. Milton

You May Also Like

1807-1907 The One Hundredth Anniversary of the incorporation of the Town of Arlington Massachusetts

Various

ISBN: 9780649420544
Paperback: 108 pages
Dimensions: 6.14 x 0.22 x 9.21 inches
Language: eng

Biennial report of the Board of State Harbor Commissioners, for the two fiscal years commencing July 1, 1890, and ending June 30, 1892

Various

ISBN: 9780649194292
Paperback: 44 pages
Dimensions: 6.14 x 0.09 x 9.21 inches
Language: eng

www.triestepublishing.com

You May Also Like

Biennial report of the Board of State Harbor Commissioners for the two fisca years. Commeneing July 1, 1884, and Ending June 30, 1886

Various

ISBN: 9780649199693
Paperback: 48 pages
Dimensions: 6.14 x 0.10 x 9.21 inches
Language: eng

Biennial report of the Board of state commissioners, for the two fiscal years, commencing July 1, 1890, and ending June 30, 1892

Various

ISBN: 9780649196395
Paperback: 44 pages
Dimensions: 6.14 x 0.09 x 9.21 inches
Language: eng

Find more of our titles on our website. We have a selection of thousands of titles that will interest you. Please visit

www.triestepublishing.com